Postmodern Ethics

Postmodern Ethics

Zygmunt Bauman

BLACKWELL
Oxford UK & Cambridge USA

First published 1993
Reprinted 1994

Blackwell Publishers
108 Cowley Road, Oxford OX4 1JF, UK

238 Main Street
Cambridge, Massachusetts 02142, USA

British Library Cataloguing in Publication Data

A CIP catalogue record for this book is available from the British Library.

Library of Congress Cataloging-in-Publication Data

Bauman, Zygmunt.
  Postmodern ethics / Zygmunt Bauman.
    p.   cm.
  Includes index.
  ISBN 0–631–18692–1. — ISBN 0–631–18693–X (pbk.)
  1. Ethics, Modern—20th century.   2. Postmodernism.   I. Title.
  BJ319.B28   1994
  170—dc20   93–16048
                                                             CIP

Typeset in 10½ on 12pt Bembo
by Photoprint, Torquay, Devon
Printed in Great Britain by Hartnolls Ltd, Bodmin

This book is printed on acid-free paper

Contents

Introduction: Morality in Modern and Postmodern Perspective

Shattered beings are best represented by bits and pieces.
                                        Rainer Maria Rilke

As signalled in its title, this book is a study of *postmodern ethics*, not of the postmodern morality.

The latter, were it attempted here, would aim at a possibly comprehensive inventory of moral problems which men and women living in a postmodern world face and struggle to resolve – new problems unknown to past generations or unnoticed by them, as well as new forms which old problems, thoroughly vetted in the past, have now taken. There is no shortage of either kind of problem. The 'moral agenda' of our times is full of items which ethical writers of the past hardly ever touched or did not touch at all, and for good reason: they were not articulated then as part of human experience. It is enough to mention, on the level of daily life, the manifold moral issues arising from the present plight of pair relationships, sexuality and family companionship – notorious for their institutional under-determination, flexibility, mutability and fragility; or the multi-tude of 'traditions', some surviving against the odds, some others resurrected or invented, which vie for loyalty and the authority to guide personal conduct – albeit without a hope of establishing a commonly agreed hierarchy of values and norms that would save their addressees from the vexing task of making their own choices. Or, at the other extreme, that of the global context of contemporary life – one may mention the risks of an unheard-of, truly cataclysmic magnitude, which arise from the criss-crossing of partial and one-sided purposes, and which cannot be fathomed in advance or stay out of sight at the time when actions are planned because of the way in which those actions are structured.

Such problems do appear in this study time and again, but solely as the background against which ethical thinking of the contemporary, postmodern age proceeds. They are treated as the experiential context in which the specifically postmodern perspective on morality is formed. It is the form in which they are seen and assigned importance when contemplated from that postmodern ethical perspective which is here the object of investigation.

The true subject–matter of this study is the postmodern perspective itself. The main assertion of the book is that in the result of the modern age reaching its self-critical, often self-denigrating and in many ways self-dismantling stage (the process which the concept of 'postmodernity' is meant to grasp and convey) many paths previously followed by ethical *theories* (but not the moral *concerns* of modern times) began to look more like a blind alley; while the possibility of a radically novel understanding of moral phenomena has been opened.

Any reader familiar with 'postmodern writings' and current writings about postmodernity will notice immediately that this interpretation of the postmodern 'revolution' in ethics is contentious, and by no means the only one possible. What has come to be associated with the notion of the postmodern approach to morality is all too often the celebration of the 'demise of the ethical', of the substitution of aesthetics for ethics, and of the 'ultimate emancipation' that follows. Ethics itself is denigrated or derided as one of the typically modern constraints now broken and destined for the dustbin of history; fetters once deemed necessary, now clearly superfluous: another illusion the postmodern men and women can well do without. If one needs an example of such an interpretation of the 'postmodern ethical revolution' one can do worse than reach for the recently published study by Gilles Lipovetsky, *Le Crépuscule du devoir* ('The Twilight of Duty') (Gallimard, 1992). Lipovetsky, a prominent bard of 'postmodern liberation', author of 'The Era of the Void' and 'Empire of the Ephemeric', suggests that we have finally entered the epoch of *l'après-devoir*, a post-deontic epoch, where our conduct has been freed from the last vestiges of oppressive 'infinite duties', 'commandments' and 'absolute obligations'. In our times the idea of self-sacrifice has been delegitimized; people are not goaded or willing to stretch themselves to attain moral ideals and guard moral values; politicians have put paid to utopias; and yesterday's idealists have become pragmatic. The most universal of our slogans is 'No excess!' Ours is the era of unadulterated individualism and the search for the good life, limited solely by the demand for tolerance (when coupled with self-celebratory and scruple-free individualism, tolerance may only express itself as indifference). The 'after-duty' era can admit of only a most vestigial, 'minimalistic' morality: a totally new situation according to Lipovetsky – and he counsels us to applaud its advent and rejoice in the freedom it has brought in its wake.

Lipovetsky, like many other postmodern theorists, commits the twin errors of representing the *topic* of investigation as an investigative *resource*; that which should be *explained* as that which *explains*. To describe prevalent behaviour does not mean making a moral statement: the two procedures are as different in postmodern times as they used to be in pre-postmodern. If Lipovetsky's description is correct and we are facing today a social life absolved from moral worries, the pure 'is' no more guided by any 'ought', a social intercourse de-coupled from obligation and duty – the sociologist's task is to find out how it has come about that moral regulation has been 'decommissioned' from the arsenal of weapons once deployed in society's self-reproductive struggles. If sociologists happen to belong to the critical current in social thought, their task will not stop at that point either. They would refuse to accept that something is right simply for being there, nor would they take it for granted that what humans do is nothing but what they think they are doing or how they narrate what they have done.

The assumption of this study is that the significance of postmodernity rests precisely on the opportunity it offers the critical sociologist to pursue the above kind of inquiry to an effect greater than ever before. Modernity had the uncanny capacity for thwarting self-examination; it wrapped the mechanisms of self-reproduction with a veil of illusions without which those mechanisms, being what they were, could not function properly; modernity had to set itself targets which could not be reached, in order to reach what reach it could. 'The postmodern perspective' to which this study refers means above all the tearing off of the mask of illusions; the recognition of certain pretences as false and certain objectives as neither attainable nor, for that matter, desirable. The hope which guides this study is that under these conditions the sources of moral power which in modern ethical philosophy and political practice were hidden from sight, may be made visible, while the reasons for their past invisibility can be better understood: and that as a result the chances of 'moralization' of social life may – who knows? – be enhanced. It remains to be seen whether the time of postmodernity will go down in history as the twilight, or the renaissance, of morality.

I suggest that the novelty of the postmodern approach to ethics consists first and foremost not in the abandoning of characteristically modern moral concerns, but in the rejection of the typically modern ways of going about its moral problems (that is, responding to moral challenges with coercive normative regulation in political practice, and the philosophical search for absolutes, universals and foundations in theory). The great issues of ethics – like human rights, social justice, balance between peaceful co-operation and personal self-assertion, synchronization of individual conduct and collective welfare – have lost nothing of their topicality. They only need to be seen, and dealt with, in a novel way.

If 'moral' came to be set apart as the aspect of human thought, feeling and action that pertains to the distinction between 'right' and 'wrong', this was by and large the accomplishment of the modern age. Through most of human history, little difference was seen or made between now strictly separated standards of human conduct, such as 'usefulness', 'truth', 'beauty', 'propriety'. In the 'traditional' way of life, rarely looked upon from a distance and thus seldom reflected upon, everything seemed to float at the same level of importance, weighed on the same scales of 'right' versus 'wrong' things to do. The totality of ways and means, in all its aspects, was lived as if validated by powers no human will or whim could challenge; life as a whole was product of Divine creation, monitored by Divine providence. Free will, if it existed at all, could mean only – as St Augustine insisted and the Church repeatedly hammered home – freedom to choose wrong over right – that is, to *breach* God's commandments: to depart from the way of the world as God ordained it; and anything that visibly deflected from custom was seen as such a breach. Being in the right, on the other hand, was not a matter of choice: it meant, on the contrary, avoiding choice – following the customary way of life. All this changed, however, with the gradual loosening of the grip of tradition (sociologically speaking – of the tight and ubiquitous, though diffuse, communal surveillance and management of individual conduct) and the growing plurality of mutually autonomous contexts in which the life of the rising number of men and women came to be conducted; in other words, with the casting of those men and women in the position of *individuals*, endowed with identities not-yet-given, or given but sketchily – and thus facing the need for 'constructing' them, and *making choices in the process*.

It is the actions one needs to *choose*, actions one has *chosen* from among others that could be chosen but were not, that need to be assessed, measured and evaluated. Evaluation is an indispensable part of choosing, of decision-making; it is the need felt by humans as decision-makers, one that is seldom reflected upon by those who act by habit alone. Once it comes to evaluating, however, it becomes evident that 'useful' is not necessarily 'good', or 'beautiful' does not have to be 'true'. Once the question of the *criteria* of evaluation has been asked, the 'dimensions' of measurement start to ramify and grow in directions ever more distant from one another. The once unitary and indivisible 'right way' begins to split into 'economically sensible', 'aesthetically pleasing', 'morally proper'. Actions may be right in one sense, wrong in another. Which action ought to be measured by what criteria? And if a number of criteria apply, which is to be given priority?

One can find in Max Weber (who more than any other thinker set the agenda for our discussion of modern experience) two logically irreconcilable accounts of the birth of modernity. On the one hand, we learn that modernity began with the *separation* between the family household and the business enterprise – a divorce which could in principle stave off the danger of the mutually contradictory criteria of efficiency and profitability (which are right and proper for business) and moral standards of sharing and caring (which are right and proper for emotionally charged family life) ever meeting on the same territory and thus casting the decision-maker in a hopelessly ambivalent position. On the other hand, we learn from Weber that the Protestant reformers turned, willy-nilly, into the pioneers of modern life precisely because they insisted that 'honesty is the best policy', that life *as a whole* is charged with moral meaning, that whatever you do, in whatever area of life, *matters morally* – and, indeed, produced an ethic which embraced it all and stoutly refused to leave any aspect of life out of sight. Undoubtedly, there is a logical contradiction between the two accounts. And yet, contrary to logic, this does not necessarily mean that one of the accounts is false. The point is precisely that modern life does not abide by the 'either/or' of logic. The contradiction between accounts faithfully reflects the genuine clash between equally powerful tendencies of modern society; a society which is 'modern' in as far as it constantly but vainly tries to 'embrace the unembraceable', to replace diversity with uniformity and ambivalence with coherent and transparent order – and while trying to do this turns out unstoppably more divisions, diversity and ambivalence than it has managed to get rid of.

We often hear that people grew individually minded, self-concerned and egotistic, as with the advent of modernity they became godless and lost their faith in 'religious dogmas'. The self-preoccupation of modern individuals is, according to this story, a product of secularization, and can be repaired either through the resuscitation of religious creed, or an idea which, though secular, would successfully claim comprehensiveness similar to that of the great religions which enjoyed a nearly total domination before being assaulted and eroded by modern scepticism. In fact, one needs to see the connections in a reverse order. It is because modern developments forced men and women into the condition of individuals, who found their lives fragmented, split into many loosely related aims and functions, each to be pursued in a different context and according to a different pragmatics – that an 'all-comprising' idea promoting a unitary vision of the world was unlikely to serve their tasks well and thus capture their imagination.

This is why modern legislators and modern thinkers alike felt that morality, rather than being a 'natural trait' of human life, is something that needs to be designed and injected into human conduct; and this is why they tried to compose and impose an all-comprehensive, unitary ethics – that is, a cohesive code of moral rules which people could be taught and forced to obey; and this is also why all their earnest efforts to do so proved to be in vain (though the less successful their past efforts proved to be, the harder they tried). They earnestly believed that the void left by the now extinct or ineffective moral supervision of the Church can and ought to be filled with a carefully and artfully harmonized set of rational rules; that *reason* can do what *belief* was doing no more; that with their eyes wide open and passions put to rest, men can regulate their mutual relationships no less, and perhaps more and better (in a more 'civilized', peaceful, rational manner) than at a time when they were 'blinded' by faith and when their untamed and undomesticated feelings ran wild. In line with this conviction, attempts were continuously made to construct a moral code which – not hiding any more behind God's command-ments – would loudly and unashamedly proclaim its 'man-made' provenance and despite this (or, rather, thanks to this), would be embraced and obeyed by 'all rational human beings'. On the other hand, the search never stopped after the 'rational arrangement of human cohabitation' – a set of laws so conceived, a society so administered, that the individuals while exercising their free will and making their choices would be likely to choose what is right and proper over what is wrong and evil.

One may say that although the existential plight of men and women under the conditions of modern life was strikingly different from what it was before, the old assumption – that free will expresses itself solely in wrong choices, that freedom, if not monitored, always verges on licentiousness and so is, or may become, an enemy of good

– continued to dominate the minds of philosophers and practices of legislators. It was the tacit, but virtually exceptionless assumption of modern ethical thought and of the practice it recommended, that when free (and, cast in the modern conditions, they could not but be free) individuals would need to be prevented from using their freedom to do wrong. And no wonder. When viewed 'from the top', by those responsible for the 'running of society', the guardians of the 'common weal', freedom of the individuals must worry the observer; it is suspect from the start, for the sheer unpredictability of its consequences, for being a constant source of instability – indeed, the element of chaos which must be bridled if order were to be secured and made safe. And the view of philosophers and the rulers could not but be a 'view from the top' – the view of those facing the task of legislating order and bridling the chaos. On this view, to assure that free individuals do what is right, some form of enforcement had to be in operation. Their untoward, potentially heinous impulses needed to be held in check – either from inside or from the outside: either by the actors themselves, through the exercise of their 'better judgement', suppressing their instincts with the help of their rational faculties – or through exposing the actors to rationally designed external pressures which would assure that 'doing wrong does not pay' and so most individuals most of the time are discouraged from doing it.

The two ways were, in fact, intimately connected. Were the individuals devoid of rational faculties, they would not react properly to external stimuli and inducements, and the efforts to manipulate rewards and punishments, however skilful and ingenious, would be wasted. Developing individual powers of judgement (training individuals to see what is in their interest and to follow their interest once they saw it) and managing the stakes in such a fashion that pursuit of individual interest would prompt them to obey the order the legislators wished to install, had to be seen as conditioning and complementing each other; they made sense only together. On the other hand, however, they were potentially at cross-purposes. 'From the top', individual judgement could never look completely reliable, and this simply for the fact of being individual and thus rooted in an authority other than that of the guardians and spokesmen of order. And individuals with a true autonomy of judgement were likely to resent and resist interference simply for being an interference. Autonomy of rational individuals and heteronomy of rational management could not do without each other; but they could not cohabit peacefully either. They were locked together for better or worse, bound to clash and struggle without end and with no real prospect of lasting peace. The conflict which their togetherness never

stopped generating kept sedimenting on one extreme the anarchic
tendency to rebel against rules experienced as oppression, and on the
other the totalitarian visions which could not but tempt the keepers of
the 'common weal'.

This *aporetic* situation (aporia: in a nutshell, a contradiction that
cannot be overcome, one that results in a conflict that cannot be
resolved) was to remain the fate of modern society, as a self-
admittedly 'man-made' artifice – but it was the trade mark of
modernity *not* to admit that the fate was irreparable. It was a
characteristic, perhaps the defining, feature of modernity that the
aporia was played down as a conflict not-yet-resolved-but-in-
principle-resolvable; as a temporary nuisance, a residual imperfection
on the road to perfection, a relic of unreason on the way to the rule of
reason, a momentary lapse of reason soon to be rectified, a sign of
not-yet-fully-overcome ignorance of the 'best fit' between individual
and common interests. One more effort, one more feat of reason, and
the harmony would be reached – never to be lost again. Modernity
knew it was deeply wounded – but thought the wound curable. And
thus it never ceased to look for a healing ointment. We may say that it
remained 'modernity' as long, and in as far as, it refused to abandon
that belief and those efforts. Modernity is about conflict-*resolution*,
and about admitting of no contradictions except conflicts amenable
to, and awaiting resolution.

Modern ethical thought in co-operation with modern legislative
practice fought its way through to such a radical solution under the
twin banners of *universality* and *foundation*.

In the practice of the legislators, *universality* stood for the
exceptionless rule of one set of laws on the territory over which their
sovereignty extended. Philosophers defined universality as that
feature of ethical prescriptions which compelled every human
creature, just for the fact of being a human creature, to recognize it as
right and thus to accept it as obligatory. The two universalities
winked and beckoned to each other without really merging. But they
did co-operate, closely and fruitfully, even if no contract was entered,
signed and lodged in the state archives or university libraries. The
legislators' coercive practices (or intentions) of uniformization supplied the 'epistemological ground' on which philosophers could build
their models of universal human nature: while the philosophers'
success in 'naturalizing' the legislators' cultural (or, rather, administrative) artifice helped to represent the legally constructed model of
the state-subject as the embodiment and epitome of human destiny.

In the practice of the legislators, *foundations* stood for the coercive powers of the state that rendered obedience to the rules a sensible expectation; the rule was 'well founded' in as far as it enjoyed the support of such powers, and the foundation was strengthened with the effectiveness of the support. For the philosophers, rules would be well founded when the persons expected to follow them believed, or could be convinced, that for one reason or another following them was the right thing to do. 'Well-founded' are such rules as offer a cogent answer to the question 'Why should I obey them?' The laying of such a foundation was seen as imperative, since autonomous individuals faced with heteronomous legal/ethical demands were likely to ask such questions – and above all, the question 'why should I be moral?' At any rate, the philosophers and legislators alike did expect them to ask such questions – as both thought or acted on the same assumption that good rules must be artificially designed rules, on the same premise that individuals when free would not necessarily volunteer to embrace good rules if unassisted, and on the same principle that in order to act morally, individuals must first accept the rules of moral behaviour, and that this would not happen were they not persuaded first that acting morally is more agreeable than acting without morals, and that the rules they are called to accept spell out indeed what moral acting is. Again – as in the case of 'universality' – the two versions of 'foundations', without ever blending, co-operated and complemented each other. Popular belief that the rules are well justified in what they do would ease the task of coercive agencies, while the relentless pressure of legal sanctions would pour blood into the dry veins of philosophical argument.

All in all, the persevering and unyielding search for rules that 'will stick' and foundations that 'won't shake' drew its animus from the faith in the feasibility and ultimate triumph of the humanist project. A society free from irremovable contradictions, a society pointing the way, as logic does, to correct solutions only, can be built eventually, given enough time and good will. The right design and the final argument can be, must be, and will be found. With such a faith, singed fingers would not hurt too much, there would be no last straws and the failure of yesterday's hopes would only spur the explorers to a yet greater effort today. Any allegedly 'foolproof' recipe could be proved wrong, disavowed and rejected – but not the very search for a truly foolproof recipe, one that will, as one of them surely must, put paid to all further search. In other words, the moral thought and practice of modernity was animated by the belief in the possibility of a *non-ambivalent, non-aporetic ethical code*. Perhaps such a code has not been found yet. But it surely waits round the next corner. Or the corner after next.

It is the *disbelief* in such a possibility that is *post*modern – 'post' not in the 'chronological' sense (not in the sense of displacing and replacing modernity, of being born only at the moment when modernity ends or fades away, of rendering the modern view impossible once it comes into its own), but in the sense of implying (in the form of conclusion, or mere premonition) that the long and earnest efforts of modernity have been misguided, undertaken under false pretences and bound to – sooner or later – run their course; that, in other words, it is modernity itself that will demonstrate (if it has not demonstrated yet) and demonstrate beyond reasonable doubt, its impossibility, the vanity of its hopes and the wastefulness of its works. The foolproof – universal and unshakably founded – ethical code will never be found; having singed our fingers once too often, we know now what we did not know then, when we embarked on this journey of exploration: that a non-aporetic, non-ambivalent morality, an ethics that is universal and 'objectively founded', is a practical impossibility; perhaps also an *oxymoron*, a contradiction in terms.

It is the exploration of the consequences of this postmodern critique of modern ambitions that constitutes the subject-matter of this study.

I suggest that the following are the marks of moral condition, as they appear once contemplated from the postmodern perspective.

1. The assertions (mutually contradictory, yet stated all too often with the same force of conviction) 'Humans are essentially good, and they only have to be assisted to act according to their nature', and 'Humans are essentially bad, and they must be prevented from acting on their impulses', are both wrong. In fact, humans are morally ambivalent: ambivalence resides at the heart of the 'primary scene' of human face-to-face. All subsequent social arrangements – the power-assisted institutions as well as the rationally articulated and pondered rules and duties – deploy that ambivalence as their building material while doing their best to cleanse it from its original sin of being an ambivalence. The latter efforts are either ineffective or result in exacerbating the evil they wish to disarm. Given the primary structure of human togetherness, a non-ambivalent morality is an existential impossibility. No logically coherent ethical code can 'fit' the essentially ambivalent condition of morality. Neither can rationality 'override' moral impulse; at the utmost, it can silence it and paralyse, thereby rendering the chances of the 'good being done' not stronger, perhaps weaker, than they otherwise would have been. What follows is that moral conduct cannot be guaranteed; not by

better designed contexts for human action, nor by better formed motives of human action. We need to learn how to live without such guarantees, and with the awareness that guarantees will never be offered – that a perfect society, as well as a perfect human being, is not a viable prospect, while attempts to prove the contrary result in more cruelty than humanity, and certainly less morality.

2. Moral phenomena are inherently 'non-rational'. Since they are moral only if they precede the consideration of purpose and the calculation of gains and losses, they do not fit the 'means–end' scheme. They also escape explanation in terms of the utility or service they render or are called to render to the moral subject, a group or a cause. They are not regular, repetitive, monotonous and predictable in a way that would allow them to be represented as *rule-guided*. It is mainly for this reason they cannot be exhausted by any 'ethical code'. Ethics is thought of after the pattern of Law. As Law does, it strives to define the 'proper' and 'improper' actions in situations on which it takes a stand. It sets for itself an ideal (rarely if ever reached in practice) of churning up exhaustive and unambiguous definitions; such as would provide clear-cut rules for the choice between proper and improper and leave no 'grey area' of ambivalence and multiple interpretations. In other words, it acts on the assumption that in each life-situation one choice can and should be decreed to be good in opposition to numerous bad ones, and so acting in all situations can be rational while the actors are, as they should be, rational as well. But this assumption leaves out what is properly moral in morality. It shifts moral phenomena from the realm of personal autonomy into that of power-assisted heteronomy. It substitutes the learnable knowledge of rules for the moral self constituted by responsibility. It places answerability to the legislators and guardians of the code where there had formerly been answerability to the Other and to moral self-conscience, the context in which moral stand is taken.

3. Morality is incurably *aporetic*. Few choices (and only those which are relatively trivial and of minor existential importance) are un-ambiguously good. The majority of moral choices are made between contradictory impulses. Most importantly, however, virtually every moral impulse, if acted upon in full, leads to immoral consequences (most characteristically, the impulse to care for the Other, when taken to its extreme, leads to the annihilation of the autonomy of the Other, to domination and oppression); yet no moral impulse can implement itself unless the moral actor earnestly strives to stretch the effort to the limit. The moral self moves, feels and acts in the context of ambivalence and is shot through with uncertainty. Hence the ambiguity-free moral situation has solely an utopian existence of the

perhaps indispensable horizon and stimulus for a moral self, but not a realistic target of ethical practice. Seldom may moral acts bring complete satisfaction; responsibility that guides the moral person is always ahead of what has been and what can be done. All the efforts to the contrary notwithstanding, uncertainty is bound to accompany the condition of the moral self forever. Indeed, one can recognize the moral self by its uncertainty whether all that should have been done, has been.

4. Morality is *not universalizable*. This statement does not necessarily endorse moral relativism, expressed in the frequently voiced and apparently similar proposition, that any morality is but a local (and temporary) custom, that what is believed to be moral in one place and time is certain to be frowned upon in another, and so all kinds of moral conduct practised so far happen to be relative to the time and place, affected by vagaries of local or tribal histories and cultural inventions; that proposition is more often than not correlated with an injunction against all comparisons between moralities, and above all against all exploration of other than purely accidental and contingent sources of morality. I will argue against this overtly relativistic and in the end nihilistic view of morality. The assertion 'morality is un-universalizable' as it appears in this book carries a different meaning: it opposes a concrete version of moral universalism which in the modern era served as but a thinly disguised declaration of intent to embark on *Gleichschaltung*, on an arduous campaign to smother the differences and above all to eliminate all 'wild' – autonomous, obstreperous and uncontrolled – sources of moral judgement. While acknowledging the present diversity of moral beliefs and institutionally promoted actions, and the past and persistent variety of individual moral postures, modern thought and modern practice considered it an abomination and a challenge and tried hard to overcome it. But it did not do so openly, not in the name of extending one's own preferred ethical code over populations which abide by different codes and tightening up the grip in which it held populations already under its rule – but surreptitiously, in the name of one all-human ethics bound to evict and supplant all local *distortions*. Such efforts, as we see it now, may take no other form than that of the substitution of heteronomous, enforced-from-outside, ethical rules for the autonomous responsibility of the moral self (and that means nothing less than the incapacitation, even destruction, of the moral self). Thus, their overall effect is not so much the 'universalization of morality', as the silencing of moral impulse and channelling of moral capacities to socially designed targets that may, and do, include immoral purposes.

5. From the perspective of the 'rational order', morality is and is bound to remain *irrational*. For every social totality bent on uniformity and the soliciting of the disciplined, co-ordinated action, the stubborn and resilient autonomy of the moral self is a scandal. From the control desk of society, it is viewed as the germ of chaos and anarchy inside order; as the outer limit of what reason (or its self-appointed spokesmen and agents) can do to design and implement whatever has been proclaimed as the 'perfect' arrangement of human cohabitation. Moral impulses are, however, also an indispensable resource in the administration of any such 'really existing' arrangement: they supply the raw material of sociality and of commitment to others in which all social orders are moulded. They have to be, therefore, tamed, harnessed, and exploited, rather than merely suppressed or outlawed. Hence the endemic ambivalence in the treatment of the moral self by societal administration: the moral self needs to be cultivated without being given a free rein; it needs to be constantly trimmed and kept in the desired shape without its growth being stifled and its vitality desiccated. The social management of morality is a complex and delicate operation which cannot but precipitate more ambivalence than it manages to eliminate.

6. Given the ambiguous impact of the societal efforts at ethical legislation, one must assume that moral responsibility – being *for* the Other before one can be *with* the Other – is the first reality of the self, a starting point rather than a product of society. It precedes all engagement with the Other, be it through knowledge, evaluation, suffering or doing. It has therefore no 'foundation' – no cause, no determining factor. For the same reason for which it cannot be wished or manoeuvred out of existence, it cannot offer a convincing case for the necessity of its presence. In the absence of a foundation, the question 'How possible?' makes no sense when addressed to morality. Such a question calls morality to justify itself – yet morality has no excuse, as it precedes the emergence of the socially administered context inside which the terms in which justifications and excuses are couched appear and make sense. That question demands that morality show the certificate of its origin – yet there is no self before the moral self, morality being the ultimate, non-determined presence; indeed, an act of creation *ex nihilo*, if there ever was one. That question, finally, assumes tacitly that moral responsibility is a mystery contrary to reason, that selves would not be 'normally' moral if not for some special and powerful cause; to become moral, selves have first to give up or curtail some other constituent of themselves (the most common being the premise that – with moral action being uncharacteristically unselfish – the element surrendered

is self-interest; what is assumed here is that being-for-the-Other rather than for-itself is 'contrary to nature'; and that two modalities of being are in opposition). Yet moral responsibility is precisely the act of self-constitution. The surrender, if any, occurs on the road leading from the moral to the social self, from being-for to being 'merely' with. It took centuries of power-assisted legal drill and philosophical indoctrination to make the opposite seem evidently true.

7. What follows is that contrary to both the popular opinion and hot-headed 'everything goes' triumphalism of certain postmodernist writers, the postmodern perspective on moral phenomena *does not reveal the relativism* of morality. Neither must it call for, or obliquely recommend, a 'nothing we can do about it' disarmament in the face of an apparently irreducible variety of ethical codes. The contrary is the case. Modern societies practise moral parochialism under the mask of promoting universal ethics. By exposing the essential incongruity between any power-assisted ethical code on the one hand and the infinitely complex condition of the moral self on the other, and by exposing the falsity of society's pretence to be the ultimate author and the sole trustworthy guardian of morality, the post-modern perspective shows the relativity of ethical codes and of moral practices they recommend or support to be the outcome of the *politically* promoted parochiality of *ethical codes* that pretend to be universal, and not of the 'uncodified' moral condition and moral conduct which they decried as parochial. It is the ethical codes which are plagued with relativism, that plague being but a reflection or a sediment of tribal parochialism of institutional powers that usurp ethical authority. The overcoming of variety through the extension of the scope and the reach of a given institutional power, political or cultural (as the modern fighters against moral relativism demanded virtually in unison) can only lead to a yet more thorough substitution of ethics for morality, a code for the moral self, heteronomy for autonomy. What the postmodern perspective succeeded in doing, having cast aside the prophesies of the imminent arrival of the power-assisted brand of universality, was to pierce through the thick veil of myths down to the common moral condition that precedes all diversifying effects of the social administration of moral capacity, not to mention the felt need of similarly administered 'universalization'. The humankind-wide moral unity is thinkable, if at all, not as the end-product of globalizing the domain of political powers with ethical pretensions, but as the utopian horizon of deconstructing the 'without us the deluge' claims of nation-states, nations-in-search-of-the-state, traditional communities and communities-in-search-of-a-tradition, tribes and neo-tribes, as well as their appointed and self-

appointed spokesmen and prophets; as the remote (and, so be it, utopian) prospect of the emancipation of the autonomous moral self and vindication of its moral responsibility; as a prospect of the moral self facing up, without being tempted to escape, to the inherent and incurable ambivalence in which that responsibility casts it and which is already its fate, still waiting to be recast into its destiny.

These themes will be followed and explored throughout the book, in each chapter from a different angle. The reader should be warned: no ethical code will emerge at the end of this exploration; nor could an ethical code be contemplated in the light of what will be found in its course. The kind of understanding of the moral self's condition which the postmodern vantage point allows is unlikely to make moral life *easier*. The most it can dream of is making it a bit more *moral*.

It has been my privilege to benefit, for the fourth time now, from the exquisite skills and dedication of David Roberts – the editor extraordinary who knows how to strike the fine balance between the stiff demands of language and respect for the unruliness of the author's incurably idiosyncratic thought . . .

1

Moral Responsibilities, Ethical Rules

If the natural world is ruled by fate and chance, and the technical world by rationality and entropy, the social world can only be characterized as existing in fear and trembling.

Daniel Bell

It is true of many things that the more they are needed the less readily are they available. This is certainly true about commonly *agreed* ethical rules, such as we can also hope to be commonly *observed*: such rules as may guide our conduct toward *each other* – ours towards others and, *simultaneously*, others' towards us – so that we may feel secure in each other's presence, help one another, co-operate peacefully and derive from each other's presence a pleasure untainted by fear and suspicion.

Just how badly we need such rules is brought home daily. Going about our daily affairs, we (well, most of us) seldom encounter untamed nature in all its pristine, untrimmed and un-tampered-with force; rarely do we meet technical artefacts in a form other than tightly sealed black boxes with simple operating instructions; but we live and act in the company of apparently endless multitude of other human beings, seen or guessed, known and unknown, whose life and actions depend on what we do and in turn influence what we do, what we can do and what we ought to do – and all this in ways we neither understand nor are able to presage.[1] In such life, we need

---

[1] In the words of Daniel Bell, in our world (one which Bell prefers to describe as 'postindustrial') 'people live more and more outside nature, and less and less with machinery and things; they live with, and encounter, only one another . . . For most of human history, reality was nature . . . In the past 150 years, reality has become technics, tools and things made by men yet given an independent existence outside man in a reified world . . . Now

moral knowledge and skills more often, and more poignantly, than either knowledge of the 'laws of nature' or technical skills. Yet we do not know where to get them; and when (if) they are offered, we are seldom sure we can trust them unswervingly. As Hans Jonas, one of the most profound analysts of our present moral predicament, observed, 'never was so much power coupled with so little guidance for its use . . . We need wisdom most when we believe in it least.'[2]

It is, essentially, this discrepancy between demand and supply that has been recently described as the 'ethical crisis of postmodernity'. Many would say that this crisis reaches far back in time, and that it ought to be properly named the 'ethical crisis of modern times'. Whatever is the case, this crisis has its practical and its theoretical dimensions.

Moral uncertainty

One of the practical dimensions of the crisis derives from the sheer magnitude of our powers. What we and other people do may have profound, far-reaching and long-lasting consequences, which we can neither see directly nor predict with precision. Between the deeds and their outcomes there is a huge *distance* – both in time and in space – which we cannot fathom using our innate, ordinary powers of perception – and so we can hardly measure the quality of our actions by a full inventory of their effects.[3] What we and others do has 'side-

---

reality is becoming only the social world' ('Culture and Religion in a Postindustrial Age', in *Ethics in an Age of Pervasive Technology*, ed. Melvin Kranzberg (Boulder: Westview Press, 1980), pp. 36–7). Bell's sweeping generalizations would turn out to be less exaggerated than they seem at first sight, if one accepted that the idea of 'reality' stands for the most trenchantly opaque, resistant and unmanageable aspect of living experience. It is the focus of that opacity which has shifted over time.

[2] Hans Jonas, *Philosophical Essays: From Ancient Creed to Technological Man* (Englewood Cliffs: Prentice Hall, 1974), pp. 176, 178.

[3] Anthony Giddens goes as far as defining modernity as 'a risk culture': 'the concept of risk becomes fundamental to the way both lay actors and technical specialists organise the moral world . . . The late modern world . . . is apocalyptic, not because it is inevitably heading towards calamity, but because it introduces risks which previous generations have not had to face' (*Modernity and Self-Identity: Self and Society in the Late Modern Age* (Cambridge: Polity Press, 1991), pp. 3–4). But in his pioneering study of the risks and hazards that 'blind action' (and in contemporary ultra-complex societies actions are, so to speak, *institutionally* blindfolded) cannot but spawn, Ulrich Beck observed that 'that which impairs health or destroys nature is not

effects', 'unanticipated consequences', which may smother whatever good purposes are intentioned and bring about disasters and suffering neither we nor anybody else wished or contemplated. And it may affect people we will never travel far enough nor live long enough to look in the face. We can do harm to them (or they may do harm to us) inadvertently, by ignorance rather than design, without anyone in particular wishing ill, acting with malice and be otherwise morally blameworthy. The scale of consequences our actions may have dwarfs such moral imagination as we may possess. It also renders impotent the few, but tested and trustworthy ethical rules we have inherited from the past and are taught to obey. After all, they all tell us how to approach people within our sight and reach, and how to decide which actions are good (and thus ought to be taken) and which are bad (and thus ought to be avoided), depending on their visible and predictable effects on such people. Even if we abide by such rules scrupulously, even if everyone around observes them as well, we are far from certain that disastrous consequences will be avoided. Our ethical tools – the code of moral behaviour, the assembly of the rules of thumb we follow – have not been, simply, made to the measure of our present powers.

Another practical dimension stems from the fact that with the exacting division of labour, expertise and functions for which our times are notorious (and of which they are proud), almost every undertaking involves many people, each one of whom performs but a small part of the overall task; indeed, the quantity of people involved is so huge that no one can reasonably and convincingly claim (or be charged with) the 'authorship' of (or the responsibility for) the end result. Sin without sinners, crime without criminals, guilt without culprits! Responsibility for the outcome is, so to speak, *floating*, nowhere finding its natural haven. Or, rather, the guilt is spread so thinly that even a most zealous and sincere self-scrutiny or repentance

---

recognizable to one's own feeling or eye'. Effects 'completely escape human powers of direct perception. The focus is more and more on hazards which are neither visible nor perceptible to the victims; hazards that in some cases may not even take effect within the lifespans of those affected, but instead during those of their children' (*Risk Society: Towards a New Modernity*, trans. Mark Ritter (London: Sage, 1992), p. 27). Such hazards are not, and cannot be a part of the calculation that precedes the act; they are absent from the motives and the intentions of action. Harmful effects of human actions are *unintentional*. It is not clear therefore how a moral person can avoid them. It is not clear either how they can be an object of even an *ex post facto* moral evaluation, which is apportioned to *motivated* actions.

of any of the 'partial actors' will change little, if at all, in the final state of affairs. For many of us, quite naturally, this futility breeds belief in the 'vanity of human efforts' and thus seems to be good enough reason not to engage in self-scrutiny and account-settling at all.

Furthermore, our life-work is split into many little tasks, each performed in a different place, among different people, at different times. Our presence in each of those settings is as fragmentary as the tasks themselves. In each setting we merely appear in a 'role', one of many roles we play. None of the roles seems to take hold of our 'whole selves'; none can be assumed to be identical with 'what we truly are' as 'whole' and 'unique' individuals. As individuals, we are irreplaceable. We are not, however, irreplaceable as players of any of our many roles. Each role has a brief attached which stipulates exactly what job is to be done, how and when. Every person who knows the brief and has mastered the skills which the job requires can do it. Nothing much would change, therefore, if I, this particular role-performer, opted out: another person would promptly fill the gap I left. 'Somebody will do it anyway' – so we console ourselves, and not without reason, when we find the task we have been asked to perform morally suspect or unpalatable . . . Again, responsibility has been 'floated'. Or, rather – so we are prompted to say – it rests with the *role*, not with the *person* who performs it. And role is not 'the self' – merely the work clothes we put on for the duration of the job and then take off again when the day shift is over. Once dressed in fatigues, all who wear them look uncannily alike. There is 'nothing personal' about the fatigues, nor about the job of work done by those who wear them.

As it were, it does not always feel like that at all; not all stains incurred on the job – 'in the course of the role performance' – stay on the work clothes alone. Sometimes we have the unsavoury feeling of some of the mud spilling on our body, or the fatigues sticking to our skin too tight for comfort; they cannot be easily peeled off and left behind in the locker. This is a painful enough worry, but not the only one.

If we succeed in keeping the lockers tightly shut, so that our roles and our 'real selves' are kept apart as we are told they can and should be, the worry does not go away: it is merely replaced with another. The code of conduct and guidelines for choices which are attached to the performance of a role do not then stretch to get hold of the 'real self'. The real self is free – a reason for rejoicing, but also for no little agony. Here, away from mere 'role playing', we are indeed 'our-selves', and thus we and we alone are responsible for our deeds. We can make our choices freely, guided solely by what we consider worthy of pursuing. As we find out very soon, however, this does not make our life easier. Relying on the rules has become a habit, and without the fatigues we feel naked and helpless. Upon the return from the world 'out there' in which others took (or assured us that they have taken) responsibility for all our works, the now unfamiliar responsibility is, for the lack of habit, not easy to bear. All too often it leaves a bitter after-taste and only adds to our uncertainty. We miss responsibility badly when it is denied to us, but once we get it back it feels like a burden too heavy to carry alone. And so now we miss what we resented before: an authority stronger than us, one which we can trust or must obey, one which can vouch for the propriety of our choices and thus, at least, share some of our 'excessive' responsibility. Without it, we may feel lonely, abandoned, helpless. And then 'in our effort to escape from aloneness and powerlessness, we are ready to get rid of our individual self either by submission to new forms of authority or by a compulsive conforming to accepted patterns'.[4]

In so many situations in which the choice of what to do is ours and apparently ours alone, we look in vain for the firm and trusty rules which may reassure us that once we followed them, we could be sure to be in the right. We would dearly wish to shelter behind such rules (even though we know only too well that we would not feel at all comfortable were we *coerced* to surrender to them). It appears, however, that there are too many rules for comfort: they speak in different voices, one praising what the other condemns. They clash and contradict each other, each claiming the authority the others deny. It transpires sooner or later that following the rules, however scrupulously, does not save us from responsibility. After all, it is each one of us on his or her own who has to decide which of the conflicting rules to obey and which to disregard. The choice is not between following the rules and breaking them, as there is no one set of rules to be obeyed or breached. The choice is, rather, between different sets of rules and different authorities preaching them. One cannot be, therefore, a true 'conformist', however strongly one might desire to shake off the vexing burden of one's own responsibility. Each act of obedience is, and cannot but be, an act of disobedience; and with no authority strong enough or bold enough to disavow all the others and claim monopoly, it is not clear the disobeying of which one is a 'lesser evil'.

With the *pluralism* of rules (and our times are the times of pluralism) the moral choices (and the moral conscience left in their

4   Erich Fromm, *The Fear of Freedom* (London: Routledge, 1960), p. 116.

wake) appear to us intrinsically and irreparably *ambivalent*. Ours are the times of *strongly felt moral ambiguity*. These times offer us freedom of choice never before enjoyed, but also cast us into a state of uncertainty never before so agonizing. We yearn for guidance we can trust and rely upon, so that some of the haunting responsibility for our choices could be lifted from our shoulders. But the authorities we may entrust are all contested, and none seems to be powerful enough to give us the degree of reassurance we seek. In the end, we trust no authority, at least, we trust none fully, and none for long: we cannot help being suspicious about any claim to infallibility. This is the most acute and prominent practical aspect of what is justly decribed as the 'postmodern moral crisis'.

Ethical quandary

There is a resonance between ambiguities of moral practice and the quandary of ethics, the moral theory: *moral* crisis rebounds in an *ethical* one. Ethics – a moral code, wishing to be *the* moral code, the one and only set of mutually coherent precepts that ought to be obeyed by any moral person – views the plurality of human ways and ideals as a challenge, and the ambivalence of moral judgements as a morbid state of affairs yearning to be rectified. Throughout the modern era the efforts of moral philosophers were targeted on the reduction of pluralism and chasing away moral ambivalence. Like most men and women living under conditions of modernity, modern ethics sought an exit from the predicament in which modern morality has been cast in the practice of everyday life.[5]

[5]   Hopes that all human conduct can be embraced by precise, hard and fast, unexceptional rules, not open to multiple interpretation, were gradually dashed, though, and all but abandoned in recent ethical writings. Instead, a curious reversal of ends and means has taken place. Rather than seeking the comprehensive code (or universal principle) of moral action that can guide all life occasions, ethical philosophers of this century tend increasingly to focus on conduct and choices that could be prescribed in an indubitable fashion. This leaves vast, and crucial, areas of life practice outside ethical concern, admitting into the focus of ethical inquiry but marginal and comfortingly trivial situations. Thus, G.E. Moore, arguably the most original and influential among the twentieth-century British ethical philosophers, having despaired of failed attempts to legislate foundations of moral conduct and suggested instead that 'if I am asked "what is good" my answer is that good is good and that is the end of the matter', that good is evident when seen and

At first the coming of pluralism (breaking the mould of tradition, escaping the tight and pernickety control of the parish and local community, slackening the grip of ecclesiastical ethical monopoly) was greeted by the thinking, debating and writing minority with joy. What was first noted was the *emancipatory* effect of pluralism: now individuals were no longer cast into immutable shape by the accident of birth, nor kept on a short string by the small parcel of humanity to which they happened to be assigned. The new feeling of freedom was intoxicating; it was celebrated triumphantly and enjoyed with abandon. Giovanni Pico della Mirandola profusely expressed the philosophers' delight 'in his conclusion that man is free as air to be whatever he likes'.[6] The image which the thinkers of the Renaissance found most fascinating and enchanting was that of Proteus, of whom Ovid wrote (*Metamorphoses* vii 7) that

> People have seen him at one time in the shape of a young man, at another transformed into a lion; sometimes he used to appear to them as a raging wild boar, or again as a snake, which they shrank from touching; or else horns transformed him into a bull. Often he could be seen as stone, or a tree . . .

'The image of man as chameleon, with that animal's mysterious powers of instant adaptation, is constant in this period to the point of platitude' is how Stevie Davies sums up the philosophical folklore of the Renaissance, the dawn of the modern era.[7] Instructing the betters

---

thus calls for no 'explanation' (indeed, explaining it in terms of something else would amount to what Moore called a 'naturalistic fallacy'), could by the end of his investigation spell out, as obviously and undoubtedly 'good', 'personal affection and the appreciation of what is beautiful in Art and Nature' (*Principia Ethica* (Cambridge University Press, 1903), pp. 10, 188). As to the ostensible followers of G.E. Moore of the 'intuitionist' school, worth quoting is the caustic comment made by Mary Warnock: we are told by them that 'we know the truths of ethics as we know the truth of mathematics, even perhaps better, but what we know suddenly seems to be rather boring . . . [T]he examples grow more and more trivial and absurd. It is difficult to imagine feeling very greatly exercised about whether to shout to revive a fainting man, whether to slow down as we approach the main road in our car, or whether to return the book that we have borrowed' (*Ethics since 1900* (Oxford University Press, 1979), pp. 43–4). Reading through the output of recent ethical philosophy with 'generalistic' ambitions shows that Warnock's verdict extends much beyond its case subject.

6 In 'Oration: On the Dignity of Man' (1572); quoted after Stevie Davies, *Renaissance View of Man* (Manchester University Press, 1978), pp. 62–3.
7 Davies, *Renaissance View of Man*, p. 77.

of his time about the art of educating their children, Erasmus assured them that humans 'are not born but fashioned'. Freedom meant the right (and the skill) to fashion oneself. Suddenly, one's fate – only yesterday bewailed for its tyranny or grudgingly surrendered to for the same reason – appeared to be pliable in the hands of the self-conscious man as clay was in the palms of a skilful sculptor. 'Men can do all things if they will', promised, enticingly, Leon Battista Alberti; 'We can become what we will', announced, with relish, Pico della Mirandola. The 'humanists' of the Renaissance, as John Carroll put it in his recent study of the historical ups and downs of their legacy, 'attempted to replace God by man, to put man at the centre of the universe, to deify him'.[8] Their ambition was nothing less than to found an entirely human order on earth, and one that would be erected entirely with the help of human capacities and resources alone.

Not all humans were equally endowed, though. Militant humanists of the Renaissance celebrated freedom of the chosen few. What Marsilio Ficino wrote of the soul – that it is suspended partly in eternity, partly in time (unlike the body, steeped in time alone) – stood as a metaphor for human society at large: the latter was split between immortal and mortal, the eternal and the passing, the lofty and the lowly, the spiritual and the material, the creative and the created, doing and suffering – the acting and the inert. On one side, there were those able to deploy the awesome human abilities in the service of freedom of self-creation and self-legislation. On the other, 'a credulous and hapless herd, begotten to servility', as John Milton described the masses. The Renaissance, the time of emancipation, was also the time of the great schism.

What the elite emancipated itself from was the 'animal' or not-sufficiently-human, ignorant, dependent, 'other side' of their selves – which became immediately projected upon *le menu peuple*, the coarse and uncouth 'masses' that in the eyes of the self-liberating elite epitomized all these hideous and repugnant marks of the animality in man. As Robert Muchembled, the incisive analyst of the 'great schism' put it, the self-civilizing elite rejected everything that appeared to them 'savage, dirty, lecherous – in order to better conquer similar temptations in themselves'. The masses, like the inner demons which the self-shaping elite wished to exorcize, were 'judged to be brutal, dirty, and totally incapable of holding their passions in check so that they could be poured into a civilized

[8] Cf. John Carroll, *Humanism: The Rebirth and Wreck of Western Culture* (London: Fontana, 1993), Prologue.

mould'.[9] It would be pointless to ask what was first, what was second: was the self-ennobling zeal boosted by the sight of the depravation in the 'others' one saw milling around, or was it rather that the 'masses' became in the eyes of the 'thinking minority' ever more alien, terrifying and incomprehensible since in its effort of self-cultivation the elite projected upon them their secret and intimate fear of crude passions, always lurking just beneath the veneer of freshly painted 'humanity'. Whatever was the case, the lines of communication between the 'higher' and the 'lower' regions of hierarchy were broken – seemingly beyond repair. The instant comprehension between them was no more, as the imagery of a continuous chain of being brought about by divine act of creation and sustained by divine grace has been elbowed out to make room for the free expansion of human powers.

In purely abstract terms, the humanist emancipation at the top could result in a more or less permanent break between two sections of society, guided by two totally opposed principles: freedom from constraints against all-embracing normative control, self-definition against plankton-like existence, self-assertive *Übermenschheit* against slave-like submissiveness to passions. Such an opposition could, however, be conjured up only in the imaginary universe of philosophers, and even there it could hardly prove to be logically sustainable. In practice, the self-enlightened elite faced the masses not just as an odious and hideous 'other' one should (and could) steer clear from, but as an object of rule and care – the two tasks intertwined in the position of *political* leadership. Lines of communication broken in the result of the great schism had to be restored, the newly dug abyss bridged. For philosophy, that practical challenge had to rebound in a feverish search for a bond spanning the two sides of the precipice, defying the temptation to confine the cherished humanity to the self-emancipated elite. Moreover, freedom of self-constitution was claimed in the name of *human* potential: were it to be claimed consistently, it would need to be argued in terms of a universal human capacity, not overtly sectarian terms. It was this blend and interplay of practical and theoretical necessities that lifted ethics to a most prominent position among the concerns of the modern era. And also made it into the *raison d'être*, as well as the stumbling-block, of much of the modern philosophy.

In the words of Jacques Domenech,

---

[9]   Roger Muchembled, *L'invention de l'homme moderne: Sociabilité, moeurs et comportements collectives dans l'Ancien Régime* (Paris: Fayard, 1988), pp. 13, 150.

when Diderot wrote, in his Essay on the reigns of Claudius and Nero, that La Mettrie was 'a writer who did not have a first idea of the true foundations of morality' – he spelled out the gravest of charges which could be raised against a philosopher of the Enlightenment.[10]

Indeed, with all their mutual disagreements, *les philosophes* were of one mind regarding the *need* and the *possibility* of laying firm and unshakable foundations of morality binding *all human beings* – people of all social stations, and of all nations and races. The sought-after foundations should owe nothing to Christian revelation; as a matter of fact to no particularistic, local tradition (Christian moral principles which referred to Divine commandments could only suit, as Helvétius insisted, 'the small number of Christians scattered over the earth'; the philosophers, on the contrary, 'are always bound to speak of the universal'). They had to be based solely on 'the nature of Man' (d'Holbach). Morality of properly human society had to be founded in a way that engaged every human *qua* human being – rely on no supra- or extra-human authorities, always burdened as it were with an additional sin of having been voiced in the name of but a small part of humanity.

The philosophers' assault against Revelation was to achieve simultaneously two effects, both constitutive of the modern revolution: de-legitimizing clerical authority on the ground of its ignorance (or a straightforward suppression) of the universal human attributes; and justifying the filling of the void thus created by the enlightened spokesmen of the Universal, now in charge of promoting and guarding the morality of nations. As *les philosophes* were fond of repeating on every occasion, it was the task of the enlightened elite to 'reveal to the nations the foundations on which morality is to be built', to 'instruct the nations' in the principles of moral conduct. The ethics of the philosophers were to replace the Revelation of the Church – with the yet more radical and uncompromising claim for universal validity. And so the philosophers were to replace the clergy as spiritual rulers and guardians of the nations.

The ethical code was to be grounded in the 'nature of Man'. This was, at any rate, the declaration of intent. It was enough to state it, however, to expose the danger which the formula of the natural foundations of ethics presented for the idea of man-made order and of the steering role which the knowledge class claimed in that order for

[10] Jacques Domenech, *L'Éthique des Lumières: Les Fondements de la morale dans la philosophie française du XVIIIᵉ siècle* (Paris: J. Vrin, 1989), p. 9. The statements of other philosophers which follow are quoted after the same source.

themselves. Were the foundations of ethics to be located in the 'nature' of 'really existing', *empirical* men and women; in the raw and unprocessed, so to speak, inclinations and impulses as revealed in the choices people actually made in the pursuit of their goals and in the intercourse with each other? Such a 'democratic' version of 'human nature' would play havoc with the philosophers' bid for spiritual leadership and all but make their services redundant. As it were, the philosophers themselves preferred to frighten their readers by painting lurid pictures of the threat to human order as such: were human conduct allowed to follow its spontaneous inclinations, no order fit for human habitation would emerge. Life would be 'nasty, brutish and short'. 'The multitude', wrote d'Alembert, was 'ignorant and stupefied . . . incapable of strong and generous action.'[11] The behaviour of the masses was incalculable in the destructive consequences of its crudity, cruelty and wild passions. At no time were *les philosophes* prominent for high regard for 'empirical' men and women. This presented them with a problem, and a difficult one – since it was on the 'nature' of such men and women that they sought to found the ethical code which was in its turn to legitimize the role of the enlighteners as ethical legislators and moral guardians.

There was just one conceivable solution to the quandary: yes, it is the nature of Man that will provide a rock-solid, and sufficient, foundation for the universally binding ethical code; but no, it is not the 'nature of men and women' as it stands at the moment, as it can be seen and recorded today, that will serve as such a foundation. This is so because what we can see and report now is *not* the manifestation of 'true human nature'. Nowhere yet has human nature been properly fulfilled. Human nature exists at present solely *in potentia*; as a possibility not-yet-born, awaiting a midwife to let it out, and not before a protracted labour and acute birth-pangs. Human nature is 'not-yet'. Human nature is its own *potential*; an unfulfilled potential, but – most importantly – *unfulfillable on its own*, without assistance of reason and the reason-bearers.

Two things had to be done first for that potential to turn into daily reality of life. First, the moral potential hidden in human beings should be revealed to them; people had to be enlightened as to the standards they were able to meet but unable to discover unaided. And second, they had to be helped in following such standards by an

---

[11]   On the intrinsically contradictory philosophers' view of the people and the unresolvable antinomies in which that view entangled the promoters of Enlightenment, see Zygmunt Bauman, *Legislators and Interpreters* (Cambridge: Polity Press, 1987), chap. 5.

environment carefully designed to favour and reward genuinely moral conduct. Both tasks evidently required professional skills – first of the teachers, second of the legislators. Their urgency placed knowledge and the knowledgeable, and those able to put in practice the knowledge of the knowledgeable, firmly in the position of supreme authority. It was on their minds and deeds that the fate of remaking human reality in tune with human nature depended.

Why should people abide by the principles disclosed to them by their teachers? In the absence of divine sanctions, now emphatically rejected, an ethical code should appeal to the needs of those who were exhorted to follow it. The desire to be moral could only have roots as earthy as the foundations on which future ethics were to be erected, and pass the test as human as the ground in which those foundations were set. Doing good had to be shown to be good for those who did it. It had to be desired for the benefits it brings – here, now, in this world. It had to justify itself as *the rational choice* for a person desiring a good life; rational because of the rewards it brings. 'Interest' and 'self-love' (*l'amour-propre*) were the names for reasons to submit to the moral enlighteners and accept their teachings. Self-love is what we each and every one of us experience and by what we are 'naturally' guided in what we do. We all wish pleasures and we all want to avoid pain; but self-love is not guaranteed to achieve what it is about, unless *enlightened* – supported and guided by properly understood self-interest. Indeed, interest *properly understood*; but the proper understanding is precisely what the raw and uncultivated mind was most conspicuously lacking. People must be *told* what their true interests are; if they do not listen or appear to be hard of hearing, they must be forced to behave as their *real* interest demands – if necessary, against their will.

People should do no harm to others because not doing harm to others agrees with their self-interest, at least in the long run – even if a crude, short-sighted person may assume the opposite. Being scorned by those with whom one lives is a plight no person could nor would be able ever to sustain, explained Voltaire, and hence 'tout homme raisonable conclura qu'il est visiblement de son intérêt d'être honnête homme' (*Traité de métaphysique*). When confronted with the facts of the matter, every *reasonable* person *must* accept that doing good to others is better than doing evil. In this acceptance, *reason* comes to the aid of *self-love*, and their encounter results in acting upon one's *properly understood* self-interest.

Reason is a shared human property, but in the case of this particular equality, as in all other cases, some humans are more equal than others. Philosophers are the people endowed with more direct access to reason, the unalloyed reason, reason unbeclouded by narrow interests; it is their task therefore to find out what sort of behaviour reason would dictate to the *reasonable* person. Having found this out, they should communicate their findings to those less endowed who cannot find them on their own, and do it with the *authority* of 'people in the know'. To the others, to whom the message is addressed, the findings come, however, in the form of Law: not a rule inherent in their own choices, but one that prompts the choice from outside. Despite the fact that reason is every person's property, the rules promulgated in the name of reason are to be obeyed after the pattern of submission to an overwhelming external force. They can be best thought of in the way we think of laws legislated by authorities armed with coercive means to enforce their instructions. Though the justification for being moral is ruggedly individualistic and auto-nomous – it refers to self-love and self-interest – the actuality of moral behaviour can only be secured by the heteronomous force of Law.

Moral judgement expropriated and reclaimed

It is in the gap between the 'really existing' individual inclinations and the assumed way people would have behaved *if* their conduct were ruled by the properly understood self-interest that the ethical code could be deployed as an instrument of social domination. Indeed, as long as there was such a gap the ethical code could be *nothing else but* invitation to, or justification of, moral heteronomy, even if the code itself appealed, as it had to, to the inborn all-human capacity for autonomous moral judgement. Each person is capable of moral choice, and this is what allows us to treat each person as the addressee of moral demand and a morally responsible subject; yet for one reason or another (be it the shared and hereditary burden of Adam's sin, or ignorance of one's own interest, or wayward passions of the animal in man) many or most persons, while choosing, do not choose what is morally good. Thus it is, paradoxically, the very *freedom* to judge and choose that necessitates an external force *coercing* the person to do good 'for his own salvation', 'for her own welfare', or 'in her own interest'.

This paradox haunted moral thinkers at least since the attack of St Augustine against the 'heresy' of Pelagius. Logically, this was indeed a *logical* paradox stretching philosophical ingenuity to its limits. There was, however, nothing paradoxical about it as far as the *actual condition* of common living went. All social institutions backed by coercive sanctions have been and are founded on the assumption that the individual cannot be trusted to make good choices (whether 'good' is interpreted as 'good for the individual', or 'good for community', or as both at the same time). Yet it is precisely the fact of the saturation of common life with coercive institutions, endowed with the sole authority of setting the standards of good conduct, that renders the individual *qua* individual principally untrustworthy. The only way in which individual freedom could have morally positive consequences is (in practice, if not in theory) to surrender that freedom to the heteronomously set standards; to cede to socially approved agencies the right to decide what is good and submit to their verdicts. This means, in a nutshell, to replace morality with legal code, and to shape ethics after the pattern of Law. Individual responsibility is then translated (again, in practice even if not in theory) as the responsibility for following or breaching the socially endorsed, ethical-legal rules.

Stated in such a general form, the morality/law dialectics presents itself as an 'existential predicament' of the human person; as an insoluble antinomy of 'individual versus group' or 'individual versus society' type. It is as such that it was most commonly reflected in both philosophical and sociological analyses, be they those of Jean-Jacques Rousseau or Herbert Spencer, Emile Durkheim or Sigmund Freud. However, the apparently universal model those ruminations produced hid the widely disparate levels of heteronomy to which various individuals were exposed, and the widely diverse degree to which they could, and did, accept that condition. Individual autonomy and heteronomy in modern society are unevenly distributed. Even if the presence of both is to be discovered in any human condition, they are found in widely divergent quantities, having been apportioned to different social positions in different measures. In fact, autonomy and heteronomy, freedom and dependence (and the imputation of moral trustworthiness that tends to be ex post facto theorized as the root of their antinomy) are among the principal factors of social *stratification*.

What the philosophical and sociological models of 'universal human condition' strove (in vain) to overcome in theory was the practical duality of moral standings in modern society, itself an instrument and the reflection of domination. In modern society, some individuals are freer than others: some are more dependent than others.

Decisions of some are allowed to be autonomous (and can be autonomous, thanks to the resources at the disposal of the decision-makers); either the decision-makers are trusted to know their interests well and thus to make proper, reasonable decisions, or the decisions they make are exempt from the competence of the socially promoted ethical code and declared 'morally indifferent' (*adiaphoric* – that is, of a kind on which ethical authorities do not feel it necessary to take a stand). Decisions of others are not allowed to be truly autonomous (and can hardly be so, considering the paucity of resources available to potential decision-makers); either they are not believed to be capable of knowing their real interests and thus act upon them, or their probable autonomous actions are defined as harmful to the welfare of the group as a whole, and thus obliquely to the actors themselves.

In a shorthand form, this duality of measures is expressed as the quandary of, on the one hand, intrinsic desirability of free decision-making, but, on the other, the need to limit freedom of those who are presumed to use it to do evil. You can trust the wise (the code name of the mighty) to do good autonomously; but you cannot trust all people to be wise. So, in order to enable the resourceful to do more good, one needs to give them yet more resources (they will, one hopes, put them to good use); but in order to prevent the resourceless from doing evil, one needs to further restrict the resources at their disposal (one needs, for instance, to give more money to the rich, but less money to the poor, to make sure that good work will be done in both cases).

Of course, neither total freedom nor total dependence are to be found anywhere in society. Both are but imaginary poles between which real situations are plotted – and oscillate. Besides, those who would like, ideally, to claim a monopoly, or at least an extra measure, of the rights to free choice on the ground of exclusive skills in rational decision-making seldom have it their way, and certainly not all the time. Freedom (the reality of it, if not the ideal) is a privilege, but a privilege hotly contested, and bound to be contested. The privilege cannot be claimed explicitly. It must be defended in a subtler fashion – by declaring freedom to be the innate property of the human condition and then claiming that not everybody can put it to a use society can possibly tolerate without incurring damage to its survival and well-being. Even in this form, however, the defence of the privilege is challenged. What is and what is not the proper use of freedom, what is beneficial, and what harmful to common welfare, is a moot issue – a subject of genuine conflict of interests and an object of mutually opposed interpretations. There is a real conflict here, and a real opposition between conditions of life, which ethical theories aiming to arrive at universal principles applicable to all ignore or gloss over to their own detriment; they end up either with a list of trivial recipes for universally experienced, but abominably insignificant or imaginary dilemmas, or with abstract models pleasing the philosopher with their logical elegance, yet largely irrelevant to the practical morality and daily decision-making in society as it is.

This sad predicament is not, to be sure, the philosophers' fault. Various humans within human society face different moral standards pressed upon them; they also enjoy different degrees of moral autonomy. The standards and autonomy alike are objects of conflict and struggle. There is no uncontested and all-powerful social agency which could (or, for this matter, would wish to) forge the universal principles, however firmly founded intellectually, into effective standards of universal behaviour. There are instead many agencies, and many ethical standards, whose presence casts the individual in a condition of moral uncertainty from which there is no completely satisfactory, foolproof exit. At the end of the road modern society has traversed in its pursuit of a Law-like, universally binding code of ethical rules, stands the modern individual bombarded by conflicting moral demands, options and cravings, with responsibility for actions landing back on her shoulders. 'What makes us modern', writes Alan Wolfe, 'is that we are capable of acting as our own moral agents'.[12] But whether or not are we modern, we live in a modern society, which leaves us little choice but being our own moral agents – even if (or rather because) there is no shortage of offers to do the job for us (in exchange for money, or freedom, or both).

At the other end of the modern era we are, so to speak, back at square one. Individuals were to be spared the agony of uncertainty in a rationally organized – 'transparent' – society in which Reason, and Reason alone, rules supreme. This, we know now, was never on the cards, and could not be. The bid to make individuals universally moral through shifting their moral responsibilities to the legislators failed, as did the promise to make everyone free in the process. We know now that we will face forever moral dilemmas without unambiguously good (that is, universally agreed upon, uncontested) solutions, and that we will be never sure where such solutions are to be found; not even whether it would be good to find them.

Postmodernity: morality without ethical code

At the time we face choices of unprecedented magnitude and potentially disastrous consequences, we no more expect the wisdom

[12] Alan Wolfe, *Whose Keeper? Social Science and Moral Obligation* (University of California Press, 1989), p. 19.

of the legislators or perspicacity of philosophers to lift us once for all from moral ambivalence and decisional uncertainty. We suspect that the truth of the matter is opposite to the one we have been told. It is society, its continuing existence and its well-being, that is made possible by the moral competence of its members – not the other way round. More exactly, as Alan Wolfe put it – morality is a practice 'negotiated between learning agents capable of growth on the one hand and a culture capable of change on the other'.[13] Rather than reiterating that there would be no moral individuals if not for the training/drilling job performed by society, we move toward the understanding that it must be the moral capacity of human beings that makes them so conspicuously capable to form societies and against all odds to secure their – happy or less happy – survival.

The probable truth is that moral choices are indeed choices, and dilemmas are indeed dilemmas – not the temporary and rectifiable effects of human weakness, ignorance or blunders. Issues have no predetermined solutions nor have the crossroads intrinsically preferable directions. There are no hard-and-fast principles which one can learn, memorize and deploy in order to escape situations without a good outcome and to spare oneself the bitter after-taste (call it scruples, guilty conscience, or sin) which comes unsolicited in the wake of the decisions taken and fulfilled. Human reality is messy and ambiguous – and so moral decisions, unlike abstract ethical principles, are ambivalent. It is in this sort of world that we must live; and yet, as if defying the worried philosophers who cannot conceive of an 'unprincipled' morality, a morality without foundations, we demonstrate day by day that we can live, or learn to live, or manage to live in such a world, though few of us would be ready to spell out, if asked, what the principles that guide us are, and fewer still would have heard about the 'foundations' which we allegedly cannot do without to be good and kind to each other.

Knowing that to be the truth (or just intuiting it, or going on *as if* one knew it) is to be postmodern. Postmodernity, one may say, is *modernity without illusions* (the obverse of which is that modernity is postmodernity refusing to accept its own truth). The illusions in question boil down to the belief that the 'messiness' of the human world is but a temporary and repairable state, sooner or later to be replaced by the orderly and systematic rule of reason. The truth in question is that the 'messiness' will stay whatever we do or know,

---

[13]   Wolfe, *Whose Keeper?*, p. 220.

that the little orders and 'systems' we carve out in the world are brittle, until-further-notice, and as arbitrary and in the end contingent as their alternatives.

Postmodernity, one may say as well, brings 're-enchantment' of the world after the protracted and earnest, though in the end inconclusive, modern struggle to dis-enchant it (or, more exactly, the resistance to dis-enchantment, hardly ever put to sleep, was all along the 'postmodern thorn' in the body of modernity).[14] The mistrust of human spontaneity, of drives, impulses and inclinations resistant to prediction and rational justification, has been all but replaced by the mistrust of unemotional, calculating reason. Dignity has been returned to emotions; legitimacy to the 'inexplicable', nay *irrational*, sympathies and loyalties which cannot 'explain themselves' in terms of their usefulness and purpose. Functions, manifest or latent, are no more feverishly sought for everything that people do to each other and to themselves. The postmodern world is one in which *mystery* is no more a barely tolerated alien awaiting a deportation order. In that world, things may happen that have no cause which made them necessary; and people do things which would hardly pass the test of an accountable, let alone 'reasonable', purpose. Fear of the void, that (according to Theodore Adorno) most acute of psychological effects of modern Enlightenment, has been blunted and assuaged (though never quelled completely). We learn to live with events and acts that are not only not-yet-explained, but (for all we know about what we will ever know) inexplicable. Some of us would even say that it is such events and acts that constitute the hard, irremovable core of the human predicament. We learn again to respect ambiguity, to feel regard for human emotions, to appreciate actions without purpose and calculable rewards. We accept that not all actions, and particularly not all among the most important of actions, need to justify and explain themselves to be worthy of our esteem.

For a modern mind, such postmodern sentiments spell deadly danger to human cohabitation. Having first defamed and disgraced human acts that have only 'passions' and spontaneous inclinations for their cause, the modern mind is appalled by the prospect of 'deregulation' of human conduct, of living without a strict and comprehensive ethical code, of making a wager on human moral intuition and ability to negotiate the art and the usages of living together – rather than seeking support of the law-like, depersonalized rules aided by coercive powers. A sufficient residue of modern sentiments has been

---

[14]   I have argued this case more extensively in 'Narrating Postmodernity' in Zygmunt Bauman, *Intimations of Postmodernity* (London: Routledge, 1992).

imparted to all of us by training, for each of us sometimes, or to some extent, to share in those fears and anxieties.

Acceptance of contingency and respect for ambiguity do not come easy; there is no point in playing down their psychological costs. And yet the silver lining of this particular cloud is uncommonly thick. The postmodern re-enchantment of the world carries a chance of facing human moral capacity point-blank, as it truly is, undisguised and undeformed; to readmit it to the human world from its modern exile; to restore it to its rights and its dignity; to efface the memory of defamation, the stigma left by modern mistrust. Not that the world will as a consequence become necessarily better and more hospitable. But it will stand a chance of coming to terms with the tough and resilient human proclivities it evidently failed to legislate away – and of starting from there. Perhaps starting from there (rather than declaring that beginning null and void) will even make the hope of a more humane world more *realistic* – and this for the reason of its *modesty*.

To let morality out of the stiff armour of the artificially constructed ethical codes (or abandoning the ambition to keep it there), means to *re-personalize* it. Human passions used to be considered too errant and fickle, and the task to make human cohabitation secure too serious, to entrust the fate of human coexistence to moral capacities of human persons. What we come to understand now is that that fate can be entrusted to little else; or, rather, that that fate may not be taken proper care of (that is, all the care offered or contemplated would prove unrealistic or, worse still, counter-productive) unless the fashion in which we go about caring takes cognizance of personal morality and its stubborn presence. What we are learning, and learning the hard way, is that it is the personal morality that makes ethical negotiation and consensus possible, not the other way round. To be sure, personal morality would not guarantee success of such negotiations. It may even make them harder and add quite a few obstacles to the course: no more will the roads be blazed by bulldozing. Most likely, it would make any agreement that may be reached inconclusive, temporary and short of universal acceptance. Yet we know now that this is precisely where things stand, where we stand, and that we could pretend otherwise only at the peril to our upright posture.

Re-personalizing morality means returning moral responsibility from the finishing line (to which it was exiled) to the starting point (where it is at home) of the ethical process. We realize now – with a mixture of apprehension and hope – that unless moral responsibility was 'from the start', somehow rooted in the very way we humans are

– it would never be conjured up at a later stage by no matter how high-minded or high-handed an effort. We feel instinctive sympathy with reminders, like that penned by P.F. Strawson more than twenty years ago, that the question 'What is the individual's interest in morality?' 'is not answered by mentioning the general interest in the existence of some systems of socially sanctioned demands'[15] (though we are no more sure that the question about *interest in morality* ought to be asked at all; we suspect it to be a kind of fraudulent question which pre-empts its answer). We also come to believe that all socially constructed replacements – like functional or procedural responsibilities – are but effete, untrustworthy, and morally doubtful (even if instrumentally efficient) substitutes. They all blunt, rather than reinforce personal responsibility – morality's last hold and hope. Belatedly we come to appreciate Vladimir Jankélévitch's suggestion that in the same way as the fact of the *cogito* makes total scepticism invalid, the fact of 'moral intimacy' must be seen as 'the ultimate instance', from which 'appeal is impossible, except in the case of bad faith'; 'Nothing replaces this intimate consent of the whole soul – neither the superficial consent that adheres to words, nor a transcendent authority which demands that it, itself, be relieved by conscience to make itself be admitted.'[16]

First to delegitimize or 'bracket away' moral impulses and emotions, and then to try to reconstruct the edifice of ethics out of arguments carefully cleansed of emotional undertones and set free from all bonds with unprocessed human intimacy, is equivalent (to use the memorable metaphor of Harold Garfinkel) to saying that if we only could get the walls out of the way we would better see what supports the ceiling. It is the primal and primary 'brute fact' of moral impulse, moral responsibility, moral intimacy that supplies the stuff from which the morality of human cohabitation is made. After centuries of attempts to prove otherwise, the 'mystery of morality inside me' (Kant) once more appears to us impossible to explain away. As Michael S. Pritchard recently intimated, expressing a widely shared mood,

> We may attempt to step outside ourselves and dispassionately try to support those [ethical] propositions from an external, objective point of view. However, as Strawson observes, no such attempt has yet succeeded,

[15] P.F. Strawson, *Freedom and Resentment and Other Essays* (London: Methuen, 1974), p. 35.
[16] From *Traité des vertus* (1968); quoted after *Contemporary European Ethics: Selected Readings*, ed. Joseph J.Kockelmans (New York: Doubleday, 1972), pp. 45–6.

and with good reason. If external justification requires us imaginatively to strip ourselves of our moral sentiments so that we may view them 'objectively', what resources will we be able to call on to conduct the examination? To do justice to the subject, we must employ our moral sensibilities, including, as they do, our sentiments. There is no neutral ground. If it is to be of any practical use for us, moral philosophy must be an 'inside job', however much one may wish otherwise.[17]

In as far as the modern obsession with purposefulness and utility and the equally obsessive suspicion of all things autotelic (that is, claiming to be their own ends, and not means to something else than themselves) fade away, morality stands the chance of finally coming into its own. It may stop being cajoled or bullied to present its credentials; to justify its right to exist by pointing to the benefit it brings to personal survival, standing or happiness, or the service it renders to collective security, law and order. This is a seminal chance, since – as we will see later – the question 'Why should I be moral?' is the end, not the beginning of moral stance, a stance which (much like Tönnies's *Gemeinschaft*) exists only in the *an sich* state, lasts only as long as it does not know of its presence as moral presence and does not reify itself into an object of scrutiny, nor subjects itself to evaluation in terms of standards not of its own. If the chance is taken, morality will be free to admit (or, rather, have no need to, bashfully, concede) its *non-rationality*; its being its own – both necessary and sufficient – reason. And this will be fine, since no moral impulse can survive, let alone emerge unscathed from, the acid test of usefulness or profit. And since all immorality begins with demanding such a test – from the moral subject, or from the object of its moral impulse, or both.

[17]   Michael S. Pritchard, *On Becoming Responsible* (University Press of Kansas, 1991), p. 10.

2

The Elusive Universality

Half a century or so ago, Robert Musil meditated in *Der Mann ohne Eigenschaften*, that most elaborate, and appropriately unfinished, farewell to the nineteenth century:

> Who can be interested any longer in that age-old idle talk about good and evil when it has been established that good and evil are not 'constants' at all, but 'functional values', so that the goodness of works depends on the historical circumstances, and the goodness of human beings on the psychotechnical skill with which their qualities are exploited?

It is an open question to what extent, and even whether, this 'historicity' of good and evil, which shook the moral preachers to their innermost selves, troubled also ordinary men and women engrossed in their daily pursuits; and whether in the times of indecision, or even in the traumatic moments when they felt lost, they would follow the philosophers in linking their incapacity to act with the fact that other people, in other times and places, drew the line between good and evil differently from them: or whether knowledge of that fact, if they had such knowledge, would trouble them greatly; whether it would add to the anxiety of uncertainty and indecision that haunted them already as they strove to control their own stubbornly unknown future; and whether this would change their ways to a noticeable extent. Not many among us seem to bother to find out just how widely (or, for that matter, how narrowly) our images of good and evil are shared, and for how long the agreement has lasted and would last; for most of us, the belief that what we do is approved by 'people like us' – 'people that count' – is all we need to sleep quietly, and to keep our conscience silent when 'they' – those '*unlike* us' – disapprove.

The intimate link between the obedience to moral rules and holding belief in their universality was in all probability mainly the philosophers' idea and philosophers' worry. One could not and would not postulate such a link unless one had already imputed to the ordinary men and women the pursuit of coherence and congruence that was the professional mark of philosophers; or had projected upon them the concerns characteristic of the powers-that-be, which use to promote their local ambitions under universalistic banners. But philosophers' worry it was indeed, and a serious one at that.

The fact that the images of good and evil do differ from one place to another and one epoch to another, and that there is little one can do about it, has not been a secret, at least since Montaigne. Few among the authors who wrote about it, however, viewed this fact with Montaigne-like resigned, yet serene and unclouded, equanimity. Most viewed it with horror, as a threat and utmost absurdity – a challenge both to the thinker and to the doer. Truth is, by definition, one – it is the errors which are countless; the same must surely apply to moral propriety, if moral precepts are to carry authority more respectable than that of the mere 'this is what *I* want; and want it *now*' foot-stamping and fist-thumping. If the moral rules preached and/or practised here and now are to carry such authority, it must be shown that other rules are not just different, but mistaken or evil: that their acceptance is an outcome of ignorance and immaturity, if not of ill will.

The urge to salvage the integrity of one's own moral vision from the débâcle that must surely come once it has been discovered that the vision is but-one-among-many was, arguably, best met with the idea of progress which dominated modern thinking for the better part of its history. The otherness (all man-made otherness, including the ethical one) was *temporalized* in a way characteristic of the idea of progress: time stood for hierarchy – 'later' being identical with 'better', and 'ill' with the 'outdated', or 'not-yet-properly-developed'. (The trifling thing left then was to assign the disapproved of phenomena to the past as their natural abode; to construe them as relics that outlived their time, and live presently but on borrowed time – and their carriers as in actual fact already dead, zombies that ought to be buried as soon as possible for their own and everybody else's sake.) Such a view fit well both the need to legitimize the conquest and the subordination of different lands and cultures, and that of presenting the growth and spread of knowledge as the principal mechanism not just of change, but of a change to the better

– of *improvement*. In V.G. Kiernan's words, 'colonizing countries did their best to cling to a conviction that they were spreading through the world not merely order, but civilization'.[1] Johannes Fabian dubbed this widespread habit 'chronopolitics': projecting the contemporary differentiation upon the time arrow, so that cultural alternatives may be depicted as 'allochronic' – belonging to a different time, and surviving into the present on false pretences, while being merely relics doomed to extinction.[2]

Universalism and its discontents

The postulate of universality was always a demand with an address; or, somewhat more concretely, a sword with the edge aimed against a selected target. The *postulate* was a reflection on the modern *practice* of *universalization* – in a way similar to that of the related concepts of 'one human nature' or 'human essence', which reflected the *intention* to substitute the *citizen* (the person with only such attributes as have been assigned by the laws of the single and uncontested authority acting on behalf of the unified and sovereign state) for the motley collection of parishioners, kinsmen and other locals. The theoretical postulate squared well with the uniformizing ambitions and practices of the modern state, with the war it declared on *les pouvoirs intermédiaires*, with its cultural crusades against local customs redefined as superstitions and condemned to death for the crime of resisting centralized management. The 'universal man', pared to the bare bones of 'human nature', was to be – in Alasdair MacIntyre's expression[3] – an 'unencumbered self'; not necessarily unaffected by the communally inspired particularisms, yet capable of cutting himself loose from the communal roots and loyalties; of lifting himself, so to speak, onto a higher plane and taking from there a long, detached and critical view of communal demands and pressures.

The requisite of recognizing as moral only such rules as pass the test of some universal, extemporal and exterritorial principles, meant first and foremost the disavowal of the temporal and territorially bound, communal pretences to make moral judgements with

[1] V.G. Kiernan, *The Lords of Human Kind* (London: Cresset Library, 1988), p. 311.
[2] Cf. Johannes Fabian, *Time and the Other: How Anthropology Makes its Object* (New York: Columbia University Press, 1983).
[3] Cf. Alasdair MacIntyre, *After Virtue*, 1981.

authority.[4] The sword used for the purpose, however, was soon found to be what it had been from the start – double-edged. True, it cut deep into the flesh of the named adversaries of the state-disapproved parochialism, but it also hurt where it was not meant to, seriously damaging the state's own sovereignty it was hoped to defend. Indeed, why should the 'unencumbered self' admit the right of the Law of the State, this state here and now, to spell out its essence? Why should it accept the call to confine itself to the state-shaped mould of citizenship?

When taken up seriously (that is, the way it is taken by philosophers, not the practitioners of legislating powers), the postulate of universality not only saps the moral prerogatives of communities now transformed into administrative units of the homogeneous nation-state, but renders the state's bid for supreme moral authority all but unsustainable. The logic of the postulate is dissonant with the practice of *any* self-confined political community; it opposes not just the specific counter-power currently in the dock on the charge of obstructing the movement toward universality, but the very Aristotelian principle of the polity as the ultimate fount and the guardian of humanity. It militates against any theory, like those of Michael Walzer or Michael Oakeshott, contemporary Aristotelians, who conceive of 'moral reasoning as an appeal to meanings internal to a political community, not an appeal to abstract principles',[5] regardless of the level at which the political community in question has been located.

Any *polis* separates, sets apart, 'particularizes' its members from members of other communities, as much as it unites them and makes alike inside its own boundaries. The 'situated' self (in MacIntyre's terms, the opposite of the 'unencumbered' one) is always set against a self *differently* situated – rooted in another *polis*. For this reason, the

---

[4] 'A statement having the verbal form of a moral judgment for which one is unable to give reasons does not express a genuine moral judgment at all' – may be taken as a prototypical expression of such view (from Marcus Singer, *Generalization in Ethics*; quoted after Neil Cooper, 'Two concepts of morality', in *Philosophy* (1966), pp. 19–33). Cooper calls such a concept of morality 'autonomous' or 'independent', as distinct from 'positive' or 'social'; this version of morality is presented for instance in H.L.A. Hart's assertion (in *Legal and Moral Obligations: Essays in Moral Philosophy*) that 'we can only understand the morality of the individual as a development from the primary phenomenon of the morality of a social group'.

[5] Michael J. Sandel, 'Introduction', in *Liberalism and its Critics*, ed. Michael J. Sandel (Oxford: Blackwell, 1984), p. 10.

universalistic demand tends to turn round against the *polis*, which wished to domesticate it and deploy in the war against its own rebels; at its logical limits, this demand cannot but incessantly gestate the opposition against *all* moral dictate, and thus spawn a radically *individualistic* stance. While promoting ostensibly universal, yet by necessity home-grown and home-bound standards, the polity finds itself opposed and resisted in the name of the selfsame principle of universalism which enlightens and/or ennobles its purpose. Promotion of universal standards then looks suspiciously like suppression of human nature and tends to be censured as *intolerance*.

To the defenders of the 'situated' self ('communitarians', as they came to be known) universalistic ambitions and universalizing practices are, of course, an outrage – vehicles of oppression, an act of violence perpetrated upon human freedom. They are, however, unacceptable also to the *bona fide*, earnest and consistent liberal universalists who are wary of any narrower-than-universal powers claiming to be the promoters of allegedly universal standards. As consistent liberals see it, morality may only be rooted in qualities and capacities possessed by individuals *qua* human persons. Ethical codes promoted in the name of groups – be it on the account of 'superior group interests' or of 'supreme group wisdom' – they would view, like Søren Kierkegaard did, as an instance of conspiracy between power-greedy chieftains on the one hand, and the dislike felt by their would-be charges for the burden of moral responsibility on the other:

> Man is by nature one of the animal creation. Therefore all human effort tends toward herding together; 'let us unite', etc. Naturally this happens under all sorts of high-sounding names, love and sympathy and enthusiasm, and the carrying out of some grand plan, and the like; this is the ususal hypocrisy of the scoundrels we are. The truth is that in a herd we are free from the standard of the individual and the ideal.[6]

This is, though, not the only reason for which the weapon of universalism may turn against those who wield it. With the universalism-promoting agencies well short of truly universal sovereignty, the horizon of 'actually existing' (or, rather, realistically intended) universality tends to stop at the state boundaries. Each sovereign authority's universalistic ambitions lead precarious existences among the plurality of sovereign authorities. Consistently universalistic can be only a power bent on identifying the human kind

[6] Søren Kierkegaard, *The Last Years: Journals, 1853–55*, trans. Ronald Gregor Smith (London: Collins, 1968), p. 31. 'No one wants to be a single person, everyone shirks from the strain' (p. 51); but 'as soon as the mass appears, God is invisible . . . God only exists for the single person' (p. 95).

as a whole with the population subjected to its present or prospective rule. Such power is unlikely to emerge in a world organized according to the principle of nation-states, and a world in which none of the nation-states could seriously entertain for long the dream of ecumenical sovereignty. Given this, the cohabitation of sovereign authorities, each with a limited domain circumscribed by its neighbours, needs and breeds solidarity of the sovereigns: an outspoken or tacit recognition of each sovereign's sole dominion within the borders of its rule 'cuius regio, eius religio' style. You tell your subjects what to do, and I shall tell mine. In the same way in which the image of universal moral rules is shaped for domestic use after the pattern of universal law promulgated by the state authorities, the supra-state moral universality is envisaged in the likeness of 'international relations': as the precipitate of diplomacy, bargaining, negotiations, search for genuine or make-believe 'points of agreement'. Whatever is agreed as 'truly universal' in the end, is more in the nature of 'common denominator', rather than 'common roots'. Behind the procedure lurks the assumption that makes it workable: that there is more than one conception of universal morality, and that which one of them prevails is relative to the strength of the powers that claim and hold the right to articulate it.

However powerful these constraints and profound the innate contradictions of the universalistic project, modernity treated all relativity as a nuisance and a challenge – above all, as a temporary irritant, shortly to be cured. However difficult the practising of moral universality proved to be, no practical difficulty was allowed to cast doubt on universality as an ideal and the horizon of history. Relativism was always merely 'current'; its persistence in spite of present efforts tended to be played down as merely a momentary hitch in an otherwise unstoppable movement toward the ideal. The dream of universality as the *ultimate destination of human kind*, and the determination to bring it forth, took refuge in the *processual* concept of *universalization*. There it was secure – as long as it could be reasonably believed that the process of universalization does take place, that the 'march of time' might be credibly viewed as unstoppable, and that it will lead to the progressive trimming down, and eventually to the smothering, of present differences. The trust in the wondrous healing skills of time – and especially its not-yet part, a part one could freely fantasize about and assign magical powers without fear of empirical test – was, after all, a most conspicuous feature of the modern mind. Diderot called modern man 'postéromane' – in love with posterity; and, as Alain Finkielkraut recently put it,

Modern man counted on the competence of the future to correct the injustices of the present. He envisaged humanity as a whole as a movement of qualities which would defy humans taken separately. He vested with the time that will arrive the confidence he had in Eternity . . . Modern man marches toward posterity.[7]

It is that belief, so characteristic of modern mentality, which has been undermined and cast out of fashion at the postmodern stage (together with the powers whose ambitions kept it alive). The postmodern version of the historiosophy of universalization is the perspective of 'globalization' – the vision of a global spread of information, technology and economic interdependency that conspicuously does not include the ecumenization of political, cultural and moral authorities (factors supposed to 'globalize' are seen as *non*-national, rather than *inter*- or *supra*-national). If anything, the new historiosophy renders the prospects of moral universality achieved by the spread of the 'civilizing process' distant and dim.

Deprived now of its past grounding in the 'civilizing mission' of the 'culturally advanced' or 'most developed' nation-states, the idea of universal morality, if it is to survive at all, may only fall back on the innate, pre-social moral impulses common to humankind (as opposed to those resulting from social processing; the end-products and sediments of the legislating/ordering/educating action), or on equally common elementary structures of human-being-in-the-world, similarly antedating all societal interference (see the next chapter). The alternative would be to concede the battlefield to the perpetual adversaries of universalism's preachers, the *communitarians*. The moment one accepts the likelihood that the plurality of cultural/moral sovereignties (as distinct from political/economic ones) will persist for an indefinite time, perhaps forever – one finds the retreat from the cold and abstract territory of universal moral values into the cosy and homely shelter of 'native community' exceedingly tempting; many would find the seduction irresistible. Hence the 'community first' vision of the human world, which for the better part of modern times was exiled to the seldom visited periphery of philosophical and political reflection, disdainfully rejected as 'conservative', 'nostalgic', or 'romantic' and consigned to oblivion by the dominant thought which proudly described itself as 'marching with time', scientific and 'progressive' – is now back with a vengeance; indeed, it comes quite close to being elevated to the canon and uncontested 'good sense' of human sciences.

---

[7] Alain Finkielkraut, *Le Mécontemporain: Péguy, lecteur du monde moderne* (Paris: Gallimard, 1991), p. 13. Finkielkraut quotes Claude Simon's words:

The re-rooting of the uprooted self

The trouble with the visions of born-again communitarians is that, much as the guards of universalism who refused to confine their vigilance to the checkpoints erected along the nation-state frontiers, the 'situated' selves refuse to be confined to the role of border guards of 'genuine communities' alone (that is, communities as imagined by the theorists). Frontiers of communities are notoriously more difficult to draw in an unambiguous fashion than are the borders of states; this is not, however, the main worry. If the identity of a community is to be defined by the grip in which it holds the selves it 'situates', and hence by the extent of the moral consensus it is capable of generating in them, then the very idea of community borders (especially the watertight, policed and impermeable borders experimented with by nation-states; but also borders in the somewhat softer sense of a jagged line circumscribing a comparatively uniform, culturally/morally homogeneous population) becomes ever so difficult, nay impossible, to uphold.

There is no *communal* authority with a power of legal adjudication comparable to that of the *state*-bound or *state*-endorsed agencies. In the absence of such an authority, a community truly able to 'situate' its members with any degree of lasting consequence appears to be more a methodological postulate than a fact of life. Whenever one descends from the relatively secure realm of concepts to the description of any concrete object the concepts are supposed to stand for – one finds merely a fluid collection of men and women acting at cross-purposes, fraught with inner controversy and conspicuously short of the means to arbitrate between conflicting ethical propositions. The moral community proves to be not so much *imagined* as *postulated*, and postulated *contentiously*. It is always the matter of one postulate set against other postulates; a *programme*, a bid to bind the future, rather than to defend or vindicate the past; above all, a bid to bind a certain number of men and women and subordinate their actions to certain choices made preferable by the effort to make the postulated existence of community real. What is described as 'moral' in the moral community are the desired effects of such subordination – the limiting and streamlining of individual choices obtained through the demand to co-operate in making the group real, disguised as a demand to keep the group alive (the demand often

---

'In the last account, in the same way in which one said once 'God will know His own', I believe we can suggest without much error that, sooner or later, in one way or another, History (or the human species) will know its own.'

expressed bluntly, and duplicitously, as the need to sacrifice individual, selfish interests for the – always putative – interest of all).

The current retreat of the state from *moral* legislation (or, rather, the abandoning of early modern ambitions to make such legislation ubiquitous and comprehensive) leaves the territory free for communal husbandry. Increasingly, the states recognize the rights of categories smaller than the nation (ethnic, territorial, religious, gender, sexual-policy based) to moral specificity and self-determination – or, rather, allow such a self-determination to happen by default more than by design. The void is filled now by competing pressures, each demanding the right to interpret the rules which derive from 'situatedness' of such selves as – so they claim – are the 'natural' domain of their ethical supervision. 'Human rights', which on the one hand are the effect of the state's abdication of certain prerogatives of its legislating powers and its past ambition of pervasive, pernickety regulation of individual life – of the state reconciling itself to the permanence of diversity within its realm – become on the other hand a war-cry and blackmail weapon in the hands of aspiring 'community leaders' wishing to pick up the powers the state has dropped. On the one hand, there is the expression of the individualization of difference, of new moral autonomy; on the other, there are disguised yet determined attempts to collectivize the difference anew and devise a new heteronomy – though both on a level different from before.

Confronted in the past with the condensed power of legal/moral 'universality' defined and enforced by the nation-state, individuals are now exposed to a cacophony of social pressures and/or instances of quasi-ethical blackmail, each aiming to expropriate the individual's right to moral choice. None of the contradictory pressures, however, appeals to a situation as comprehensive as the one of the citizen, of the state subject, used to be. Normally, the complex 'human targets' are reduced to just one facet picked up as the rock on which the postulated community is to be built; just one aspect of the multi-faceted identity of the individual is addressed. This one aspect is, however, proclaimed to be pivotal, to determine the individual's situation as a whole, to be destined to dwarf and outweigh all other aspects – thus exonerating the individual beforehand from all future disobedience to the pressures that may quote them. What is demanded is a kind of loyalty that should marginalize or render null and void the competitive demands of obedience, anchored in other aspects of the multi-faceted identity. The self needs to be first lopped and trimmed, dissected, and then reassembled, in order to become truly 'situated'. The theory of the situated self, and an ideology serving the community-construction which that theory reflects and assists, reverses the true logic of the process. Far from being a 'natural given', 'situatedness' is socially, and *controversially*, produced; it is always an outcome of competitive struggle, and – more often than not – of individual choice.

The state-legislated morality and the diffuse moral pressures of the self-appointed spokesmen of postulated communities are unanimous on one point: they both deny or at least curtail the individual moral discretion.

Both strive to substitute heteronomous ethical duty for autonomous moral responsibility. Both intend to expropriate the individual from moral choice; or at least from exercising free choice in such areas of life as are considered relevant to the 'common weal': in case of conflict, they want the individuals to opt for the action that promotes the common cause – over and above all other considerations ('The interest of all ought to prevail over interests of each'). Both are wary of individual initiative. Both bear ill the attachments and loyalties that individuals spin on their own, in the process of spontaneous, uncontrived and non-policed intercourse. Both view with suspicion, as a fertile soil for resistance and sedition, the web of interpersonal bonds – and wait for the occasion to tear it apart.

For reasons referred to before, the enmity towards 'spontaneous' and autonomous, individually begotten morality is, in the case of postulated communities, much more vigilant, intense and pugnacious than in the case of a well-entrenched, secure and self-confident state. Militant intolerance stems from insecurity, which in the case of the postulated communities is endemic and incurable. Postulated communities are insecure *because* they are but postulated; yet they lack confidence even more for the reason of remaining postulated *in perpetuity*, whatever they do to solidify their present and insure their future; as Cornelius Castoriadis put it, 'in the deepest recesses of one's egocentric fortress a voice softly but tirelessly repeats "our walls are made of plastic, our acropolis of papier-mâché"'.[8] Having no other ground except the submissiveness of the converted, the presence of communities must be renewed daily. There is no time to rest; even a momentary lapse of vigilance may result in irreversible dissipation. And so, expectedly, there are no limits to cruelty and oppression which may be committed on the road leading from the determined postulation to precarious existence. The most ruthless and murderous suppression of individual autonomy

[8] Cornelius Castoriadis. 'Reflections on Racism', trans. David Ames Curtis, *Thesis Eleven*, vol. 32 (1992), p. 9.

happens to be perpetrated today in the name of 'human rights', expropriated and collectivized as 'rights of a minority' (but always a minority desiring to be the majority, or at least desiring the right to behave like one). The refusal to accept the enforced interpretation of 'situatedness' is condemned as the act of subversion and treason; let the traitors expect no mercy.

In the same way as the clarion call of 'unencumbered' self served all too often to silence the protest against the suppression of moral autonomy by the unitary nation-state, the image of 'situated' self tends to cover up the 'communitarian' practices of similar suppression. Neither of the two is immune to misuse; neither is properly protected against being harnessed to the promotion of moral heteronomy and the expropriation of the individual's right to moral judgement.

The moral limits of ethical universality

What makes both concepts eminently usable for the promotion of ethical heteronomy is the fact that what any vision of group-universal morality tacitly assumes (whether the group in question is co-terminous with the human species as a whole, or a nation-state, or a postulated community), is that moral conduct may indeed be expressed in rules which can be given universal form. That is, that moral selves may be dissolved in the all-embracing 'we' – the moral 'I' being just a singular form of the ethical 'us'. And that within this ethical 'we', 'I' is exchangeable with 's/he'; whatever is moral when stated in the first person remains moral when stated in the second or third. As a matter of fact, only such rules as withstand this 'depersonalization' are seen as meeting the conditions set for *ethical* norms. That morality can be only *collective* in one way or another – as an outcome of either the authoritative legislation or of the allegedly non-deliberate, yet equally powerful *a priori* communal 'situating' – is hence tautologically 'evident'. Its truth has been guaranteed in advance by the way moral phenomena have been defined and singled out.

And yet the premises can survive only as long as they remain tacit, and thus uncontrolled. At a closer look, they do not appear either immediately obvious or even safe to accept.

Take the first premise – that when considering moral phenomena, we are free to follow the grammatical injunction to treat the 'we' as the plural form of 'I'. This is, however, a travesty of morality – objects Emmanuel Lévinas. He explains:

To show respect cannot mean to subject oneself; yet the other does command me. I am commanded, that is recognized as someone capable of realizing a work. To show respect is to bow down not before the law, but before a being who commands a work from me. But for this command to not involve humiliation – which would take from me the very possibility of showing respect – the command I receive must also be a command to command him who commands me. It consists in commanding a being to command me. This reference from a command to command is the fact of saying 'we', of constituting a party. By reason of this reference of one command to another, 'we' is not the plural of 'I' (Nous n'est pas le pluriel de Je).[9]

There would be a smooth way leading from many 'I's to the collective 'we' only if one could posit all 'I's as by and large identical, at least in respect of an attribute which assigns the units as members of one set (like 'we, the blond-haired', or 'we, the graduates of X University', or 'we, the supporters of Leeds United') – and therefore, again in this respect, exchangeable; 'we' becomes a plural of 'I' only at the cost of glossing over I's multi-dimensionality. 'We' is then a sum, a result of counting – an aggregate of ciphers, not an organic whole. This is not, however, the case of the 'moral party'. If the idea of supra-individual totality may at all apply to the world of morality, it may only refer to a whole knit together, and continuously knit together, out of the commands that are given and received and followed by the selves which are moral subjects precisely *because each one of them is irreplaceable*, and because their relations are *asymmetrical*.

Attitude *before* the relations; one-sidedness, *not* reciprocity; a relation that cannot be reversed: these are the indispensable, defining traits of a moral stance. 'In the relation to the Face, what is affirmed is asymmetry; in the beginning, it does not matter who the Other is in relation to me – that is his business.'[10] This sentence of Lévinas can be read as a definition of the Face: Face is encountered if, and only if, my relation to the Other is *programmatically* non-symmetrical; that is, not dependent on the Other's past, present, anticipated or hoped-for *reciprocation*. And morality is the encounter with the Other as Face. Moral stance begets an essentially *unequal* relationship; this inequality, non-equity, this not-asking-for-reciprocation, this disinterest in mutuality, this indifference to the 'balancing up' of gains or rewards – in short, this organically 'unbalanced' and hence non-

[9] 'The Ego and the Totality' ('Le Moi et la Totalité'), in Emmanuel Lévinas, *Collected Philosophical Papers*, trans. Alphonso Lingis (The Hague: Martinus Nijhoff, 1987), p. 43. (*Entre nous: Essais sur le penser-à-l'autre* (Paris: Grasset, 1991), p. 49.)

[10] Emmanuel Lévinas, 'Philosophie, Justice et Amour', in *Entre nous*, pp. 122–3.

reversible character of 'I versus the Other' relationship is what makes the encounter a moral event.

Lévinas draws a most radical conclusion from Kant's solution to the mysteries of 'moral law inside me', but only such radicalism may give justice to Kant's conception of morality as a posture guided solely by the concern for the Other *for the Other's sake*, and the respect for the Other as a free subject and the 'end in itself'. Other, milder versions of post-Kantian ethical theory can hardly match the enormity of the moral demand which Kant's conception entails. For Martin Buber, for instance, what sets the I-Thou relationship apart from the I-it (one in which the Other does not appear as a moral subject) is from the start the *dialogical* character of the encounter, or the anticipation of a dialogue; I-Thou has an 'address and response' structure,[11] a structure of ongoing conversation, in the course of which the partners incessantly exchange the roles, address each other and respond to each other in kind. It is the symmetry of attitudes and responsibilities that gives the relation its I-Thou character, being present in it from the start, as a postulate or categorical expectation; if I treat you as Thou rather than It, it is precisely because I stipulate (expect, work towards) being also treated by you as your Thou.[12] Heidegger's *Mitsein* similarly carries the assumption of symmetry from the start. I am with the Other in as far as 'we' – I and the Other – 'are in it together'. Since it is merely the commonality of ontological predicament that 'unites' us, no wonder critics charged Heidegger with the non-substantiality of any ethics that may be derived from such impoverished, content-less togetherness, a togetherness *before* morality, togetherness that does not already entail moral engagement and commitment; and with an irreparable ethical neutrality (and neutrality, morally speaking, is indistinguishable from indifference) that inevitably follows the grounding of togetherness in *Mitsein*. '*Miteinandersein*', Lévinas comments caustically,

> being-with-another, is but a moment of our presence in the world. It does not occupy central place. *Mit* means to be aside of . . . it is not to confront the Face, it is *zusammensein*, perhaps *zusammenmarschieren*.[13]

---

[11] Cf. Maurice Friedman, *Martin Buber's Life and Work: The Early Years, 1878–1923* (London: Search Press, 1982), pp. 314–15.

[12] Comp. Emmanuel Lévinas, 'Philosophie, Justice et Amour', p. 122.

[13] Emmanuel Lévinas, 'Philosophie, Justice et Amour', p. 135. Note the striking affinity between Heidegger's vision of *Miteinandersein* and Kafka's recurrent theme of wondrously yet mysteriously co-ordinated pairs, visible yet incomprehensible – a theme to which he obsessively returns in countless forms: the two assistants of K., Blumfeld's two helpers, two hopping but

'Being with' is symmetrical. What is blatantly non-symmetrical, what makes the partners un-equal, what *privileges* my position by emancipating it from its dependence on whatever stance the Other may take, is *being for* – 'être-pour-l'autre', the mode of being that precludes not only the solitude (which *Mitsein* has also ruled out) but also indifference. (Solitude and indifference, Lévinas remarks, are deficient forms of being-for-other, and so they obliquely confirm it, much as sloth and unemployment, being deficient forms of an existence based on work, confirm the significance of labour.)[14] I am for the Other whether the Other is for me or not; his being for me is, so to speak, his problem, and whether or how he 'handles' that problem does not in the least affect my being-for-Him (as far as my being-for-the-Other includes respect for the Other's autonomy, which in its turn includes my consent not to blackmail the Other into being-for-me, nor interfere in any other way with the Other's freedom). Whatever else 'I-for-you' may contain, it does not contain a demand to be repaid, mirrored or 'balanced out' in the 'you-for-me'. My relation to the Other is not reversible; if it happens to be reciprocated, the reciprocation is but an accident from the point of view of my being-for.

The 'we' that stands for a 'moral party' is not, therefore, a plural of 'I' – but a term which connotes a complex structure that ties together units of sharply unequal standing. In a moral relationship, I and the Other are not exchangeable, and thus cannot be 'added up' to form a plural 'we'. In a moral relationship, all the 'duties' and 'rules' that may be conceived are addressed solely to me, bind only me, constitute me and me alone as an 'I'. When addressed to me, responsibility is moral. It may well lose its moral content completely the moment I try to turn it around to bind the Other. As Alasdair MacIntyre pithily expressed it, 'The man might on moral grounds refuse to legislate for anyone else than himself':[15]

---

numb girls, and finally – as if the *summa* of the series – two celluloid balls of tightly synchronized movements . . . What all those pairs have in common is that they are seen *from outside* as apparently moving in unison, but do not audibly account for their movements; the correlation between movements is all what a *detached* observer, an *uninvolved* observer and an *uncommitted* one, can find out about them. Blumfeld's helpers speak to each other only when watched by Blumfeld from the other side of the window-pane which stifles all sound . . .

14   Emmanuel Lévinas, 'Mourir pour . . .', in *Entre nous*, p. 225.
15   Cf. Alasdair MacIntyre, 'What Morality is Not', in *Philosophy* (1957), pp. 325–35. Lévinas, to be sure, goes further than that, promoting such a refusal to the defining feature of the 'moral grounds'.

A moral hero, such as Captain Oates, is one who does more than duty demands. In the universalizable sense of 'ought' it does not therefore make sense to assert that Captain Oates did what he ought to have done. To say of a man that he did his duty in performing a work of supererogation is to contradict oneself. Yet a man may set himself the task of performing a work of supererogation and commit himself to it so that he will blame himself if he fails without finding such failure in the case of others blameworthy.

Because it insists on the universality of moral rules which it is meant to support (and hence on mutual exchangeability of moral subjects), Kant's categorical imperative may make certain conduct a moral duty – if it is interpreted as setting out the *sufficient* condition for moral behaviour; but if treated as the description of the *necessary* condition for moral command, it also absolves conscience for failing to follow many a crucial moral impulse. The moral person and the object of that person's moral concern cannot be measured by the same yardstick – and this realization is precisely what makes the moral person moral.

'I am ready to die for the Other' is a moral statement; 'He should be ready to die for me' is, blatantly, not. Neither is a command that *the others* should sacrifice their lives for the homeland, the party, or any other cause, however worthy – though my own readiness to give up *my own* survival, so that some idea would not die without issue, could make me a moral hero. The readiness to sacrifice for the sake of the other burdens me with the responsibility which is *moral* precisely for my acceptance that the command to sacrifice applies to me and me only, that the sacrifice is not a matter of exchange or reciprocation of services, that the command is *not universalizable* and thus cannot be shrugged off my shoulders so that it falls on someone else's. Being a moral person means that I *am* my brother's keeper. But this also means that *I* am my brother's keeper whether or not my brother sees his own brotherly duties the same way I do; and that I am my brother's keeper whatever other brothers, real or putative, do or may do. At least, I can be properly his keeper only if I act *as if* I was the only one *obliged*, or even likely, to act this way. I am always the one who carries that straw which will break the back of the camel of moral indifference. It is this uniqueness (not 'generalizability'!), and this non-reversibility of my responsibility, which puts me in the moral relationship. This is what counts, whether or not all brothers of the world would do for their own brothers what I am about to do.

Were I to look for standards by which my moral responsibility ought to be measured to match my moral impulse, I *would not* find them in the rules which I may reasonably demand others to follow.

'The I always has one responsibility *more* than all the others';[16] only on this assumption is a '*moral* party', as distinct from contractual partnership, thinkable and realizable. My responsibility is always a step ahead, always greater than that of the Other. I am denied the comfort of the already-existing norms and already-followed rules to guide me, to reassure me that I have reached the limit of my duty and so spare me that anxiety which I would account for as 'guilty conscience'. If my responsibility can be at all expressed as a rule, it will be (like in the famous Kafka parable of the door to the Palace of Justice through which no one ever entered, as it had been kept open but for a single penitent and was bound to be closed the moment he died) just a *singular* rule, a rule which for all I know and care has been spelled out for me only and which I heard even if the ears of others remained blocked. 'Appel de la sainteté précédant le souci d'exister'; 'Souci comme sainteté, ce que Pascal appelait amour sans concupiscence'; 'Le moi de celui qui est élu à répondre du prochain . . . Unicité de l'élection!';[17] I have been chosen by this responsibility which I bear alone – and thus my standards cannot be ordinary, statistically average, or commonly shared. The saints are *unique* people, people who do things other people shirk – being too afraid, or too weak, or too selfish to do them – and things which one would not in good conscience demand that they do, since doing them goes beyond and above 'sheer decency' or 'the call of duty'. Such things can the saints demand to be done only by themselves, and demanding those things to be done by themselves while *not* demanding them to be done by others is what makes them the saints they are. The standard by which I (I only) may measure my (mine only) action or responsibility is the standard of saintliness: a standard only I can set for myself and cannot brandish in front of other people as the measure of their morality. What Lévinas means by 'standard of saintliness' is a standard over and above the shared, universal, conventional or statistically average measure of moral decency. A standard – so be it – of the impossible, of the unattainable; a utopia which may only leave any actual accomplishment lagging pitiably behind, forever woefully non-satisfactory.

No uniformity either at the far end of the care taken, responsibility exercised – not even at the end as *imagined* the moment responsibility is entertained. Responsibility does not have 'purpose' or 'reason' (it is

[16]   Emmanuel Lévinas, *Ethics and Infinity: Conversations with Philippe Nemo*, trans. Richard A. Cohen (Pittsburgh: Duquesne University Press, 1985), p. 99.
[17]   Lévinas, 'Mourir pour . . .', pp. 228–9.

not an effect of 'will' or 'decision'; not something that can be, at will, assumed or not, and non-existent if not assumed; it is rather the *impossibility* of not being responsible for this Other here and now that constitutes my moral capacity). But converting the object of responsibility to my standard, taking him or her into my possession, putting under my command, making identical with myself in this or any other respect, and thus stripping him or her of *their* responsibility, which constitutes *their* alterity, their *uniqueness* – is most certainly not the outcome my responsibility may pursue or contemplate without denying itself, without ceasing to be a moral stance. Our 'moral party' is not one of fusion, of identity, of joint submission to a 'third term' (that is, to neither I nor Thou, but certain impersonal principles which everyone must needs obey), of dissolving my saintliness and your alterity in a common standard that obliterates the individuality of us both (and that includes the standard of reciprocity, of equal treatment, of balanced exchange). Moral collectivity is 'le face-à-face sans intermédiaire', not the one which post-Platonian ethical philosophers sought: not a communion in which moral subjects sink and submerge in a collective representation of a shared ideal, a 'we' 'qui, tournée vers le soleil intelligible, vers la vérité, sent l'autre à côté de soi, et non pas en face de soi'.[18]

The solitude of the moral subject

No universal standards, then. No looking over one's shoulders, to take a glimpse of what other people 'like me' do. No listening to what they say they do or ought to be doing – and then following their example, absolving myself for not doing anything else, nothing that others would not do, and enjoying a clear conscience at the end of the day. We do look and listen, but it does not help – at least does not help *radically*. Pointing my finger away from myself – 'this is what people do, this is how things are' – does not save me from sleepless nights and days full of self-depreciation. 'I have done my duty' may perhaps get the judges off my back, but won't disband the jury of what I, for not being able to point my finger at anybody, call 'conscience'. '*The duty of us all*' which I *know*, does not seem to be the same thing as *my responsibility* which I *feel*.[19] I would earnestly wish to

[18]   Emmanuel Lévinas, *Le temps et l'autre* (Presses Universitaires de France, 1979), pp. 88–9.
[19]   The condition of *not* being haunted by scruples is quite easy to obtain, to be sure. In fact, we all obtain it, and find ourselves in it, most of the time. But 'most of the time' we move outside the realm of moral action into the

get rid of that gnawing worm of self-distaste which some of us call guilt, some others call sin. I am told by some well-wishers that I may never again feel *wrong* if I learn how to be always *correct*. I am told by some others that though no safeguards are truly reliable, I can still repent and thus make the past record clean again.[20] Yet however desperately I cling to the hope such counsels proffer, this hope will hardly emerge unscathed from the next, yet untried, test.

Only rules can be universal. One may legislate universal rule-dictated *duties*, but moral *responsibility* exists solely in interpellating the individual and being carried individually. Duties tend to make humans alike; responsibility is what makes them into individuals. Humanity is not captured in common denominators – it sinks and vanishes there. The morality of the moral subject does not, therefore, have the character of a rule. One may say that the moral is what *resists* codification, formalization, socialization, universalization. The moral is what remains when the job of ethics, the job of *Gleichschaltung*, has been done.

There are several attributes which morality should have possessed in order to be universalizable – but which it does not have.

First, a *purpose*. Having a purpose divides the deeds into the expedient and the useless. Purpose supplies the measure and criterion of choice. It makes deeds into alternatives and permits one to compare them, to state a preference and to act on it. Purpose allows one to improve on expediency; it prompts the thinking person to opt for more expedient actions and fight the temptation to engage in less expedient ones. Many desirable states have suggested themselves or have been suggested as 'purposes of morality'.

Insurance against future risks, for instance: I ought not hesitate to

---

area where conventions and etiquette, going through the codified and thus easily learnable and readable motions, as well as the simple rule of respecting the other's privacy and making respect visible through turning one's eyes the other way and not looking the other in the face, will do. The rest of the time, though, we are in morally charged situations, and that means being on our own. True, these are *liminal* situations, and yet they are the soil in which moral subjects germinate, grow, blossom and fade – like the existential *extrema* of death, love and parenthood, and all the countless situations on which they cast their gigantic and dense shadow.

[20] It is tempting to suggest that it was all along this ineradicable and unquenchable experience of 'not having done enough', of the existential impossibility of unclouded self-satisfaction, of the insatiable demands of responsibility, that supplied the ore from which was cast first the image of 'original sin', and later that of 'birth trauma' or other equally stubborn 'psychological complexes' of early, far-away, unreachable childhood.

jump into the river to rescue a drowning stranger – 'Suppose that one day I myself will need to be rescued'. 'Cheats – those who take help but refuse to give it – never prosper, for their cheating is noticed and punished.' The logic of evolution, the form which evolution gave to survival, can vouch for it: 'if there are advantages in being a partner in a reciprocal exchange, and if one is more likely to be selected as a partner if one has genuine concern for others, there is an evolutionary advantage in having genuine concern for others'.[21] Or, just a shade more bluntly: 'It is generally believed, for good reason, that the practice of morality is in the interest of business, and this is one justifiable motive for acting in accordance with morality.'[22] Passing on genes for the sociobiologists, leading the firm from strength to strength for the tutors of businessmen, or just personal survival for all the rest, is the purpose of a moral stance: it *pays* to have concern for others, since it is reasonable to suppose that the others will appreciate, offer credit of confidence and trust, and eventually repay in kind, perhaps with interest added. Somewhere deep down is the once obsessively brandished (by religions), now shyly eclipsed (by the scientific spirit) promise: the good are rewarded (in that other, or in this, world), the bad are punished (with hell, or survival problems). Being moral means investing in the future, and especially saving for the rainy day. It means binding the unbound, controlling the uncontrollable, making the unknown habitable – perhaps even hospitable.

Or the survival of 'something greater', more awe-inspiring, more worthy than myself – my kin, my nation, my Church, my Party, and the ideas they stand for, guard, and make immortal, immortalizing themselves in the bargain. United we stand, 'we' need to stick together, care and succour each other, help each other in the hour of need, behave like brothers do or should, so that we have a better chance of survival than 'them', our enemies or competitors. Helping each other may require a sacrifice, and making sacrifice is what

---

[21]   Peter Singer, *The Expanding Circle: Ethics and Sociobiology* (New York: Farrar, Straus & Giroux, 1981), pp. 17, 44.

[22]   Tom L. Beauchamp and Norman E. Bowie, *Ethical Theory and Business* (Englewood Cliffs: Prentice Hall, 1988), p. 5. Yet considerations of expediency stay in mind throughout; as Thomas M. Garvett and Richard J. Klonowski (*Business Ethics* (Englewood Cliffs: Prentice Hall, 1986), p. 13) inform their readers: 'often, to be sure, we are in a position where we cannot prevent evil or can prevent it only at a disproportionate price. In such situation, we may be excused temporarily.' Morality, like anything else in business, is ultimately the matter of costs and gains.

morality is about. It does not matter whether I benefit from my sacrifice now or in the future, in or after life. What does matter is that I have made my contribution to the continuance of that group by whose success the good and the right is measured. Calculation of expediency, in this case, has been *made for me* by someone in authority. Effectiveness of my action is not a bet, morality not a gamble – I have been assured that I have done my bit and that I am right having done it. This assurance is the bait which the spokesmen for the 'something greater' use keenly and to great effect. Given the torments of moral uncertainty, guarantees of righteousness are temptations difficult to resist.

What both suggestions imply is that morality is a rational stance to take, since it has a purpose; and that this purpose is self-preservation: survival or immortality, on the individual or collective level. Morality 'makes sense'. Morality is 'in order to'. Moral acts are *means to an end*. It is the end that counts. Morality is the handmaiden of existence, briefed by the reason that monitors it. Morality is what a reasonable being, being reasonable and a being, would choose. A moral stand is what a calculating person would prefer each time s/he has done the accounts right. Calculation *precedes* morality . . . Or does it? Must morality justify itself in terms of something other than itself? Does it not cease to be morality once it feels the need, or is forced to, apologize for what it has prompted? On the other hand, are deeds suggested by the calculation of survival necessarily moral? And is the deed not moral just for the fact of having no survival value?

Thus reciprocity is the vital attribute morality does not possess – but should possess if one wished it to be universalizable. The duty of one partner is not the other partner's right; neither does the duty of one partner demand an equivalent duty on the side of the other. A stance does not wait to become moral until it has been reciprocated and thus turned into an ingredient of dual or multiple *relationship*. Nor is it the expectation, however vague, of being reciprocated that makes it moral. The contrary, rather, is the case: it is equanimity with which the subject views the question of repayment, reward, or equal standard that renders him or her, for as long as such equanimity lasts, a moral subject.

Reciprocity may be immediate or delayed; specific or generalized. Reciprocity of a *business transaction*, for instance, is both immediate and specific. The exchange of services must occur either simul-taneously or be completed on a clearly stated date, and the services exchanged must be seen by both sides as by and large balancing each other out within this transaction here and now. A business trans-action is a self-enclosed episode; calculation of its propriety is neither affected by past transactions nor does it temper or otherwise prejudice future ones. Each business transaction starts, so to speak, in a void, and ends there. It is difficult to confuse business transactions with moral relationships; at the utmost, one can say (as Durkheim did when he insisted on 'noncontractual conditions of contract') that without trusting the partner's readiness to keep his word and to act on his promises – often represented as the sign of moral rectitude – no business transaction would be possible. Even this oblique connection between transaction and morality is, however, questionable, as pernickety legal regulations and threats of stern penalties envelop the conduct of the partners to the extent of making their moral postures all but invisible and above all irrelevant, while making the breach of promise a 'bad business' in a quite tangible, calculable sense.

There are, however, other kinds of reciprocity – non-immediate, non-specific, or neither immediate nor specific. *Gift-giving*, for instance, is quite often a form of non-immediate reciprocity: reward is neither discussed nor consciously calculated at the moment the offering is made – in the long run, however, one expects gifts to be reciprocated, and in quantities judged to be needed to maintain parity. The readiness of gift-giving is not likely to survive indefinitely unless this expectation comes true. Unlike the case of the business transaction, profit is not the motive of the gift; more often than not it is benevolence that triggers the action. More importantly yet, gift-giving is not an episodic, not a self-contained act. On the contrary, it makes sense – as Claude Lévi-Strauss has shown[23] elaborating on Marcel Mauss's idea of *le don* – when seen as a tool of establishing stable and peaceful relationship between otherwise mutually isolated and/or hostile persons or groups. But similarly to business transactions, 'fairness' and 'equity' are the measures of propriety and success (whatever that may mean) of gift-giving. As in the former case, reciprocity is assumed in gift-giving from the start; accordingly, if a moral consideration is involved at all, it is focused on the recipient, not the giver. It is the recipient whom the gift-giving renders the bearer of a 'moral duty': namely, the duty to reciprocate (this time, indeed, undoubtedly, moral – in the sense of 'merely moral'; that is, not ordained, sustained, or deputized for, by legal rules and legally prescribed sanctions). Whatever moral obligation appears in this context, arises at the far end of the gift-giving act, as its consequence, not the beginning.

[23] Cf. *Les Structures élémentaires de la parenté* (1955); English (revised) edition under the title *Elementary Structures of Kinship*, trans. James Harle Bell and John Richard von Sturmer (Boston: Beacon Press, 1969).

And there is as well a kind of reciprocity which is neither immediate nor specific; a *generalized* reciprocity, with no time limit attached; of a kind which we mentioned briefly before, when pondering the idea that 'it pays' to be good to others since others are more likely to be good to those who earned the opinion of being good to others . . . Kindness will be, eventually, repaid by someone, hopefully in excess, and not necessarily by those persons to whom the kindness was done, nor necessarily in the same form or context. Generalized reciprocity is not as easy to monitor for 'equity' as gift-giving. For this reason it may in principle go on for a long time even if returns have not matched the outlay. (In practice, it is rather the other way round: generalized reciprocity evades close monitoring on both sides, and so makes fraud and pretence into 'rational', and always tempting, propositions. This weakness of generalized reciprocity is a standing invitation to legal interference and the main reason for which 'mere moral decency' is seldom relied upon as a solid foundation of any collective endeavour, and certainly not trusted as a building material for a stable structure of society.)

Whatever is the case, however, expectation of reciprocity (even if a delayed one, and of a diffuse kind) is firmly locked on the side of the motives, and as long as this is the case the action it prompts stems from other roots than moral impulse; the circumstance not easy to detect and recognize, since the conduct inspired by considerations of generalized reciprocity may look, for an outside observer, strikingly similar to disinterested generosity.

Neither can morality be described as *contractual* (another absence which makes it non-universalizable), and for quite similar reasons. The gist of the contract is that the duties of the partners have been negotiated, defined and agreed *before* any action is undertaken. What the partners are expected to do, what they may be called to do, what they may be reprimanded for not doing – is all spelled out and circumscribed in advance. It is required of both partners – no less, but no more either – that they fulfil their respective 'contractual obligations'. Attention of both partners is to be focused on *the task at hand* – the delivery of a certain commodity, the performing of a certain job, the exchange of a certain service for a certain sum of money – not on *each other*. Their interest in each other neither needs, nor is encouraged to reach beyond the performance of the contractually agreed task. For all they care and are supposed to care, each is but an agent or a carrier or an operator of the services or commodities delivered. There is nothing 'personal' about either of them. Partners are not persons, not individuals. Their obligations could be performed by others, if need be; if it is I who does it, it is merely because

I signed the contract. I am no more than a legal construct, patched together from the paragraphs of the agreement. In their impersonal, contractual capacity, partners need not be, and usually are not, interested in each other's welfare; none is called to care for the interest of the partner in contract. Contracts are entered in order to safeguard or enhance one's own well-being. The entering has an explicit purpose; and that purpose is plainly selfish.

What more than anything else sets the contractually defined behaviour apart from a moral one, is the fact that the 'duty to fulfil the duty' is for each side dependent on the other side's record. I am obliged to abide by the contract only as long, and in as far, as the partner does the same. It is my partner's action, not my own, that I watch and scrutinize and evaluate first. My partner must 'deserve' or 'earn' the fulfilment of my obligation; at least he must not do anything to become 'undeserving'. 'He has not done his part' is the only argument I need to be excused from my own obligation. It is, so to speak, in the power of my partner to set me (by design or by default) 'free', to 'unbind' me from my duties. My duties are *heteronomic*. And so are, by proxy, my contractual actions, and in the end I, the actor, a fictional compact of contractual obligations.

Furthermore, in contractual relationship my obligations are strictly confined; enclosed within the set of actions that can be *enforced*. 'This is my duty' means not much more than 'In the case where I fail to do it, I shall be penalized'. The idea of duty has here an extrinsic meaning, but no intrinsic one. Without a sanction attached, there is no duty. Good will here follows the fear of punishment, and what I do in the end is always the matter of weighing the discomfort of fulfilling the obligation against the inconvenience of penalty for dereliction. This circumstance further exacerbates the heteronomic character of contractual behaviour. Granted, the entering of a contract may be depicted as the expression of my status as an independent decision-maker. From then on, however, there is 'nothing personal' about my actions. Once bound by contract, my actions are 'remotely controlled' by punitive sanctions, administered by the agencies of enforcement. My actions can no more be one-sidedly referred to my own, individual stance; anyone 'in my position', that is in a situation defined by the terms of contract, would be expected to behave like this, and be forcefully brought in line in a case where the expectations have not been fulfilled.

There is a common denominator to all those attributes which actions properly called 'moral' do not possess. What unites purpose-fulness, reciprocity and contractuality is that all three imply *calculability* of action. They all assume that thinking precedes doing;

definition precedes the task; justification precedes the duty. The three
attributes presuppose action that is the outcome of rational decision-
making, or at least can be such an outcome if the actors put
themselves to it. In the light of Max Weber's definition of rationality,
we may say that the actions which the listed attributes refer to are
rational, in the sense of being accountable in terms of means and ends.
As the adequacy of means, and propriety of their selection, can in
principle be objectively evaluated against the ends these means are
meant to serve – the actions under consideration are also objective in
the sense of being *impersonal*: their choice is the work of reason which
is no one's personal property, and different choices can be explained
solely in terms of the difference between knowledge and ignorance,
or reasoning skills versus mental ineptitude. It is precisely this
impersonality of rational action that permits its portrayal as a rule-
guided action, and an action following rules that are universal in
theory and universalizable in practice.

I suggest, on the contrary, that morality is endemically and
irredeemably *non-rational* – in the sense of not being calculable, hence
not being presentable as following impersonal rules, hence not being
describable as following rules that are in principle universalizable.
The moral call is thoroughly personal; it appeals to my responsibility,
and the urge to care thus elicited cannot be allayed or placated by the
awareness that others do it for me, or that I have already done my
share by following to the letter what others used to do. Rules would
tell me what to do and when; rules would tell me where my duty
starts and where it ends; rules will allow me to say, at some point,
that I may rest now as everything that had to be done has been done,
and thus allow me to work permanently and on all occasions toward
such a point of rest which, as I am told, exists and can be reached. If
rules are missing, however, my plight is much harder, since I cannot
gain reassurance by faithfully following the standards I can observe in
others, memorize and imitate. As a moral person, I am alone, though
as a social person I am always *with* others; just as I am free though
entrapped in the dense web of prescriptions and prohibitions. (As
Maurice Blanchot put it, 'everyone here has his own prison, but in
that prison each person is free'.)[24] 'Being *with* others' can be regulated
by codifiable rules. 'Being *for* the Other' conspicuously cannot. In
Durkheim's terms, though in defiance of Durkheim's intuitions, we
could say that morality is the condition of perpetual and irreparable
anomie. Being moral means being abandoned to my own freedom.

[24] Maurice Blanchot, *Vicious Circles*, trans. Paul Aster (New York: Station
Hill, 1985), p. 10.

I am moral *before* I think. There is no thinking without concepts (always general), standards (general again), rules (always potentially generalizable). But when concepts, standards and rules enter the stage, moral impulse makes an exit; ethical reasoning takes its place, but ethics is made in the likeness of Law, not the moral urge. What we call ethics Jean Fourastié dubbed 'morales des savants', which he contrasted with 'morales du peuple'. The latter, he suggested, 'is very close to instinct. Unlike the morality of the sages, it does not proceed through reasoning and demonstrating'.[25] He also proposed that morality ('morales du peuple') is a 'morality of the sacrifice' – that is, it reveals itself to be such when judged retrospectively by its effects. It cannot be accounted for as pursuit of happiness, nor – however obliquely – defence of the actor's interests.

What follows is that if solitude marks the beginning of the moral act, togetherness and communion emerge at its end – as the togetherness of the 'moral party', the achievement of lonely moral persons reaching beyond their solitude in the act of self-sacrifice which is both the hub and the expression of 'being *for*'. We are not moral thanks to society (we are only ethical or law-abiding thanks to it); we live in society, we *are* society, thanks to being moral. At the heart of sociality is the loneliness of the moral person. Before society, its law-makers and its philosophers come down to spelling out its ethical principles, there are beings who have been moral without the constraint (or is it luxury?) of codified goodness.

---

[25] Jean Fourastié, *Essais de morale prospective* (Paris: Goutier, 1966), p. 29.

3

The Elusive Foundations

L'humain est un scandale dans l'être, une 'maladie' de l'être pour les réalistes . . .

Emmanuel Lévinas

The moral self is also a self with no foundation. To be sure, it has its moral impulse as the ground on which to stand – but this is the only ground it has. And moral impulse would be hardly considered by philosophers to be worthy of the name of the foundation. For those in charge of Law and Order (those who distinguish, through their laws, order from disorder), moral impulse is not a sort of ground on which anything of importance and stability can be erected: like a slushy marshland, it must first be thoroughly drained to be turned into a building site. Philosophers would not believe that anything so subjective, elusive, erratic as moral impulse can reliably found anything; if people do behave in a way which may be described as moral, and go on behaving like that in a more or less regular way, there must be some more potent reasons for being so. It could be (as Leo Strauss suggested in 1953) nature or history; something that is always and everywhere the same for all humans and must be therefore *discovered*, or something that changes from time to time and place to place having been first collectively created. In both cases, though, single individuals would be always confronted with a species-wide or community-wide 'ought', always more powerful than their own inclinations; they will be goaded or guided, inspired or limited by something outside each individual's power. Morality may be only *heteronomous*.

Philosophers and the administrators of order alike would view a self leaning solely on the moral impulse with considerable suspicion. There is no way one can guess what such a self will be doing; given such a self, 'everything may happen'. For the guardians of order and the philosophers alike, the world in which everything may happen (read: a world of which they cannot say, with authority, what will, and what will not, happen) is an affront to the mind and red alert for the man of action.

Throughout the modern era, echoing the concerns of the order-builders, philosophers deeply distrusted the moral self. That selves cannot be left to their own resources, that they have no adequate resources to which they can be, conceivably, left – was an assertion which did not depend for its truth on empirical findings; it did not generalize from reality, but defined the way in which (in the case of the guardians of order) reality was to be shaped and (in the case of the philosophers) was to be thought about and interpreted. Since mistrust was built from the start into the shape of the world in which the selves acted, and into the narratives accounting for their action, the assertion of moral insufficiency of the self could stay safely outside the territory where empirical testing is done. It did not matter whether the assertion was true or false; what did matter was that the condition under which one could find out, God forbid, whether the assertion was true, had been, thank God, staved off – by the thinkers, through thinking it out of the realm of the thinkable, and by the practitioners of order, by ordering it out of order. Thinkers and practitioners joined forces in the pursuit of the joint task of disavowing whatever impulse may be animating the self as a 'moral' impulse.

Building on distrust

More often than not, common weal is thought of in a modern society as an artifice of human deliberation and deliberate action. Even if that action aims only to reveal what nature 'wants' or 'requires' people to be and to do, and then making sure that this is exactly what they will be doing, the job cannot be expected to be done by individuals themselves, following blindly, unthinkingly, without assistance, their 'natural inclinations'. The perfection of human order, the quality of human cohabitation, is measured by the distance at which it has moved away from the 'natural order of things', now dubbed, with a mixture of derision and apprehension, 'the law of the jungle'. (It is that mythical jungle, the mirror image of the inner demons of our own, socially fabricated law, which – like the portrait of Dorian Gray – shows all the cruel contortions kept under the smooth skin of our own face, so that this skin, at least in our own eyes, may stay smooth.) It is contrary to reason – indeed, unimaginable – that such an order, the synonym of order as such, the only order we can think of in the world already construed as an artifice – could have its roots lodged in the natural soil – in nature acting on its own, uncultivated and unsupervised. A *constructed* common weal is too fragile and too insecure a building to be left to the care of moral impulses of its residents. (Would an architect worth her salt leave the implementation of her design to non-professional dabblers?) At best, the natural impulses stand some chance of becoming genuinely moral if operated 'under a new management': if put to a good use by agencies more reliable and trustworthy than their original owners. Social powers, like medieval alchemists, can transubstantiate the raw ore of natural inclinations into the pure gold of moral intentions; but unlike in the alchemists' case, the gold that sediments in the socially improvised crucible is the only moral gold that can be found in the whole universe; there is no morality outside the walls of the alchemists' cave, called society.

Jeremy Bentham, arguably more than any other thinker responsible for the agenda of modern ethical philosophy, believed – true to the Hobbesian inspiration – that 'human beings are . . . deficient in altruism and therefore require the threat of coercion to encourage them to seek majority interests rather than their own'.[1] Bentham believed (in T.L.S. Sprigge's pithy rendition) that human 'natural' motives of pursuit of happiness and avoidance of pain – by themselves devoid of moral significance –

> are simply the raw material of human psychology with which the legislator or social engineer must deal. The important thing is to create a society in which the motives people actually have will operate so as to generate good intentions, such as will normally produce good actions, that is, ones which augment happiness.[2]

For Bentham and his followers, as well as for most of his detractors, *moral* intentions and acts could be only the fruit of social engineering. Engineers called to perform the job come in two kinds: there are either rulers, who state the law of the land and enforce it in order to coerce the selfish happiness-seekers to give thought to the happiness of those around them. Or there are moral thinkers, whose twofold task is to advise the rulers how to manipulate socially distributed pleasures and pains so as to render the submission more likely, and to convince the coerced that they will give justice to their

---

[1]   As interpreted by R.S. Dowrie and Elisabeth Talfer in *Respect for Persons* (London: Allen & Unwin, 1969), p. 42.
[2]   T.L.S. Sprigge, *Theoretical Foundations of Ethics* (London: Routledge, 1988), p. 16.

happiness-seeking urge if they submit to the coercion without resisting.

The feverish search for the 'foundations' of moral rules could be only prompted and kept urgent by the latter task – of convincing. Indeed, coercion by the law stands a chance of being accepted with a minimum of murmur only if the law in the name of which coercion had been threatened could be shown to be more than just a whim of the legislators. It must represent something stronger than caprice, even the caprice of the strong; something that not simply ought to be accepted, but which a sane person cannot *not* accept; something that binds with the same overwhelming powers of necessity those who are called to obey and those who call them to obey. More importantly yet (though this consideration is seldom brought into enough light to supply conscious motives for the search) we can imagine moral commandments as 'grounded' only if they come in the likeness of the Law, that is in the form of *principles* one can spell out, articulate, list, take a stock of. It is, after all, the very act of discursive conception, the activity of formulating and detailing, that grounds the prescriptions and the prohibitions of the Law as principles to guide action, and by proxy grounds the actions themselves. There could be no morality without moral principles – as no act could be moral unless it meant acting *on a principle*.

Fairness, Rawls insists, 'is not at the mercy, so to speak, of existing wants and interests'.[3] In saying this, he is not alone. There is wide agreement among the writers on ethics of the most diverse schools of thought that entrusting the fate of what the people in authority and those who do their thinking for them would be prepared to describe as 'fairness' to the 'existing' (that is, un-processed) 'wants' and

---

[3] John Rawls, *A Theory of Justice* (Oxford University Press, 1971), p. 261. Alan Wolfe (*Whose Keeper? Social Science and Moral Obligation* (University of California Press, 1989), p. 125) takes issue with Rawls's indefatigable search for principles that in his view should override 'lesser' grounds of human interaction, pointing out that 'principles' have little use, and still less practical effect, in the business of life: 'In a world where people raise children, live in communities, and value friendships, a moral theory that demands rational cognition to the degree that Rawls's does is little help and may well be a burden. It teaches people to distrust what will help them most – their personal attachment to those they know . . .' What Wolfe failed to note, or at least to make plain, is that teaching such a distrust is not a mistake, not a symptom of sociological naivety, but precisely the purpose, acknowledged or latent, of the accolade bestowed on 'principles' in the hierarchy of moral criteria in which allegedly erratic sympathies and impulses to be concerned are confined solidly to the bottom rank.

'interests', would amount to abandoning them 'to the mercy'. And so the statements to this effect, like the following, picked up almost at random, abound through the ethical writings of our time:

> If my fundamental values and final ends are to enable me, as surely they must, to evaluate and regulate my immediate wants and desires, these values and final ends must have a sanction independent of the mere fact that I happen to hold them with a certain intensity.[4]

> A man cannot be said to have adopted the moral point of view unless he is prepared to treat the moral rules as principles rather than mere rules of thumb, that is, to do things *on principle* rather than merely act purposively, merely to aim at a certain end. And, furthermore, he must act on rules which are meant for everybody, and not merely for himself or some formed group.[5]

> Liberal democracies are the territory of moral pluralism which allows individuals to entertain radically diverse conceptions of goodness and human perfection. In such a situation, moral philosophy must . . . distil, solely by the force of rationality, a formal kernel of the universal obligations, moral precisely in the sense of being detached from beliefs and traditions . . . This requirement posits in principle a radical separation between rationality and historical rootedness . . .[6]

Readers will surely note, in the quoted and similar arguments, the abundance of phrases like 'it cannot', 'it must', 'they surely must' which more often than not convey the author's inability to supply any reason for the opinion voiced except for the intuition of what is 'sensible' or the horror of whatever the author considers to be 'incongruent'. The most gallant warriors of the war against the moral intuitions of *hoi polloi* rely heavily, and with gusto, on legal intuition of their own. This is, however, merely a formal observation, which would not by itself matter much if not for the substance of reasoning to which it is most intimately related. The substance that truly matters, and in the name of which the staunch defenders of correct reasoning are ready to resort to the subterfuge of *petitio principii*, is the mistrust of the autonomous moral subject; that is, a moral subject whose autonomy is grounded in something other than the internalization of principles already endorsed by an authority which claims to be speaking for 'everybody'. The true message conveyed by the

[4]   Michael J. Sandel, 'Justice and the Good', in *Liberalism and its Critics*, ed. Michael J. Sandel (Oxford: Blackwell, 1984), p. 159.
[5]   Kurt Baier, *The Moral Point of View* (Ithaca: Cornell University Press, 1958), p. 210.
[6]   Monique Canto-Sperber, 'Pour la philosophie morale', in *Le Debat*, vol. 72 (1992), p. 49. Admittedly, Canto-Sperber distances herself from the sharpest expressions of the programme she sympathizes with and is ready to make

assertion that only a conduct monitored by principles may be recognized as moral, and the demand that a pre-conative and supra-conative foundation must be unravelled and demonstrated for such principles, is that the conduct as it 'just happens to occur' tends to be *un*-principled and *un*-founded. The most immediate effect and achievement of the foundation-building was the proclamation of the non-existence or insufficiency of any other grounds on which moral choices and moral acts may be based; the more agitated and anxious the efforts of construction were, the more pronounced (and, hopefully, more convincing) would be the mistrust of the autonomous moral judgement, the uncertainty of the moral subject, the need the moral subject felt for an authoritative guidance.

The sought-after foundations were as a rule conceived in the image of legal authority, entitled to make binding pronouncement on the legal status of persons and their acts; an authority having the power to decide the rights and the wrongs of the case, and so set apart the approved from the disapproved acts. Overwhelmingly, the wager was made on reason (postulated as a universal human attribute, or rather an attribute every human was capable of acquiring – thus having no excuse for not having acquired it) and rules, or more precisely on *reason-dictated rules* and *rule-guided reason* (for all intents and purposes, reason and rule-guidance tended to be treated as synonymous). Most ethical arguments followed unstintingly Kant's invalidation of emotions as morally potent factors: it has been axiomatically assumed that feelings, much as acting out of affections, have no moral significance – only choice, the rational faculty, and the decisions it dictates can reflect upon the actor as a moral person.[7] In fact, virtue itself meant for Kant and his followers the ability to stand up to one's emotive inclinations, and to neutralize or reject them in the name of reason. Reason had to be un-emotional, as emotions were un-reasonable; and morality was cast fairly and squarely in that

some concession to the sceptical mood of our times. And so she says two pages later that 'It seems to me that the principal questions which pose themselves regarding those obligations are the questions of their discovery, definition and "stabilization", not the question of foundation' – whatever that may mean, and in whatever way, if any, it differs from the orthodox self-apology of the foundation-seekers/builders.

[7] In Lawrence A. Blum's rendition (*Friendship, Altruism and Morality* (London: Routledge, 1980), p. 169): 'The claim that our emotions and feelings can reflect on us morally is contrary to one of the deepest strains of thought within the Kantian view, according to which only our capacity for choice – our will – can reflect on us morally; feeling and emotions, in respect of which we are entirely passive, cannot reflect on a person morally.'

un-feeling dominion of reason. Just as well that it had been put there, since reason, unlike feelings, was precisely that mechanism of action which could be legislated about. Kant's fear of emotions haunted his search for moral autonomy; reason was, after all, the aperture through which heteronomous pressures might penetrate the 'motivational inside' of actors' choices. Appointing reason as the sole faculty relevant to moral evaluation of action pre-empted the questions of morality as *rule-governed*, and rules as *heteronomous*.

Just how much the wager on reason was prompted by the desire to tame and domesticate the otherwise obstreperous moral sentiments through lodging them safely in a straitjacket of formal (or formalizable) rules, is shown by the tendency of the balance between reason and rules to shift constantly to the side of the rules: to the 'deontological' conception of morality, according to which in order to know whether the act was morally correct or not, one need not bother to find out whether the consequences of the act were 'good' (defining the 'good' independently of the question whether or not the rules have been followed faithfully would be a tall order anyway, given the virtual identification of moral conduct with the government by the rules) − it is enough to know whether the acting was in agreement with the rules prescribed for that sort of action. Criteria of morality gravitated therefore to pure 'proceduralism', which in its extreme form declared the moral conscience of the actor totally out of court and managed to separate the means from the ends, goodness of behaviour from the goodness of its outcome, the question of morality from the question of 'doing good'. As a matter of fact, the consistently deontological conception of morality, with its emphasis on procedure rather than effects and motives, struck the question of 'doing good' out of the moral agenda altogether, replacing it with the question of *discipline*. It cast the gate wide open for the manipulation of the moral impulse, expropriation of the individual right to autonomous moral judgment, and the denigration of moral conscience − all this with potentially disastrous consequences. As C.H. Waddington warned thirty years ago,

> the wars, tortures, forced migrations and other calculated brutalities which make up so much of recent history, have for the most part been carried out by men who earnestly believed that their actions were justified, and, indeed, demanded, by the application of certain basic principles in which they believed . . .[8]

[8]   C.H. Waddington, *The Ethical Animal* (London: Allen & Unwin, 1960), p. 187. Waddington goes on to comment that in view of the omnipotence of the heteronomous rules in streamlining human behaviour a question may be

Since Waddington penned these words, the lasting topicality of his warning has been confirmed many times over. De-substantiation of the moral argument in favour of proceduralism does a lot for the subordination of the moral agent to the external legislating agency, yet little or nothing at all for the increase of the sum total of good; in the final account it disarms the forces of moral resistance to immoral commands – very nearly the only protection the moral self might have against being a part to inhumanity.

The long search for secure foundations of moral conduct here comes full circle. Mistrusting the sentiments declared *a priori* as fickle and mercurial, the seekers of foundations put their wager on the rational decision-maker they set to extricate from the shell of erratic emotions. This shifting of the wager was intended to be the act of liberation; following the emotions was defined as unfreedom (whatever one cannot help doing even if reason would suggest not doing it, must have been a result of compulsion capable of overriding all argument), and consequently the emancipation was tantamount to exchanging the dependence of action on feelings for its dependence on reason. Reason is, by definition, rule-guided; acting reasonably means following certain rules. Freedom, the trade mark of a moral self, came to be measured by the strictness with which the rules were followed. By the end of the day, the moral person has been unhooked from the bonds of autonomous emotions only to be put in the harness of heteronomous rules. The search that starts from the disbelief in the self's moral *capacity* ends up in the denial of the self's *right* to moral judgement.

Morality before freedom

Commenting on Cain's answer/question 'Am I my brother's keeper?' to God's challenge 'Where is your brother?', Emmanuel Lévinas writes:

asked 'whether our present development of the super-ego does not represent an over-specialisation, comparable to the excessive body-sizes of the later dinosaurs, or the freaky adaptation of certain parasites which fits them to live on only one host'. I have explored elsewhere the role of procedural reductionism, prominent for its tendency to overemphasize the organizational discipline over independent moral judgement of the performers, in making possible the participation of otherwise 'moral' persons in the collective perpetration of morally outrageous acts, and in particular in the specifically modern forms of genocide (Zygmunt Bauman, *Modernity and the Holocaust* (Cambridge: Polity Press, 1989)).

One should not treat Cain's response as a mockery of God, or as a response of a little boy: 'This is not me, this is him.' Cain's response is sincere. Only the ethical is absent there; the answer is solely from ontology; I am I and he is he. We are beings ontologically separate.[9]

Ontologically, each one of us is separate from any other; and Cain had the right to feel indignant at God's question. Something must first happen to bring us together, into a kind of relationship in which the question 'Where is your brother?', if addressed to me, will sound natural. This 'something' may be a list of duties that someone in authority has composed and instructed me to obey: 'You are obliged to be interested in your brother's movements'; or, more demandingly: 'You are obliged to see to it that no harm is done to your brother'. Alternatively, this 'something' may be a contract which I and my brother agreed to enter and duly signed or swore, so that we have become, to some extent, agents and representatives of each other, and our respective fates or some of their aspects have been tied together. If nothing of this sort had happened, Cain was well within his rights when he expressed bewilderment and took umbrage when hearing God's question. It was God's business, after all, to justify the propriety of questioning Cain about Abel's whereabouts.

Ontologically, we are at best *with* each other. Side by side may even be physically close, literally rubbing each other's shoulders – and yet infinitely remote: two separate and self-enclosed beings, Leibnizian monads of sorts, each existing through guarding its *ipseité* (Paul Ricoeur), its identity-with-itself, its boundary, its space. Paradoxically, being *with* means being *apart*. 'He is but the not-me, the place he occupies is a place where I am not.' The separation, the distance between us will never vanish. The gap may only be bridged: by my knowledge of him, by my counting of the possible profits and potential dangers his presence portends, or by my giving him what he wants and getting from him what I want. We may be kind to each other or we may fight each other. We can coexist in peace or we can set ambushes for each other. All this said or done, we will still remain but side-by-side. Moreover, bridges may be dismantled. Bridges must therefore be protected. To keep them intact one needs solid mortar and vigilant guards. Also, perhaps, a severe penalty for acts of sabotage. One needs *Law*. Or one needs *Ethics*, which only masquerades as Morality while aping the Law. Law – with its heteronomy and coercive power – is the only point one can arrive at when starting from the 'being with' of ontologically separate beings.

[9]   Emmanuel Lévinas, 'Philosophie, justice et amour', in *Entre Nous: Essais sur le penser-à-l'autre* (Paris: Grasset, 1991), pp. 128–9.

Lévinas knows that, and hence he announces, while pondering on Heidegger's *Miteinandersein*: 'it is not with the preposition *mit* that the original relation with the Other ought to be described'.[10] *Mit* is what constitutes ontology. Ontology is the territory without morality. From the perspective of ontology, moral relationship can be only a later addition, an artifice, never fully legitimate, forever an alien and awkward body, forever questionable and cast in a position in which apology is constantly demanded and never really accepted: one cannot derive the 'ought' from the 'is'; one cannot argue values starting from the facts. Facts are neither good nor bad; true facts are neutral and must remain neutral to stay true; 'facts of the matter' do not include evaluations . . . Whoever starts from ontology does not embark on founding morality. One embarks instead on disqualifying morality as 'given' before being and before facts, and hence renders its replacement with Law and Law-like Ethics a foregone conclusion.

But morality *is* given, though it is given precariously, in a posture that resists synthesis, that does not survive synthesis, that melts and fades at the point at which the synthesis takes over. What is constructed out of the ontological circumstance of 'being with' is not morality, though the architects and the builders do their best to present it as such, so that nothing else could claim the title. Morality is *before* ontology; *for* is before *with*:

> the irreducible and ultimate experience of relationship appears to me in fact to be elsewhere: not in synthesis, but in the face to face of humans, in sociality, in its moral signification. But it must be understood that morality comes not as a secondary layer, above an abstract reflection on the totality and its dangers; morality has an independent and preliminary range. First philosophy is an ethics . . .
>
> The relationship between men is certainly the non-synthesizable par excellence. One can also wonder if the idea of God, especially such as Descartes thinks it, can be made part of a totality of being, or if it is not, much rather, transcendent to being. The term 'transcendence' signifies precisely the fact that one cannot think God and being together. So too in the interpersonal relationship it is not a matter of thinking the ego and the other together, but to be facing. The true union or true togetherness is not the togetherness of synthesis, but a togetherness of face to face.[11]

First philosophy is an ethics . . . Ethics comes *before* ontology . . . Moral relationship comes *before* being . . . What does all this mean? What may 'before' mean when being, ontology, are not yet? Is not

[10] Emmanuel Lévinas, *Le temps et l'autre* (Paris: Presses Universitaires de France, 1979), p. 19.

[11] Emmanuel Lévinas, *Ethics and Infinity: Conversations with Philippe Nemo*, trans. Richard A. Cohen (Pittsburgh: Duquesne University Press, 1985), p. 77.

the time sequence (to which words like 'before' and 'after' refer) at home in ontology only? Do not simultaneity and succession, 'before' and 'later', appear only together with the ontological being? This is, precisely, the point: the 'before' of moral condition is a *non-ontological* before, a condition with which ontology does not interfere; or a condition in which that interference is rejected and ignored so it is as well as not-being-there, and the authority of ontology, also the authority over 'before' and 'after', over 'together' and 'alone', is not recognized and loses its hold. In that condition, 'before' does not signal the orderliness of being, a being that has been ordered, given structure. Rather, it stands for the rejection of all ordering bustle, of all structure that casts beings 'in the place they belong'. 'Before' in the absence or in spite of ontology may have only *moral* sense, and that sense is: *better*. 'Face to face' is *better* than 'with'. 'With' has a practical advantage over 'face to face', the same advantage tough reality of being has over inchoate shoots of possibility. Having the advantage, however, means at most being stronger, not better.

And so morality is posited here not as a hero of etiological myth, not as an imaginary 'primordial' being of sorts; not as a different kind of being, another being before the being we know, a mythical 'pre-ontological' state of the self; not as a being that *precedes* the ontological 'being *in time*' ('preceding' is conceivable solely as an eminently ontological notion). The 'before' of morality is instituted not by the absence of ontology, but by its demotion and dethroning. Morality is a *transcendence* of being; morality is, more precisely, the *chance* of such a transcendence. The moral self comes into its own through its ability to rise above being, through its defiance of being; through the choice of 'face to face' over 'with'; through the refusal to accept that the grip of being is indeed an 'iron grip'; through living the 'face to face' with the Other *as if* being, that being we know from ontology, had no voice, or if it had voice, that voice could be ignored, did not need to be obeyed. As Lévinas's translator, Richard A. Cohen, expressed it,

> Ethics does not have an essence, its 'essence', so to speak, is precisely not to have an essence, to unsettle essences. Its 'identity' is precisely not to have an identity, to undo identities. Its 'being' is not to be but to be *better than being*. Ethics is precisely ethics by disturbing the complacency of being (or of non-being, being's correlate). 'To be or not to be', Lévinas insists, is *not* the question.[12]

---

[12] In Lévinas, *Ethics and Infinity*, p. 10. Many a sentence struggling to convey the idea of ethical 'being before being' sounds awkward in a fashion that cannot be repaired. The language we use (the only one we can use) is a

Morality has no 'ground', no 'foundation' (again, two uncompromisingly ontological notions, untranslatable into the language of morality, having no referents in the moral world 'before' ontology, in the 'otherwise than being'). It is born and dies in the act of transcendence, in the self-elevation over 'realities of being' and 'facts of the case', in its not-being-bound by either. Confronting the Other not as a person (*persona*: the mask worn to signify the role played, that role having been first described and prescribed in the scenario), but as the *face*, is already the act of transcendence, since everything that appertains to the Other in her capacity of being is absent from the Other as Face. 'The face is not a force. It is an authority. Authority is often without force.' The face 'is what resists me by its opposition and not what is opposed to me by its resistance . . . The absolute nakedness of a face, the absolutely defenseless face, without covering, clothing or mask, is what opposes my power over it, my violence, and opposes it in an absolute way, with an opposition which is opposition in itself.'[13] The Other has no power over me; or, rather, if she has such power – if she has already spoken the command which I must obey – it would be no longer a face, but an ontological being, the hard-and-fast reality of resistance and tug-of-war. The Other is a face in as far as I lead the way, spearhead her command, anticipate it and provoke; as I command her to command me. The Other is an authority since I am willing to listen to the command before the command has been spoken, and to follow the command before I know what it commands me to do. 'By herself' (if there was such a state), the Other is weak, and it is precisely that weakness that makes my positioning her as the Face a moral act: I am fully and truly *for* the Other, since it is I who give her the right to command, make the weak strong, make the silence speak, make the non-being into being

---

sedimentation of life organized under the auspices of ontology's unchallenged domination. It is a language shaped to report and to account for *being*, construed the way ontology defines it; the concept of 'being' and all its correlates and derivatives convey matter-of-factly ontology's right to define. One may be helped to struggle through and away from the resulting difficulty by remembering that in Lévinasian ethical discourse 'being' appears, as Derrida would say, *sous rature*.

[13] 'The Paradox of Morality: an Interview with Emmanuel Lévinas by Tamara Wright, Peter Hayes and Alison Ainley', trans. Andrew Benjamin and Tamara Wright, in *The Provocation of Lévinas: Rethinking the Other*, ed. Robert Bernesconi and David Wood (London: Routledge, 1988), p. 169; Emmanuel Lévinas, 'Freedom and Command', in *Collected Philosophical Papers*, ed. Alphonso Lingis (The Hague: Martinus Nijhoff, 1987), pp. 19, 21.

through offering it the right to command me. 'I am for the other' means I give myself to the Other as hostage. I take responsibility for the Other. But I take that responsibility not in the way one signs a contract and takes upon himself the obligations that the contract stipulates. It is I who take the responsibility, and I may take that responsibility or I may reject it, but as a moral person I am taking this responsibility as if it was not me who has taken it, as if the responsibility was not for taking or rejecting, as if it was there 'already' and 'always', as if it was mine without ever being taken by me. My responsibility, which constitutes, simultaneously, the Other as the Face and me as the moral self, is *unconditional*.

> The responsibility for the other can not have begun in my commitment, in my decision. The unlimited responsibility in which I find myself comes from the other side of my freedom, from a 'prior to every meaning', an 'ulterior to every accomplishment', from the non-present par excellence, the non-original, the anarchical, prior to or beyond essence.[14]

Being unconditional means not to depend on the merits of the case or the quality of the Other. My responsibility is not the desert the Other has earned and 'has the right' to claim. It is not even something I owe the Other for the services rendered. It is not a remuneration or compensation for anything, as nothing has yet happened and the 'moral party' between me and the Other starts only now. Morality is the *absolute beginning*.

The reader will be bewildered by now, most probably put off as well, by the eerie nebulousness, 'unreality' of that description. Surely the Other is not merely a face, but at best *somebody's* face? Surely there is a person behind every face, a person with the normal load of virtues as well as vices, accomplishments and failures, achievements and neglects, good will and malice, likeability and repulsiveness? Surely our togetherness has a previous history, even if until this encounter here and now I have not been aware of it? Surely the 'Face' as described here is a fiction, and a fiction I am supposed to conjure up entirely on my own, while – as if to make things more baffling still – pretending that it was there all the time?

The unfounded foundation

Yes, the reader has the right to incredulity, just as Cain was in the right when shrugging off, as irrelevant or absurd, God's inquisition.

---

[14] Emmanuel Lévinas, *Otherwise than Being, or Beyond Essence*, trans. Alphonso Lingis (The Hague: Martinus Nijhoff, 1981), p. 10.

In a morality that comes *before* being there is nothing to justify my responsibility, and still less to determine that I am responsible, that the responsibility is mine; determination and justification are features of being, of the ontological being; the only being which there is, after all. And the reasonable reader will be right to point out that 'before being' does not *exist*, and even if it did we would know nothing about it anyway – not in the way we 'know' about 'facts'. Yes, all this is evidently true (with ontology supplying all the evidence one would ever need). And yet there is no other place for morality but *before being*; that is, let us repeat, in that realm–not–realm which is *better* than being. And that realm has to be found by the moral self, as there are no beaten and signed tracks leading to it. Responsibility conjures up the Face I face, but it also creates me as moral self. Taking responsibility as if I was already responsible is an act of creation of the moral space, which cannot be plotted elsewhere or otherwise. This responsibility which is taken 'as if it was already there' is the only foundation morality can have. A frail foundation, one must admit. But here you are: take it or leave it . . .

Ethically, morality is before being. But ontologically there is nothing before being, as ontologically also the 'before being' is another being. Morality is 'before being' only in its own, moral sense of 'before'; that is, in the sense of being 'better'. But in the ontological sense, the sense which gets the upper hand whenever the two senses compete in the realm of being, the realm we are all in – being is before morality; the *moral* self can be no other than a moral *self*. Ontologically, morality can come only *after* being, that is either as a determined outcome of being, or as a rule obliged to admit priority of being by willing to justify itself in being's terms. And moral selves (that *otherwise* than being, not *another* being) are ontologically inseparable from fleshy, animated objects called human beings. Ontologically, those objects come *before* moral selves. 'Why should the other concern me? . . . Am I my brother's keeper? These questions have meaning only if one has already supposed that the ego is concerned only with itself, is only a concern for itself. In this hypothesis it indeed remains incomprehensible that the absolute outside-of-me, the other, would concern me.'[15] The awesome truth about morality is that *it is not inevitable, not determined* in any sense which would be considered valid from the ontological perspective; it does not have 'foundations' in the sense that perspective would recognize. The ethics that leaps into the Great Unknown of 'before being' does not do it in order to find or build foundations that no

[15] Lévinas, *Otherwise than Being*, p. 117.

expedition starting from 'being' has managed to reveal or build. Ethics looks in the 'before' of being not because it hopes that the sought-after foundations hide there, but because it knows that it is precisely *the act of looking there* which founds the moral self, being as it were the only foundation morality can ever have and the only one it will ever afford.

> There is a utopian moment in what I say; it is the recognition of something which cannot be realised but which, ultimately, guides all moral action . . . There is no moral life without utopianism – utopianism in this exact sense that saintliness is goodness.[16]

And yet the query would not go away and has to be confronted. What makes the difference between an active utopia, a utopia capable (*just capable*) of generating moral action (though not always, and with no assurance of success), and the idle and abstract utopian fantasy? Is there something inside the being that prompts the ontological self to wander into the exile of the 'otherwise than being' and thus make itself into a moral self? Lévinas describes that journey as 'awakening' (*l'éveil*) which is prompted and contained by, or contains, the birth of the self. Awakening does not refer to the confrontation with *myself* as 'another self', but to that Husserlian sight of the Other in which the *Körper* becomes *Leib*, live body, spiritual body, body 'with subjectivity'. Only in Lévinas's analysis that wondrous event which for Husserl is itself non-epistemological (non-cognitive), but the beginning of all epistemology (of the *possibility* of epistemology) – is instead a pre-ethical event which is the beginning of all morality (of the *possibility* of morality). In this event, 'the primordial sphere loses its priority, the subjectivity wakes up from its egology: from egoism and egotism'. This event is 'the possibility of sobering up where I, facing the Other, am liberated from myself, wake up from dogmatic slumber'. 'Everything is from the start in the accusative . . . I am "in myself" through the others.'[17] The awakening is not in the 'I am I', but in the 'I am *for*'.

It is still awakening, though. Or, more poignantly yet, the sobering up. One may awake, one may not. One may sober up, but one may stay besotted. And both awakening and sobering up point to a two-way passage. If one can awake or sober up, one can as well fall asleep and get inebriated. Uncertainty rocks the cradle of morality, fragility haunts it through life. There is nothing necessary in being

16 'The Paradox of Morality', p. 178.
17 Emmanuel Lévinas, 'La Philosophie et l'éveil', in *Entre Nous*, p. 103; *Otherwise than Being*, p. 112.

moral. Being moral is a chance which may be taken up; yet it may be also, and as easily, forfeited.

The point is, however, that losing the chance of morality is also losing the chance of the self. If 'everything is from the start in the accusative' – there would be no self, unless it started from accusative, from 'being for'. Awakening to being for the Other is the awakening of the self, which is the *birth* of the self. There is no other awakening, no other way of finding out myself as the *unique* I, the one and only I, the I different from all others, the *irreplaceable* I, not a specimen of a category.

Jean-Paul Sartre suggested that ego is born of self-knowledge, but that this self-knowledge is triggered by the gaze of the Other: a scrutinizing gaze, evaluating gaze, 'objectifying' gaze. The Other looks upon me as an object, and by doing so has compromised my subjectivity; he made me into 'being as such', a being among other beings, an object among other objects, a thing constituted by His, the Other's, interests and relevancies. This is not so much discovery, as being discovered; an assault which prompts my resistance. My 'awakening' to myself (if Sartre used that phrase) would be unthinkable unless as an act of resistance. I can become a self, an ego, only when gathering my strength *against* the Other, fighting for the liberty the Other threatens. For Sartre, rupture is the birth-act of my subjectivity. Subjectivity is *estrangement* . . . Not so, says Lévinas. The self may be born only out of *union*. It is through stretching myself *towards* the Other that I have become the unique, the only, the irreplaceable self that I am.

> To be human means to live as if one were not a being among beings . . . It is I who support the Other and am responsible for him . . . My responsibility is untransferable, no one could replace me. In fact, it is a matter of saying the very identity of the human I starting from responsibility . . . Responsibility is what is incumbent on me exclusively, and what, humanly, I cannot refuse. This charge is a supreme dignity of the unique. I am I in the sole measure that I am responsible, a non-interchangeable I, I can substitute myself for everyone, but no one can substitute himself for me.[18]

It is such responsibility – utterly, completely unheteronomous, radically unlike the responsibility on behest, or obligations stemming from contractual duty – that makes me into I. That responsibility does not 'derive' from anything else. I am responsible not because of what I know of the Other, of her virtues, of what she has done or what she could do to me or for me. It is not up to the Other to prove to me that I owe her my responsibility. Only in that stout and proud

[18] *Ethics and Infinity*, pp. 100–1.

refusal of 'having a reason', of 'having a foundation', responsibility sets me free. This emancipation is not contaminated with submission, even if it results in my giving myself up as a hostage of the Other's weal and woe. Ambivalence lies at the heart of morality: I am free as far as I am a hostage. I am I in as far as I am for the Other. Only, once that ambivalence is papered over or banished from sight, egoism may be set against altruism, self-interest against common weal, the moral self against socially endorsed ethical norm.

Life, though, is carried in that 'after the split', when ambivalence has been already transformed into binary opposition, conflict and struggle of interests. It is from such life that one needs to 'awake', 'sober up', in order to reach *back* into that messy, incongruent, non-rational *ambivalence* which truly founds the moral self. Moral self would look for foundations in the 'after of ambivalence' in vain. In that 'after' it could find only compromise that leaves egoism unscathed and interests opposed – a compromise urged to apologize as a surrender, as a lesser evil, as an unavoidable, though regrettable, self-sacrifice. Foundations can be found only in retreat from that orderly and well reasoned and logical being. And, ultimately, in the 'sobering up' to the fact that morality is neither orderly nor logical; that it has the ambivalence as its sole foundation.

The unbearable silence of responsibility

Moving back to that incurable ambivalence of 'for the Other' means also moving away from the comforting security of being to the fearsome insecurity of responsibility. If I leave behind the well-trimmed, shapely existence of interests that can be clearly circum-scribed, articulated and calculated, the duties that can be learned and rights that can be tested and defended through courts, I surrender the comfort of life insured against guilt, of the benign involvement detoxicated into conventions which ask no more than to be followed. In the words of Knud E. Løgstrup, the formidable Danish ethical philosopher, 'what is normally expected of us in everyday living is not concern for a person's life but for the things which belong to conventional courtesy. Social convention has the effect of reducing both the trust that we show and the demand that we care for the other person's life'. Conventions make life comfortable: they safeguard life lived in the pursuit of self-interest. It only seems, on the surface, that following conventional courtesy is the instrument of togetherness. In fact, separation is the effect. We use conventions 'as a means for keeping aloof from one another and for insulating ourselves'. This use already makes conventions attractive, and the living-with as conventional courtesy seductive. There is, however, another merit, which makes conventionality more tempting yet: the social norms

> give comparatively precise directives about what we shall do and what we shall refrain from doing. We are normally able to conform to these directives without ever having to consider the other person, much less take care of his life.[19]

Now I am right, now I am wrong; in both cases I know exactly where I stand, it is always either here or there, *tertium non datur*. Social norms, rules, conventions are about security and tranquil conscience. 'Everyone does it', 'This is how things are done' is the preventive, and effective, medicine for guilty conscience. True, I have lost my autonomy as a side-effect. But what I gained is not to be dismissed lightly.

How troublesome is facing up, instead, to that pre-ontological demand which conventions help us to conveniently forget. *That* demand is *unspoken*. The Other, as we remember, is not a force, but a face: the Other resists me simply by being the Other, by her opposition – does not oppose me by her resistance (resistance is something I am prompted to fight against and overcome; it is the lack of resistance that truly disarms). The Other is 'only' authority, and authority does not need force. So the command to care, to 'be for', had been given before it was spoken, and it would have been given even if it was never spoken and was to remain silent forever. As Løgstrup points out,

> The demand, precisely because it is unspoken, is radical . . . Regardless of how significant or insignificant that which is to be done appears on the surface, the demand is radical because in the very nature of the case no one but he alone, through his own unselfishness, is able to discover what will best serve the other person . . . The demand has the effect of making the person to whom the demand is directed an individual in the precise sense of the word . . . The radicality manifests itself also in the fact that the other person has no right himself to make the demand.[20]

[19] Knud E. Løgstrup, *The Ethical Demand*, trans. Theodor I. Jensen (Philadelphia: Fortress Press, 1971 [orig. 1956]), pp. 19, 20, 58. Following conventions calls for no thought, and certainly for no involvement: 'No one is more thoughtless than he who makes a point of applying and realising once-delivered directions . . . Everything can be carried out very mechanically; all that is needed is a purely technical calculation' (p. 121). This is, Løgstrup insists, why there can be no such thing as 'Christian morality'. If Jesus has 'broken the silence of the demand' (p. 115) – the moral substance is taken out of the ethical form.
[20] Løgstrup, *The Ethical Demand*, pp. 46–7.

The 'demand', unlike the comfortably precise order, is abominably vague, confused and confusing, indeed barely audible. It forces the moral self to be her own interpreter, and – as with all interpreters – remain forever unsure of the correctness of intepretation. However radical the interpretation, one can be never fully convinced that it matched the radicality of the demand. I have done this, but could I not do more? There is no convention, no rule to draw the boundary of my duty, to offer peace of mind in exchange for my consent never to trespass. And there is not even the hope that the Other, entrusted to my responsibility, may help. The Other has no right to demand . . . If she did voice her demands, she would just be invoking and enacting rights and obligations, norms and rules (so that we can go both to the court and litigate) or flexing her muscle (so that we can fight). But neither lawsuit nor fisticuffs are likely to placate a demand which stays stubbornly silent where the conventions are voluble and vociferous. It is precisely the radicality arising from the unspokenness that makes the demand rock-hard, indestructible, unconditional – just the foundation on which the moral self may rest its insecure security, its uncertain certainty . . .

To be frank, this is not the kind of foundation ethical philosophers dreamt of and go on dreaming about. It leaves quite a lot to be desired, and this is perhaps why the seekers for the building site of Law prefer to look the other way. No harmonious ethics can be erected on this site – only the straggly shoots of the never ending, never resolved moral anxiety will on this soil grow profusely. This foundation promises anything but architectural harmony and the residents' peace of mind. And yet it is moral *anxiety* that provides the only substance the moral self could ever have. What makes the moral self is the urge to do, not the knowledge of what is to be done; the unfulfilled task, not the duty correctly performed. 'But it all adds up to the fact that a person can never be entirely sure that he has acted in the right manner', concludes Løgstrup.[21] Indeed. This uncertainty with no exit is precisely the foundation of morality. One recognizes morality by its gnawing sense of unfulfilledness, by its endemic dissatisfaction with itself. *The moral self is a self always haunted by the suspicion that it is not moral enough.*

Speaking of the moral responsibility of anyone who survived the horrors of the Holocaust, one of the most active and dedicated rescuers of Nazi victims, Władysław Bartoszewski, concluded that 'Only those who died bringing help can say that they have done enough.' This verdict will not bring much succour to those who

---

[21] Løgstrup, *The Ethical Demand*, p. 114.

survived, at whom it was aimed: it sounds like a life-long confinement to guilt. After all, many helped the victims, but fewer were ready to become victims themselves. The Vatican has recognized the exceptionality, the abnormality of radical self-sacrifice by proclaiming Father Kolbe, who went to his death to save the life of another Auschwitz prisoner, a saint. Talmudic sages did not have doubts either: this is what they said in *Trumot* (8:10):

> Ulla bar Koshev was wanted by the government. He fled for asylum to Rabbi Joshua ben Levi at Lod. The government forces came and surrounded the town. They said: 'If you do not surrender him to us, we will destroy the town. Rabbi Joshua went up to Ulla bar Koshev and persuaded him to give himself up. Elijah used to appear to Rabbi Joshua, but from that moment on he ceased to do so. Rabbi Joshua fasted many days, and finally Elijah revealed himself to him. 'Am I supposed to appear to informers?' he asked. Rabbi Joshua said: 'I followed the law'. Elijah retorted: 'But is the law for saints?'

Saints are saints because they do not hide behind the Law's broad shoulders. They know, or they feel, or they act as if they felt, that no law, however generous and humane, may exhaust the moral duty, trace the consequences of 'being for' to their radical end, to the ultimate choice of life or death. This does not mean that in order to be moral one must be a saint. It does not mean either that moral choices are always, daily, matters of life and death: most of life is carried on at a safe distance from the extreme and from the ultimate choices. But it does mean that morality, to be effective in non-heroic, mundane life, must be cut out to the heroic size of the saints; or, rather, hold the saintliness of the saints for its only horizon. Moral *practice* can have only *impractical* foundations. To be what it is – moral practice – it must set itself standards which it cannot reach. And it can never placate itself with self-assurances, or other people's assurances, that the standard has been reached. It is, ultimately, the lack of self-righteousness, and the self-indignation it breeds, that are morality's most indomitable ramparts.

4

The Moral Party of Two

One by one, modernity stripped man of all 'particularistic' trappings and pared him to the (assumed) 'all-human' core – that of the 'independent, autonomous, and thus essentially non-social moral being'.[1] From the start, modernity set out to free man from all 'historical influences and diversions that ravage his deepest essence' so that – it was hoped – 'what is common to all, man as such, can emerge in him as his essence'.[2] 'Man as such' was, of course, a code name for a human being subordinated to, and moved by, one power only – the legislating power of the state; while the emancipation that had to be performed so that 'the essence' could shine in all its pristine purity stood for the destruction or neutralization of all *pouvoirs intermédiaires* – 'particularizing' powers sabotaging the job the 'universalizing' power of the modern state strove to perform. The battle to uncover 'human essence' was just one among many battles waged in the war for the right to legislate, and to legislate *monopolistically*. Or, rather, the war to replace the 'dead hand' of custom and tradition (a hand in fact very much alive thanks to the locally entrenched mechanisms of controlled reproduction) with the will of the state as the sole legislator. Other – customary, traditional – forms had to be crushed and disposed of, so that the bare body and soul of the 'man as such' could be dressed in the new, this time designer-made, clothing.

---

[1] Louis Dumont, *Essays on Individualism: Modern Theory in Anthropological Perspective* (University of Chicago Press, 1986), p. 25.
[2] Georg Simmel, 'Freedom and the Individual', in *On Individuality and Social Forms*, ed. Donald N. Levine (University of Chicago Press, 1971), p. 219–20.

Peeled of the shell of its 'natural' bonds, the 'essence' of 'man as such' proved to be, among other things, an asocial loneliness. The leading thinkers of the new artificially designed order, like Hobbes or Locke, envisaged an individual related to society at large (read: the nation-state) only externally and instrumentally: they did not see the fact of 'being a part of society' as having the capacity 'to change or alter individuals in any fundamental or meaningful way', but believed social institutions 'to exist in order to preserve, protect and defend the self-interest of individuals'.[3] In this view, however, the individual was freed from all obligations towards other human beings (except, that is, those spelled out and enforced by the sole power competent to legislate 'the law of the land'). In Simmel's incisive summary,

> All relations with others are thus ultimately mere stations along the road by which the ego arrives at its self. This is true whether the ego feels itself to be basically identical to these others because it still needs this supporting conviction as it stands alone upon itself and its own powers, or whether it is strong enough to bear the loneliness of its own quality, the multitude being there only so that each individual can use the others as a measure of his incomparability and the individuality of his world.[4]

The hermetically closed, lonely monad is abandoned among the multitude of others who are close to hand yet infinitely remote and estranged beyond repair, seeking in every intercourse merely a chance to nourish his identity . . . Modern society specialized in the refurbishment of the social space: it aimed at the creation of a public space in which there was to be *no moral proximity*. Proximity is the realm of intimacy and morality; distance is the realm of estrangement and the Law. Between the self and the other, there was to be distance structured solely by legal rules – no distorting influence of anything spontaneous and unpredictable, no room for powers as unreliable and resistant to universal legislation as those of the wayward moral impulse. It was hoped that legal rules would be obeyed in as far as they appealed to the *self*-interest of those called to obey, and promised to deliver the best service there is or could be: legal rules were to assist and encourage the individuals to seek what suits their self-interest and promised to show how to do it. The legally defined individual was one who had interests which were not the interests of others. The

---

[3]   Jean Bethke Elshtain, 'Liberal Heresies: Existentialism and Repressive Feminism', in *Liberalism and the Modern Polity: Essays in Contemporary Political Theory*, ed. Michael J. Gargas McGrath (New York: Marcel Dekker, 1978), p. 35.
[4]   Simmel, 'Freedom and the Individual', p. 223.

distance between the self and the other was stretched beyond the risk of collusion by the separation and (always possible) conflict between individual interests.

Once exiled from their natural abode, that of proximity, affections could be redirected to the abstract, imagined totality of the nation-state (in Reinhold Niebuhr's vocabulary, individual altruism could be re-forged into group egoism). This would leave the immediate vicinity of the individual, the company of others in which life was lived, morally desiccated. The partly planned, partly unanticipated effect of all this was, so to speak, a secondary moral illiteracy: the individual's inability to cope with the presence of the Other and the affection that presence – mysteriously and illegitimately, as it now appeared – evoked. In a world construed of codifiable rules alone, the Other loomed on the outside of the self as a mystifying, but above all a confusingly ambivalent presence: the potential anchorage of the self's identity, yet simultaneously an obstacle, a resistance to the ego's self-assertion. In modern ethics, the Other was the contradiction incarnate and the most awesome of stumbling-blocks on the self's march to fulfilment.

, If postmodernity is a retreat from the blind alleys into which radically pursued ambitions of modernity have led, a postmodern ethics would be one that readmits the Other as a neighbour, as the close-to-hand-*and*-mind, into the hard core of the moral self, back from the wasteland of calculated interests to which it had been exiled; an ethics that restores the autonomous moral significance of proximity; an ethics that recasts the Other as the crucial character in the process through which the moral self comes into its own. As Alain Renaut has postulated, to remedy the neglects of modern ethical philosophy the new ethics would need to focus on inter-subjectivity, as the 'limitation imposed on monadological individualism'.[5] In this sense, Lévinas's is the postmodern ethics. As François Laruelle suggested, Lévinas is 'le penseur de l'Autre'; 'Lévinas "invente" un Autre radicalement éthique, il dit l'Autre par quoi il fut interpellé avant même de pouvoir en énoncer les manières.'[6] Or, in the words of Marc-Alain Ouaknin: Lévinas's ethics is a 'humanisme de l'Autre homme'. His ethics is postmodern since it is moved by

> the strategy of opening, which breaks the monadic immanence and makes the subject into one-that-steps-outside-of-itself, the subject of self-

[5]   Alain Renaut, *L'Ère de l'individu* (Paris: Gallimard, 1989), p. 61.
[6]   François Laruelle, 'Irrécusable, irrecevable', in *Textes pour Emmanuel Lévinas*, ed. François Laruelle (Paris: Jean-Michel Place, 1980), p. 9.

transcendence. For Lévinas, it is that shooting-up [*surgissement*] of inter-subjectivity that constitutes the subject, not the other way round.[7]

In a postmodern ethics, the Other would be no more he who, at best, is the prey on which the self can feed to replenish its life-juices, and – at worst – thwarts and sabotages the self's constitution. Instead, he will be the gatekeeper of moral life. In Lévinas's own words, 'the humanity of man, subjectivity, is a responsibility for the other, an extreme vulnerability. The return to the self becomes an interminable detour . . .' And what these words speak about is a responsibility for the Other which arrives before the Other herself had the time to demand anything; responsibility 'that is unlimited for not measured by commitments, to which assumption and refusal of responsibilities refer'.[8] Responsibility before commitments have been entered into, a responsibility that is the *a priori* measure of all commitments, rather than being *a posteriori* measured by them.

The asymmetry of I–Thou

In a most dramatic reversal of the principles of modern ethics, Lévinas accords the Other that priority which was once unquestion-ably assigned to the self.

> Intersubjective relation is a non-symmetrical relation. In this sense, I am responsible for the Other without waiting for reciprocity, were I to die for it. Reciprocity is *his* affair . . . I am responsible for a total responsibility, which answers for all the others and for all in the others, even for their responsibility. The I always has one responsibility *more* than all the others.[9]

> The knot of subjectivity consists in going to the other without concerning oneself with his movement toward me. Or, more exactly, it consists in approaching in such a way that, over and beyond all the reciprocal relations that do not fail to get set up between me and the neighbour, I have always taken one step more toward him . . . The neighbour concerns me before all assumption, all commitment consented to or refused . . . I am as it were ordered from the outside, traumatically commanded, without interiorizing by representations or concepts the authority that commands me. Without asking myself: What then is it to me? Where does he get his right to command? What have I done to be from the start in debt?

[7]   Marc-Alain Ouaknin. *Méditations érotiques* (Paris: Balland, 1992), p. 129.
[8]   Emmanuel Lévinas, 'No Identity', in *Collected Philosophical Papers*, trans. Alphonso Lingis (The Hague: Martinus Nijhoff, 1987), p. 149.
[9]   Emmanuel Lévinas, *Ethics and Infinity: Conversations with Philippe Nemo*, trans. Richard A. Cohen (Pittsburgh: Duquesne University Press, 1985), pp. 98–9.

The face of a neighbour signifies for me an unexceptionable responsibility, preceding every free consent, every pact, every contract.[10]

No freedom is absolute, all–embracing, limitless. There is no way
of lifting oneself from one kind of dependency except with the lever
of another. Each struggle for liberation results, if triumphant, in the
replacement of one constraint, painful and vexing, with another – yet
untried or seen as a lesser evil. Each freedom celebrated is a freedom
from the dependency most feared, not dependency as such. Modern
emancipation held as its ideal the *socialized man*, guided by rules
rationally processed, clearly spelled out, legally endorsed and thus
rebaptized as the Law of the Land, which would replace dependence
on the unruly and uncontrolled, uncodified and thus 'blind' forces of
individual instincts and emotions (for Durkheim, for instance, taking
off the constraining shackles of societally imposed norms would
uncover not a free individual, but a slave of animal passions). On the
other hand, freedom of the self who has been given back the right to
act, with no shame and no need for apology, on her own moral
responsibility, can only mean abandoning oneself to a moral command that knows no relief and always demands more than the self
can, or is willing, to deliver.

The realm of being, the realm of rules, is also the realm of
meanings. Things and acts are expected to carry meanings and to
possess meanings: to be *owners* of meanings, and – ownership being a
relationship of exclusion – to have meanings which other things and
acts do not have. Responsibility, in as far as it remains moral only, in
as far as no attempt has yet been made to exhaust it in a list of
obligations and conceded duties, does not have meaning in that sense.
The face which responsibility confronts demands through its meaninglessness, through the unfulfilledness of its potential to assume and
carry meanings. It will be only later, when I acknowledge the
presence of the face as my responsibility, that both I and the
neighbour acquire meanings: I am I who is responsible, he is he to
whom I assign the right to make me responsible. It is in this creation
of meaning of the Other, and thus also of myself, that my freedom,
my *ethical* freedom, comes to be. And it is precisely because of the
one-sidedness, the non-symmetry of responsibility, because of the
condensation of creative power totally on my side, that freedom of
the ethical self is perhaps, paradoxically, the only freedom which is
free from the ubiquitous shadow of dependence.

The realm of moral command to be responsible (and thus to be

[10]   Emmanuel Lévinas, *Otherwise than Being, or Beyond Essence*, trans.
Alphonso Lingis (The Hague: Martinus Nijhoff, 1981), pp. 84, 87, 88.

free), Lévinas calls 'proximity'. Once more, the term – with its spatial connotations – is *sous rature*: there is nothing really spatial about proximity, certainly not in the sense of physical space, not even in the sense of social space (that of the density of mutual knowledge). The closeness of proximity does not refer to the shortening of distance, to the two beings coming arm to arm or cheek to cheek (literally or metaphorically), to contiguity or the merger of identities. It does not refer to anything relative that can be plotted and measured. 'Proximity' stands for the unique quality of the ethical situation – which 'forgets reciprocity, as in love that does not expect to be shared'. Proximity is not a very short distance, it is not even the overcoming or neglecting or denying distance – it is, purely (though not at all simply), 'a suppression of distance':

> The relationship of proximity cannot be reduced to any modality of distance or geometrical contiguity, nor to the simple 'representation' of a neighbour; it is already an assignation, an extremely urgent assignation – an obligation, anachronously prior to any commitment. This anteriority is 'older' than the a priori.

The 'absolute and proper meaning' of proximity, simply (or not simply at all) 'presupposes "humanity"'.[11] Proximity of the neighbour is 'obsessive' – the kind of immediacy which is 'slipping the stage of consciousness, not by default but by excess, by the "excession" of the approach'. Proximity is 'beyond intentionality'.[12] Intention already presupposes a measured space, a distance. For intention to be, there had first to be separation, time to reflect and ponder, to 'make up one's mind', to proclaim and announce. Proximity is the ground of all intention, without being itself intentional. Maurice Blanchot suggested that in ethical relationship the Other is 'the attention'.

> Attention is waiting [*L'attention est l'attente*]: not an effort, tension, nor mobilization of knowledge around a certain thing with which one is preoccupied. Attention waits. It waits without haste, leaving empty what is empty and avoiding but the haste, the impatient desire and, even more, the horror of void that prompts us to fill the emptiness prematurely.[13]

Such an attention, such *waiting*, is not possessive; it does not aim at dispossessing the Other of her will, of her distinctiveness and identity

---

[11] Lévinas, *Otherwise than Being*, pp. 82, 100–1, 81.
[12] Emmanuel Lévinas, 'Language and Proximity', in *Collected Philosophical Papers*, p. 119.
[13] Maurice Blanchot, *L'Entretien infini* (Paris; Gallimard, 1969), p. 174.

– through physical coercion, or the intellectual conquest called 'the definition'. Proximity is neither a distance bridged, nor a distance demanding to be bridged; not a preambula to identification and merger, which can, in practice, only be an act of swallowing and absorption. Proximity is satisfied with being what it is – proximity. And is prepared to remain such: the state of permanent attention, come what may. Responsibility never completed, never exhausted, never past. Waiting for the Other to exercise her right to command, the right which no commands already given and obeyed can diminish.

Aporia of proximity

To attend, to wait in such a fashion, is a daunting task. It strains the self to the limits of endurance; it comes too close to these limits for the possibility that the transgression may be avoided. How long can one wait, if no end is promised, if the waiting is from the start denied the comfort of the fulfilment to come? No wonder that thinking starts with responsibility feverishly seeking its own denial. The temptation to ask 'Am I my brother's keeper?' is inscribed in being one. Erich Fromm's 'escape from freedom' is nowhere so over-whelming an impulse as in the state of the erstwhile, pre-ontological responsibility, where freedom is at its most absolute and thus least bearable.

But the power of the Other is revealed in its denial. What was so tempting as the promise of liberation (from merciless, insatiable responsibility and interminable waiting) only uncovers the Other as my dependence. Now I am truly a hostage (to merciless, insatiable pretentions of the Other and her interminable fretting). If in the state of proximity the Other was the *authority* which grounded my responsibility – my freedom, my uniqueness – now she becomes a *force*, a resistance; that power out there that draws a boundary around my freedom, that lies in ambush to rob me of whatever freedom I would wish to keep. The frailty of the Other aroused the moral self in me; her forcefulness and militancy, on the other hand, cast me on the battleground and keep me there. As before, though, the end is not in sight. The struggle, like the waiting, knows of no end, admits of no once-for-all resolution.

Since it is in the state of proximity that the responsibility, being unlimited, is least endurable – it is also in the state of proximity that the impulse to escape responsibility is at its strongest. Hence the paradox: the same condition that sustains disinterested attention gives birth to the most pitiless of struggles (no war is as ruthless, leaves so little room for magnanimity, as one of desperation, one without hope of winning). The same soil breeds love and hatred; the most humane of loves and the most inhuman of hatreds. The terrain of responsibility is also, inevitably, the site of cruelty. Only the limit-lessness of cruelty can (or so logic whispers) out-balance (short of out-balancing – silence, or banish out of sight) the unconditionality of ethical command. Proximity is the terrain of morality's most dazzling glory; but also of its most ignoble defeats.

Humanity turns into cruelty because of the temptation to close the openness, to recoil from stretching out towards the Other, to fight back the relentless, since voiceless, push of the 'unspoken command'. This is a conflict, a genuine one, a conflict experienced many times over by anyone finding generosity too onerous, and the unconditional priority of Other's weakness over my strength too demanding for being accepted in perpetuity. Indeed, the conflict is so common and so 'normal' that it is impossible to contemplate the 'innateness' of the moral impulse without simultaneously admitting the endemic nature of aggression. Hence the notorious endlessness-cum-inconclusiveness of the debate between the thinkers who believe that 'by nature' humans are good, and those who assert the 'naturalness' of evil. Each side of the debate has ample evidence to support its argument – too ample for the other side to feel confident. Indeed, the condition of proximity, the birthplace of the moral self, tends to be from the start torn apart by the impulse to stay and the impulse to escape. The wrestling match between the state of opening and the urge of closure starts well before reason, and the ethical rulings which reason is so apt to churn up, start to intervene.

Unconditional demand is disarmed once proximity is replaced with reason-mediated distance; inattention then takes the place of attention, impatience replaces the waiting. It is now attention and waiting that need to be brought about and put in place: argued, 'made a case for', shown to be proper and 'have good reasons'. Here we enter the realm of *being*, that *otherwise than morality*, that kingdom of essences and rules. We also enter the realm of *conflicts* that hope for resolution and seek *resolutions* – through victory or compromise, and through keeping the game *within the rules*. Before conflicts and conflict-resolution there is, however, the aporia of the unconditional demand itself; not a conflict, since conflicts are contradictions that may be resolved (or are believed to be resolvable), but precisely an *aporia* – that is, a state entangled in a contradiction *without* solution: a condition which cannot fulfil itself without self-denial, that cannot but be undermined by its very effort at self-perfection, self-completion . . . A condition whose drive to self-destruction stems from its inborn necessity to strive for perfection.

Attention to the Other as an-other, as that frailty which provokes my strength, as that other presence which resists me by its opposition (before it had, or before I gave it, the chance of opposing me by its resistance), comes *before* knowledge. As a matter of fact, it ends the moment knowledge comes; at any rate, with the coming of knowledge it changes beyond recognition: it is now a reasoned decision rather than an impulse, it demands (or shows) explanations and guarantees. Yet it was that attention-before-knowledge which set me on the road to knowledge and gave me the first push. Being-for-the-Other means listening to the Other's command; that command is unspoken (this is precisely why my responsibility is unlimited), but my being-for demands that I make it speak. My knowledge is the only way I have to make it speak. If being-for means acting for the Other's sake, it is the Other's weal and woe that frame my responsibility, give content to 'being responsible'. I am responsible for attending to the Other's condition; but being responsible in a responsible way, being 'responsible for my responsibility', demands that I *know* what that condition is. It is the Other who commands me, but it is I who must give voice to that command, make it audible to myself. The silence of the Other commands me to speak-for, and speaking-for-the-Other means having knowledge of the Other.

Even if this was not its intention (and most certainly not its conscious intention, its design), attention prompts me to inquire into the condition of the Other I attend to. I embark on the search for the content of the command. But I cannot find that content in any way except through 'representing', putting it together as *my knowledge*. What I 'find' is *the Other's* command as I have articulated it; my representation of the Other's voice. The 'finding' sets a distance between the Other as she-may-be-for-herself and the Other I am for – the distance which was not there before. My 'being for' is now *mediated*. The erstwhile innocent proximity is no more . . . And this happens even if my representation of the command is identical with the command itself. (What would such an identity mean anyway? As if I could know that this is the case and if I could know how to find out whether this is the case . . . The resonance between the command and its representation will also ever be, after all, *my* construction.) The distance – inevitably, because of being a distance – holds out non–identity as its perpetual corollary. Identity may be deceptive, putative; whether genuine or fantasized, it will be always *imputed*. But the representation of command is the only form in which I hear the command distinctly; the only command on which I can *act*.

The Other is recast as my creation; acting on the best of impulses, I have stolen the Other's authority. It is I now who says *what* the command commands. I have become the Other's plenipotentiary, though I myself signed the power of attorney in the Other's name. 'The Other for whom I am' is my own interpretation of that silent, provocative presence. And so I may come to think (I am already *thinking*) that what I have come to see is not what I like, or is not what I need to bother myself with excessively; the 'Am I my brother's keeper?' question follows swiftly and 'naturally', and the 'moral party' is over. True, I may still proceeed where my moral impulse prompts me to go; I may still follow the command, acknowledge my responsibility. It will be now, though, a command to serve my interpretation, responsibility for the weal and woe of the Other 'as seen in interpretation'. Another question may follow – still from inside the moral party, but already auguring its demise: 'Am I not a better judge of what is good for her?' The Other may fail to recognize herself in the interpretation; if she stays silent, as inside the moral relationship she would, I will have no means to learn of the disagreement; if she breaks the silence, acquires a voice of her own provoked by the sound of my voice, and so begins to resist, it is now her self-reading against my reading-for-her; and if I want to make sure that my responsibility has been exercised in full, that nothing has been left undone, overlooked or neglected, I will feel obliged to include in my responsibility also the duty to overcome what I can see as nothing else but her ignorance, or *mis*-intepretation, of 'her own best interest'. If anything, my responsibility seems to be, gratifyingly, enhanced: naivety, imprudence, improvidence of the Other underlines my insight, prudence and circumspection.

Following its own logic, imperceptibly and surreptitiously, without fault of mine or ill will, care has turned into power. Responsibility has spawned oppression. Service rebounds as a contest of wills. Because I am responsible, and because I do not shirk my responsibility, I must force the Other to submit to what I, in my best conscience, interpret as 'her own good'. There is no point in accusing me of greed or possessiveness, even of egotism: I still act *for the Other's sake*, I am still a moral self, unconcerned with self-interest, not counting my costs, ready for sacrifice. 'There is really no other thing I am to do, since I am responsible' – so I will respond to the charges.

This is the genuine aporia of moral proximity. There is no good solution in sight. If I do not act on my interpretation of the Other's welfare, am I not guilty of sinful indifference? And if I do, how far should I go in breaking the Other's resistance, how much of her autonomy may I take away? As Bertrand Russell said on another occasion, the trouble with this road on which each step leads to the next is that one does not know at what step to start screaming . . . There is but a thin line between care and oppression, and the trap of unconcern awaits those who know it, and proceed cautiously as they beware of trespassing . . .

Morality as caress

'Postmodern ethics', suggests Marc-Alain Ouaknin, 'is an ethics of caress.'[14] The caressing hand, characteristically, remains open, never tightening into a grip, never 'getting hold of'; it touches without pressing, it moves obeying the shape of the caressed body . . .

Emmanuel Lévinas first used the allegory of caress in 1947, thirty years before completing his magnum opus, *Otherwise than Being*. The vision of caress as the paradigm of moral relationship appeared first, long before the first premonition of the pre-ontological space of ethics, before the phenomenological exploration of proximity and articulation of responsibility-without-limits. In its primary sense, the caress is the activity of erotic love; it visualizes what in love escapes vision, it lends itself to description the way love does not. In description, the caress stands for love. In the history of Lévinas's ethical philosophy, erotic love supplied the frame in which 'being for' in general, the moral condition as such, was to be plotted. Or, to put it another way, the moral stance, as represented in Lévinas's ethical teaching, is a metaphor of erotic love: simultaneously generalizing and particularizing, a mother-category and a specific case of love at the same time.

Caress moves into the centre of Lévinas's vision in the context of his analysis of the striking parallelism between future and the Other. Future, the genuine future, future that has-not-been-yet (unlike the future existing in the anticipation, Bergson's-Heidegger's-Sartre's future, 'the present future'), is what *cannot* be grasped in any fashion. The exteriority of the future is totally unlike spatial exteriority precisely because no stretching of the hand will be enough to grasp it. The future 'falls upon us' and 'overwhelms us'. In other words, 'L'avenir, c'est l'autre'. Regarding the future, like regarding the Other, the subject 'ne peut rien pouvoir' – 'cannot be capable of anything'. The future, like the Other, is (in its act of confrontation, in its face-to-face), simultaneously 'given' and 'hidden'. No equivalent, not even a likeness, of the future can possibly be found in the present,

---

[14]   Ouaknin, *Méditations érotiques*, p. 129.

in that-which-I-grasp, that-which-can-be-grasped. Between the present and the future, an abyss. The future is always a new birth, an absolute beginning. And so is the Other.

Erotic love recognizes this absolute alterity; more than that, it is the absoluteness of alterity that makes erotic love possible.

> The pathos of love consists in the insurmountable duality of beings. Love is a relationship with that which is forever concealed. This relationship does not neutralize the alterity, but conserves it. The pathos of desire rests in the fact of being two. The other as other is not an object bound to become mine or become me; it retreats on the contrary into its mystery.[15]

Intentionality of loving desire is aimed not at a 'future fact', but at the future as such, at its absolute otherness and perpetual elusiveness. The caress, the activity of desire, has no intention of 'possessing, catching, knowing'; if that were the case, the caress would aim at annihilating the alterity in the Other and thus at self-destruction. The caress is 'like a play with something that hides, a play without any project or plan, played with something not meant to become ours or us, but with something other, always other, forever inaccessible, always to come. The caress is the attention paid to pure future, a future without content.'[16] Erotic love is the relationship with the alterity, with mystery, with the future – with what in this world, in which there is everything, is never there . . .

One may argue, with Edith Wyschogrod,[17] that Lévinas's pre-ontological ethics could not be founded on the faculty of seeing or hearing, but only on the sense (or, rather, meta-sense, arch-sense) of touch – that 'pure approach, pure proximity', that 'nearness of being'. One should add nevertheless that more than ethics may be founded in the phenomenon of touch. Caress and physical assault (reaffirmation of alterity, and invasion of the body's privacy) are *both* instances of touching, and – as so many court cases have shown – notoriously difficult to distinguish from each other. The caress is the gesture of one body reaching towards another; already, from the start, in its inner 'structure', an act of *invasion*, let it be just tentative and exploratory. Being invited or welcome is not its necessary condition. Neither is its reciprocation and mutuality. But this

---

[15]   Cf. Emannuel Lévinas, *Le Temps et l'autre* (Paris: Presses Universitaires de France, 1991), pp. 64, 68, 71–2, 78.

[16]   Lévinas, *Le Temps et l'autre*, p. 82.

[17]   Cf. Edith Wyschogrod, 'Doing before Hearing: On the Primacy of Touch', in *Textes pour Emmanuel Lévinas*, ed. François Laruelle (Paris: Jean-Michel Place, 1980), pp. 179–203.

'multifinality', this underdetermination of the outcome, this possibility to ramify into appropriation and violence – is not a fault, not
an *accidens* of the caress, but its *attribute*, its constitutive feature; it is,
after all, what sets apart *touching* (that one-sidedness but . . .) from
seeing or hearing (that one-sidedness pure and simple), and this is
why one can build the 'ethics of love' (or, having assumed that love is
the pattern after which the moral stance as such is shaped and judged,
also the 'ethics of the Other' in general) on the faculty of tactility, but
not on those of seeing or hearing.

At the heart of the caress we find, once more, ambivalence. No
wonder it has been custom-made as the pattern of love, that
condition which owes its wondrous capacity of bringing together the
separate, of sharing fears and doling out joys, precisely to its innate
and inextricable ambivalence. Indeed, were the love just the recognition of 'insurmountable duality of beings', how would it differ
from sheer callousness and indifference? What would bar it from
degenerating into the narcissism of self-concern? Yes, the 'pathos of
love' acknowledges the duality of being as more than a temporary
failure, more than what thus-far-has-remained-unsurmounted; it
accepts the duality as insurmountable. And yet it cannot give
expression to that acceptance in any other way but by attempting,
from the beginning and as long as love lasts, to deny what it has
assumed – to surmount the insurmountable: to make the partner's
sufferings one's own, to 'suck in' the partner's sentiments, to partake
of the partner's being ('to love is to be changed into likeness with the
beloved'), as Kierkegaard suggests,[18] to make two bodies into one, to
transform the boundary between bodies into the seam that holds
together one body. Without that codicil which demands that the
duality should be lived as a challenge, to be felt as a too-tight collar,
perceived as a condition one cannot contemplate with equanimity –
love would not be love, but alterity pure and simple. Dropping the
codicil; this is how love wilts, fades and dies. Listen to Max Frisch:

> Because our love has come to an end, because its power is expended, that
> person is finished for us . . . We withdraw from our willingness to
> participate in further manifestations. We refuse him the right that belongs
> to all living things to remain ungraspable, and then we are both surprised
> and disappointed that the relationship has ceased to exist. 'You are not',
> says he or she who has been disappointed, 'what I took you for'. And what
> was that?
>   For a mystery – which after all is what a human being is – for an exciting

---

[18] Søren Kierkegaard, *The Last Years: Journals, 1853–1855*, trans. Ronald
Gregor Smith (London: Collins, 1968), p. 186.

puzzle of which one has become tired. And so one creates for oneself an image. This is a loveless act, the betrayal.[19]

True, the pathos of love feeds on mystery. But the mystery it feeds on is one it hopes to crack. Curiosity is the hope of knowledge – and when the hope wanes, curiosity gives way to indifference. A mystery too hermetic, dismissive of all cajoling and molestations to allow itself to open, loses its seductive power. But so does a mystery only too willing to throw itself open, to stop being a mystery, to exhaust itself in a no-surprise routine. Thus, on two sides of the 'insurmountable duality' vicious snares wait for hapless love. Love may be poisoned by curiosity tired of the forever postponed satisfaction, or by the boredom of curiosity slaked. To avoid the first snare love may 'take the initiative into its own hands' and put, surreptitiously, its own 'solution' in place of the puzzle. To escape the second snare, love needs only to retreat. In both cases, the cure for love's aporia is non-love.

These are traps lined up along love's outer limits, spawned not by any external imposition, but by love's own inner urges, the cravings which love, being love, cannot do without. Once in the traps, or moved solely by the wish to escape them, love fades or dies. But what happens when the snares are still no more than an outside chance, and love is still on its own? Ambivalence is the daily bread of love. Love needs a duality that stays insurmountable. But love lives by trying to surmount it. Success, though, is the death knell of love. Love lives off its failure. Under the circumstances, love's daily labours are palliatives, half-solutions, quasi-solutions, solutions which breed the need of new solutions. A vision of what the partner may be like when truly free is formed only to be shattered the next moment by the partner's 'actually existing' freedom; one needs to make the vision stick – after all, free flourishing of the partner is what love is about (it would not be love were it not conducting itself as if that were the case); as if following Rousseau's audacious recipe, one needs to force the partner to be free . . . Yet a partner forced is no more free, and thus no more respected, and thus no more worthy of concern . . . As Jeffrey Blustein aptly observed, 'intimate relations lend themselves especially easily to manipulative and paternalistic

[19]   Max Frisch, *Sketchbook, 1946–1949*, trans. Geoffrey Skelton (New York: Harcourt Brace Jovanovich, 1977), p. 17. 'The lover's solitude', remarked Roland Barthes, 'is not a solitude of person . . . it is a solitude of system: I am alone in making a system out of it' (*A Barthes Reader*, ed. Susan Sonntag (London: Jonathan Cape, 1982), p. 453).

failures of respect'.[20] The more intimate are the relations, the more vulnerable they are. Love's labours are lost before they started.

There is an ambivalence, an aporia at the heart of love. What makes love unsustainable is precisely that ideal intention without which love cannot be . . . The intention of love, of all care, is the happiness of its object. But it is, it must be, the lover's vision of happiness that is posited as the horizon of love's effort. The first, the existential necessity, militates against, and is thwarted by, the second, the pragmatic necessity. Young Lukács expressed this aporia poignantly, though perhaps inadvertently, when he put side by side, on the same page, two equally indispensable, yet jarringly incompatible, characteristics of love. 'To love: to try never to be proved right.' And: 'Love in such a way that the object of my love will not stand in the way of my love'.[21] Self-determination, the lover's gift to the partner proclaimed in the first sentence, is cancelled in the second. The first sentence announces the lover's surrender. The second is the manifesto of the lover's domination. The problem is that they are both aspects of the same relationship; their co-presence is the *sine qua non* of love.

In a splendid study of pets as products of love, Yi-Fu Tuan finds that 'affection is not the opposite of dominance'; that, more confusingly still, 'affection itself is possible only in a relationship of inequality': 'the word *care* so exudes humaneness that we tend to forget its almost inevitable tainting by patronage and condescension in our imperfect world'. Affection is not an adornment, the tempering or mollification of inequality – it is inequality's constant and most profuse source. In the surge to implement itself in full, to reach completeness and perfection, affection and care – the affectionate care, love – tempts the carer, the lover to reduce the object of love and care 'to simulacra of lifeless objects and mechanical toys'.[22] Indeed, once lifeless, the object of love would not, surely, 'stand in

---

[20]   Jeffrey Blustein, *Care and Commitment: Taking the Personal Point of View* (Oxford University Press, 1991), p. 176. And this is precisely, in Blustein's view, because love is a 'species of disinterested care' (p. 148). The greater the care, the greater the intimacy, mutual dependency and vulnerability – and the loss of respect, and then the loss of disinterested care, follow.

[21]   György Lukács, 'The Foundering of Form against Life', in *Soul and Form*, trans. Anna Bostock (Cambridge, Mass: MIT Press, 1974), p. 34. As long as the relationship stays alive, writes Lukács, 'it is now the one who is right, and now the other; now the one who is better, nobler, more beautiful, and now the other'. As long as that see-saw goes on rocking, however, the object of love does stand in love's way . . .

[22]   Yi-Fu Tuan, *Dominance and Affection: The Making of Pets* (New Haven: Yale University Press, 1984), pp. 1–5.

the way of my love' . . . In their pursuit of perfection (perfection of their love, which they project as the perfection of those whom they love), lovers tend to turn themselves into artist-gardeners, and their partners into gardens where their art is displayed. And in the smooth continuity of steps, one hardly ever knows when to start screaming . . .

The intimate dialectics of love and domination were noted already a century ago by Max Scheler. *Agape* (counterposed to *Eros*, never truly 'unmotivated'[23] because always tainted with the sin of con-cupiscence) is the Christian ideal of love. God's love is the perfect pattern by which inept human imitations are to be measured: but God is all-powerful. He surely does not love 'in order to' – to gain something for Himself that He has not possessed before. His love, *agape*, is all giving and no taking – and so should be all love that tries to emulate Christ's example. Love is thus a 'free renunciation of one's own vital abundance', manifestation of the sense of security, fullness, strength, plenitude of power. In the act of love, 'the noble stoops to the vulgar, the healthy to the sick, the rich to the poor, the handsome to the ugly, the good and saintly to the bad and common, the Messiah to the sinners and publicans'.[24] Scheler wrote his vision of *agape* in response to Nietzsche, who painted in hellish black what in Scheler shines in angelic whiteness: to Nietzsche (see, especially, his *Antichrist*), *agape* was but an oppression born and bred by *ressentiment* – rancour and spite aroused by the sight of resolute and self-confident *difference*. Were Scheler willing, however, to think through his own, ostensibly anti-Nietzschean, portrayal of love, he would not find much to quarrel about. 'Stooping to' the weak by the self-confident strong is in the end the birth-act of domination and hierarchy: the re-forging of difference into inferiority. Scheler's *agape*, like Nietzsche's, is from the start tainted with patronizing and condescension, only in that duplicitous and self-deceptive way which Nietzsche tried bluntly to unmask.

Ill health is love's normality. As the lovers themselves, love dies because of its 'pre-programmed' mortality, not because of con-tingent, in principle avoidable, diseases. Love's death is the product

[23] Cf. Anders Nygren, *Agape and Eros*, trans. Philip S. Watson (Philadel-phia: Westminster Press, 1953), p. 75. 'Motivated' love, says Nygren, is human; spontaneous and 'unmotivated' love is Divine. But it is the task of humans to strive to lift their love to Divine standard.
[24] Max Scheler, *Ressentiment*, trans. William W. Holdheim (New York: Free Press, 1961), pp. 86–8. Love is 'essentially expansion'; love is 'descent' to the weak which 'springs from a spontaneous overflow of force'.

of love's life activities. Each malady may be curable – but the cure is but a subterfuge that is another malady. One trouble that cannot be healed is the ambivalence, love's essence. Take that ambivalence away, and love is no more. And yet all patented, expert-recommended medicines for love's ailments attempt to do just that.

Maladies and remedies and more maladies of love

Goaded by its own ambivalence, love is by nature restless: a constant urge to transgress and to transcend what has been reached. Transcendence is not necessarily a dash forward, though it seems so at the time; in retrospect, it looks more like 'doing all the running it can just to stay in the same place' – a condition of not retreating. Love has to draw ever new supplies of energy in order to stay alive. It has to restock itself and reassert every day anew: once accumulated, the capital is eaten up fast if not daily replenished. Love is, therefore, insecurity incarnate. Assuming that insecurity is for most people an uncomfortable condition and in the long run unendurable, two strategies can be reasonably expected to be pursued – of *fixation*, and of *flotation*.

Fixing. The effort to emancipate relationship from erratic and flickery sentiments, to make sure that – whatever happens to their emotions – partners will go on benefiting from love's gifts: the other partner's concern, care, responsibility. An effort to reach the state in which one can go on receiving without giving more, or giving no more than the established pattern demands.

Floating. The refusal to concede the arduousness of the task and the hard labour involved. The strategy of 'cutting one's losses', of 'not throwing good money after bad', of giving up trying and looking elsewhere for another try once the gains seem to have fallen below the level of expenses needed to secure them. In this strategy, insecurity is escaped rather than fought, in the hope that security may be found, at a lesser cost and with less onerous an effort, elsewhere.

Both strategies had (and still have) their practitioners and their philosophers.

The first strategy, that of fixation, aims by and large at the substitution of rules and routines for love, sympathy and other sentiments considered too unreliable and costly to ground a secure relationship. The classic formulation of this strategy was supplied by Kant at the threshold of the modern era and has since been tacitly accepted as the axiom on which the strategy of fixation is founded. In Downie and Talfer's rendition, for instance, we can do without (sympathy), for if we are to believe Kant, it is possible to do one's duty without sympathy . . . It may be possible to go through the outward motions of actions which conform to duty without active sympathy.[25]

The same idea has been explicated, yet more lucidly, in Francesco Alberoni's and Salvatore Veca's popular study of moral altruism:

We cannot oblige ourselves to love somebody . . . Our reason, on the other hand, is capable of conceiving the duty as a necessity. If the spontaneity of loving sentiment fails, morality would nevertheless be possible thanks to the existence of duty. Duty fills the void left by love . . . Since we cannot count on love, that spontaneous sentiment, we voluntarily accept its equivalent which has the same practical consequences. Morality forces us to act *as if* we were in love. Duty is a 'look-alike' of love.[26]

Duty replaces love, as the comfortably familiar routine replaces frantic effort and adventure. Love is an uphill struggle, duty is effortless – when practised consistently, it turns into habit. Doing what routine demands may not be pleasant at all. This is, however, a different kind of unpleasantness from the one caused day by day by the chronic incompleteness and uncertainty of love: this is an unpleasantness one can bear with, precisely for its routine character:

[25]   R.S. Downie and Elisabeth Talfer, *Respect for Persons* (London: Allen & Unwin, 1969), pp. 25–6. The authors add, however, that 'creative and imaginative exercise of moral life' (whatever this may mean), is 'not possible without active sympathy' (p. 26). 'Active sympathy' is defined by the authors, after W.G. Maclagan, as 'practical concern for others' – unlike the 'passive sympathy', which denotes only empathy and emotional identification. The sympathy which the authors consider to be a condition of 'creative and imaginative' moral life is, therefore, of the same ontological status as the rules: it uses intellectual faculties of the moral actors as its building materials.
[26]   Francesco Alberoni and Salvatore Veca, *L'Altruisme et la morale* (Paris: Ramsay, 1990), p. 77. The authors suggest that while morality of love is one of joy, morality of duty is one of effort (p. 79). This is not, however, what has been suggested by our own analysis. A more suitable juxtaposition could be made, perhaps, between continuous effort on the one side, and routine and habituation on the other.

In their sharp and insightful narrative of modern love's predicament (*Das ganz normale Chaos der Liebe* (Frankfurt am Main, 1990), Ulrich Beck and Elisabeth Beck-Gernsheim declare the counsels and therapies contained in the 'Home First Aid Kit' of modern rationality to be 'part of the illness which they are meant to cure'; the spontaneity they seek, the resonance of feelings, are contrary to the promise curbed. 'Contractual certainty cancels what it were to make possible: love' (p. 205). This is because the symbolic art, seductiveness, resoluteness of love all *grow* with its impossibility (p. 9). 'Love', says Beck, is 'communism in capitalism' (p. 232).

nothing else looms on the horizon: there seems to be no alternative; one is spared the agonizing hesitation of the crossroads. This is a tranquil unpleasantness, one that breeds sadness but does not spur into action. The unpleasantness of a cemetery, one is tempted to say. Indeed, duty is the death of love – of its splendours as well as its torments . . .

The following is a beautiful passage from Lukács's early essay in which the fatal link between certainty and death is traced in all its awesome – deadly – certainty:

> Someone has died. And the survivors are faced with the painful, forever familiar question of the eternal distance, the unbridgeable void between one human being and another. Nothing remains they might cling to, for the illusion of understanding another person is fed only by the renewed miracles, the anticipated surprises of constant companionship . . . [E]verything one person may know about another is only expectation, only potentiality, only wish or fear, acquiring reality only as a result of what happens later; and this reality, too, dissolves straightaway into potentialities . . .
>   The truth, the formality of death, is dazzlingly clear, clearer than anything else, only, perhaps, because death alone, with the blind force of truth, snatches loneliness from the arms of possible closeness – those arms which are always open for a new embrace.[27]

Death means that nothing will happen any more. No miracles, no surprises – no disappointments either. The death of the loved one is the safety of the lover; now the lover is free, really and fully free, without a single 'but', to paint the portrait of the beloved using his own palette – and only now that freedom has been fully and truly attained. But what comes from under his brushes will forever remain a portrait of the dead – a death mask. The final embrace, the two-in-one of which love, being love, always dreamed and which inspired all its many labours, has at last arrived. But the moment is death, and the site is the graveyard.

Duty is a rehearsal of that death; a routinized rehearsal, daily repetition-before-the-fact; today's life colonized by the death of tomorrow; an attempt to steal the tranquillity, the death's charity,

---

[27] György Lukács, 'The Moment and Form', in *Soul and Form*, pp. 107–8, 109. Let us note, however, that love is 'death bound' also when it avoids flirting with the completion – indeed, *in the result* of such an avoidance. 'The condition of all genuine love is the desperately difficult willingness to let go, not once but over and over again: to let go of the stereotypes and expectations that break lover and beloved in crippling straitjackets; to let go of your control, and even in some senses of your claim upon the other person; to let them be free to be themselves, and you to be yourself . . . The

when still uncontaminated by finality, the death's chicanery. For all practical intents, the beloved is now dead – and so is the love of the lover. Not as a blow of fate, though; but as the last station in the love's pilgrimage to self-perfection. The 'outsideness' of routine has been an 'inside' tendency of love all along. Indeed, it is being such a tendency that kept love alive; a necessary condition of love's possibility. Love cannot really fulfil itself without fixation. Short of fixation, it remains unsure of itself, unsatiated, fearful and restless. It is that restlessness that makes it love – only it would not really be love if it admitted it and accepted it with no resistance. To be love, it had to take fixation (love forever, come what may; for better or worse; till death do us part) for its ideal, and thus treat thirst and fluster as the signs of its own imperfection. And yet the closer it comes to the ideal, the less is left of it; love's ideal is its grave, and love can arrive there only as a corpse. It is as if Thanatos drove the chariot of Eros.

Perhaps this is not the bane of love alone. It seems that love shares the consequences of its aporetic character, of the 'ambivalence at the core', with many other intentions, similarly driven by a *telos* that they can reach only at the cost of life. It seems that love is but a case (arguably, one of the more spectacular, romantic and inspiring cases) of that more general human predicament of which Jean-François Lyotard wrote:

> shorn of speech, incapable of standing upright, hesitating over the objects of its interest, not able to calculate its advantages, not sensitive to common reason, the child is eminently the human because its distress heralds and promises the things possible.[28]

– humanity being thus a state of perpetual childhood and never fully fulfilled possibility – though all the efforts that mark human existence are aimed at 'maturation', leaving that childhood behind. Humanity is bound to implement itself in the perpetual effort to run away from its predicament . . .

Jacques Derrida wrote of intentionality of linguistic acts in a fashion which love's peregrinations would fit without qualification. Intention, says Derrida,

> necessarily can and should *not* attain the plenitude toward which it nonetheless inevitably tends. Plenitude is its *telos*, but the *structure* of this

---

way of love is a contract series of little deaths; and physical death is only the ultimate letting-go' (Gordon Mursell, *Out of the Deep: Prayer as Protest* (London: Darton, Longman & Todd, 1989), pp. 38, 39).
28 Cf. Jean-François Lyotard, *The Inhuman: Reflections on Time*, trans. Geoffrey Bennington and Rachel Bowlby (Cambridge: Polity Press, 1991), pp. 2–7.

telos is such that if it is attained, it as well as intention both disappear, are paralyzed, immobilized, or die . . .

Plenitude is the end (the goal), but were it attained it would be the end (death) . . .

[P]lenitude is what at once *orients and endangers* the intentional movement . . . There can be no intention that does not tend toward it, but also no intention that attains it without disappearing with it.[29]

What allows language to steer clear of the danger, to survive its own suicidal tendency which nevertheless is its *spiritus movens*, is – so Derrida suggests – *iterability*; that curious repetition/non-repetition, a 'happening again' which is not repeating what happened before, that ability of locutions to be separated from the intentional context which gave them birth, and apparently 'repeated' – only apparently, though, as each 'repetition' is inevitably a renewal, a rebirth, a rejuvenation, sucking in the life juices of other contexts and other intentions (locutions are *iterated*, not *re*-iterated). The endemic ambivalence of iterability, rather than dreamt-of fixity of *Eindeutigkeit*, is the only prevention, or antidote, against the dangers inherent in the endemic ambivalence of the intention's *telos*. Reduced to the essentials, this would not be great news, however: what it means, in a nutshell, is the banal observation that the only foolproof preventive medicine against death is life (the selfsame life that is, and cannot not be, life-toward-death).

The urge of fixation (the desperate attempt to reach the plenitude before death will bring it unsolicited) only unravels the ambivalence inside and the incurable precariousness of love that follows. Love is precarious and bound to remain such as long as it is moved by loving intention, and thus the thirst for fixation will be never slaked. Ethical legislators felt it (intuited, even if they abstained from giving an account of the intuition), and their most energetic and imaginative projects sided with the love's overwhelming desire to escape its own fragility, to hold its object, lovable because mysterious and ungraspable, firmly – instead of 'merely' caressing. Curiously, it was enough for the ethical legislators to lift the natural proclivity of love to the heights of an abstract principle, and then call the actors to follow the principle rather than their proclivities, to achieve (in theory, and in practice preceded by that theory) just that: the ghostly apparition of love after death; galvanization of the corpse, with the prod of principles, into spectral imitation of the moves once made by the living body prompted by its loving impulse. No other ethical

[29] Jacques Derrida, 'Afterword: Towards an Ethic of Discussion', trans. Samuel Weber, in *Limited Inc.* (Evanston: Northwestern University Press, 1988), pp. 128–9.

philosophy performed the feat more thoroughly than utilitarianism, which made out of love's original intention – the care for the happiness of the Other – the overriding precept of all reasoned action. On the face of it, utilitarianism erected scaffolding of steel to firm up the brittle edifice built on love impulses. But on the face of it, only. As Stuart Hampshire's verdict goes,

> the original sense of the sovereign importance of human beings, and of their feelings, has been converted by exaggeration into its opposite; a sense that these original ends of action are, or may soon become, comparatively manageable problems in applied science . . .
> The utilitarian habit of mind has brought with it a new abstract cruelty in politics, a dull, destructive political righteousness.[30]

The gentle touch of love becomes an iron grip of power. Nothing except the vocabulary (or, more exactly, the rhetoric) of love and care has survived the transformation. 'Care for the other', 'doing it for the sake of the other', 'doing what is best for the other' and similar, love motives are now the legitimizing formulae of domination. Most of the time, they accompany bureaucratically simplified routines of conscience-clearing: what I describe here is but a variant of, in Michel Foucault's terms, the domination typical of 'pastoral power', one of the most insidious of the many shapes of domination, as it blackmails its objects into obedience and lulls its agents into self-righteousness by representing itself as self-sacrifice in the name of 'the life and salvation of the flock'. But on not too infrequent an occasion they supply a welcome excuse for cold and relentless cruelty with which 'the best interests' of the others are pushed through their throats. Whatever is the case, emotions are all but gone. Utilitarian recipe for universal happiness differs from loving care the way the latest tariff of welfare handouts differs from sharing a meal. In the ascent to the standards of routinized care, love is the first ballast to be thrown overboard.

Fixation is not an undiluted disaster, though; not for all, at any rate. For many a recipient of services love may render, fixed routine may be a genuine, perhaps the only, shelter against love's vagaries. For a weaker side of the love relationship the choice may be not between the live body and the skeleton of love, but between being loved (in whatever shape or form) and being abandoned. Love is, as we remember, an inherently precarious relationship for anyone involved; but seldom is the degree of precocity equal for both sides.

[30] Stuart Hampshire, 'Morality and Pessimism', in *Public and Private Morality*, ed. Stuart Hampshire (Cambridge University Press, 1978), pp. 3, 4. In the hands of utilitarian philosophers, morality becomes, says

Both partners go perpetually through the torments of uncertainty, yet in all likelihood one of them would feel yet more insecure than the other; for the less secure partner the compromise of routinized and rule-fixed care may be a lesser evil. One may argue, therefore, that routinization of the care element in love (though not love itself; love, as we have seen, bears no routine) does carry some protection for the weak (this is why the strong, on the whole, resist it and refuse to accept it unless forced). Injecting the volatile erotic impulse with the solidifying mixture of marriage laws, or tying down the capricious parental drives with the norms defining family duties, provide the most evident cases in point. One may expect that it will not be the weak who will gladly accept the alternative strategy, that of the *flotation*, as the medicine against love's undependability.

Flotation is the proposition most telling to the ears of the strong. It mollifies love's torments through lowering the stakes and permitting an exit before things get unbearably hot. Love is a continuous joy, but also a continuous sacrifice; flotation promises to preserve the first without the need to pay the heavy price of the second. Or, rather, it limits the payments to the time when joys, received or still hoped for, go on outweighing the pain of the expenses. And this applies equally to both partners: both enter the relationship freely, and each is free to opt out. Equality is in this case, to be sure, the ideology of the stronger partner and but a self-deception of the weaker one. The love relationship cannot be created unless *both* partners agree; for finishing it, however, the decision of one partner is sufficient. The feelings and desires of the other partner do not count any more. Flotation is no cure for domination, love's constant trap.

In a recent study of Anthony Giddens we find the most comprehensive survey and the most coherent analysis to-date of the contemporary trends in love forms. It pinpoints with precision the ever more prominent place occupied by flotation (not Giddens's term) among love strategies prevalent under contemporary, late-modern or post-modern, conditions. The practice of flotation is well grasped by two of Giddens's concepts: *pure relationship*, and *confluent love*.

> A pure relationship has nothing to do with sexual purity, and is a limiting concept rather than only a descriptive one. It refers to a situation where a social relation is entered into for its own sake, for what can be derived by each person from a sustained association with another; and which is continued only in so far as it is thought by both parties to deliver enough satisfactions for each individual to stay within it . . .

Hampshire, 'a kind of psychical engineering which shows the way to induce desired or valued states of mind'.

Confluent love is active, contingent love, and therefore jars with the 'for-ever', 'one-and-only' qualities of the romantic love complex.[31]

In neither of the two definitions is there a reference to moral motives or ethical significance (indeed, there are no 'ethics' or 'morality' entries in the otherwise scrupulously detailed index of the book devoted to the current transformations of intimacy). And justly so, since the destination of 'pure relationship' and 'confluent love' is to serve as the warp and the woof in the conceptual net in which certain important contemporary experience, that is today's experience of certain important men and women, (important because articulate, vociferous, standard-setting) could be best caught. It is this experience that provides the material for Giddens's analysis, which in that 'double hermeneutics' which, as Giddens explained in his previous works, is the job of sociology, sets itself the task of the 'second degree' hermeneutics. (If the English word 'experience' had not beaten flat together the two senses which the German language keeps apart, one would be able to say that Giddens's method is to lift the notoriously ineffable *Erleben* of the actors to the level of *Erfahrung*, where it can be discursively articulated and, so to speak, 'rationalized'.) In that primary experience which provides both the resource and the topic for Giddens's analysis, moral considerations are indeed conspicuous by their absence. It is one of the most striking characteristics of postmodern intimacy, that is the kind of intimacy sought and practised by men and women who carry the postmodern life-style, that it tends to set itself free from moral compulsions known to simultaneously motivate and constrain the I-Thou love relationships.

We may say that by analogy with science, which established its identity through prohibition and elimination (through banning from its language all teleological terms), postmodern experience of intimacy derives its identity from eliminating all reference to moral duties and obligations. Indeed, for the experience of intimacy to be postmodern, the criterion of 'what can be derived by each person from the association' must be enough to account for the cases of intimacy, much like the criterion of 'what is the case' was to be the sole one used for the representation of reality to be scientific. And, thus, 'drawing satisfaction' by each partner is the meaning of the relationship being 'for its own sake', and the only justification that can be given to keep alive the intimate relation.

This is, basically, a reproduction of Plato's concept of φιλια (a

---

[31] Anthony Giddens, *The Transformation of Intimacy: Sexuality, Love and Eroticism in Modern Societies* (Cambridge: Polity Press, 1992), pp. 58, 61.

relationship compressing into one what we today call love and friendship), which assumed that a proper object of affection must be useful to the subject of affection, 'useful' in the sense of supplying what the subject otherwise would lack and miss; a man sufficient unto himself, i.e. a man who lacks nothing and needs nothing, will therefore love no one. Also, a man whose needs have been satisfied (or whose object of affection has stopped supplying the missing goods) has no reason to go on with his love.[32] (This is exactly what I mean here by the 'flotation of love'). Giddens's 'pure relationship' is pure not just for the fact of being emancipated (in the self-awareness of the partners, even if not objectively) from the social functions which intimate relations were once meant to serve, but also, and I would say primarily, for the fact of neutralizing moral impulses as well as eliminating moral considerations from the partners' definitions and accounts of their intimacy. 'Pure relationship', I would suggest, is the intimacy of persons who suspend their identity of moral subjects for the duration. Pure relationship is a de-ethicized intimacy.

What the relationship-in-search-of-purity has disposed of first are the bonds of moral duty: that constitutive act of all morality, my (unlimited) responsibility for the Other. It is only when reponsibility is disposed of that one can seek, and practise, the escape from love's aporias through the expedient of flotation. In my responsibility for the other, being responsible for my *impact* on the Other plays a crucial, indeed, *the* bonding role. There are the effects of my own 'stretching out', of my caressing touch, to be considered; I may have solicited reciprocity in love, I may have succeeded in opening up my partner towards me, I may have made my partner dependent on my response to her response to my caress. In this way my responsibility grows instead of diminishing in the course of being exercised; moral demands grow while obeyed, just like appetite grows with eating. The trace left by love's history thickens and widens with time and becomes ever more difficult to efface. My moral duties to the partner in love multiply and swell as the *consequence* of my love. I am

---

[32] Cf. A.W. Price, *Love and Friendship in Plato and Aristotle* (Oxford: Clarendon Press, 1989), pp. 4–6. The interpretation is based mostly on the text of *Lysis*. It follows also – obliquely – from the same text, that, since according to Lysis persons most similar to each other are also most filled with enmity, strife and hatred, the affection – once it has fulfilled its 'function,' (that is, satiated the needs of the subject of the affection) – will tend to turn into mutual enmity of the former partners; where they were different yesterday, they are similar today . . .

responsible for the effects of my love (and this is even if I leave out of account, as the partners in a 'pure relationship' often do, my responsibility for the 'side-effects' my love may spawn – like, for instance, children most obviously affected by the ebbs and flows of their parents' 'confluent love'). My love is *consequential*, and I accept it together with the *new and growing* responsibilities which follow. But the postmodern form of intimacy is possible only on the condition that this consequentiality is denied, or refused conative significance, or has its authority rejected.

Pure relations (because they are pure in the above sense) and confluent love (because it is confluent) are by nature 'lived through' as episodic, however long they may prove to last in the end. Being lived as episodic means, of course, that they are assumed *not* to be 'till death do us part' and are managed accordingly; that they are thought of as having an imminent, though for the time being undefined, end-point; and that they are at every moment of their duration but 'until further notice'. But being episodic means something else as well: namely, that whatever happens today does not bind the future, that nothing solid is sedimented, that togetherness of the partners does not 'accumulate' with time, being instead fully exhausted in the intimacies of successive current moments. Being episodic means, in other words, being of no consequence – at least of no *lasting* consequence (that is, a consequence lasting longer than the 'drawing of satisfaction').

The ambivalence of fixation, as we saw before, consists in displaying simultaneously the prospects of security and of serf-like dependence. The ambivalence of flotation consists, on the contrary, in combining the promise of freedom with the spectre of insecurity. All too often, the regaining of freedom by one partner has the earthquake effect on the other partner's chances. Floated love leaves in its wake a thick precipitate of misery.

But the expediency of flotation rests not just in the possibility of escaping unilaterally a love entanglement felt to be too harrowing; if this were the only thing the flotation could do, escape would have been neither an attractive proposition nor a genuine escape at all, as the price in terms of wounded moral responsibility (which may be muted by the conventions of confluent love but never truly ex-tinguished) would be too high for the gains being seen as worth trying. The expediency of flotation is real only if the right to unilateral renunciation extends over the moral nature of the relation; if, in other words, each partner may not only terminate the love relationship, but also announce the moral insignificance of the act, together with the moral insignificance of the now estranged Other.

At the end of confluent love, such a condition of moral irrelevance can be only set up by an act which is in itself immoral. As Lévinas insisted on many occasions, the justification of the Other's pain is the beginning and the hard core of all immorality;[33] and the conventions of pure relationship are so construed that they allow the right to the freedom to escape to justify the pain of the person one has escaped from. On the other side or beyond the bounds of confluent love extends the world in which rules of etiquette and procedural norms replace moral impulses and in which most daily acts are not eligible for moral condemnation. For lovers, though, the only path to that world leads through the cruelty of an immoral act.

Let us note that, although it is the pain visited upon the Other, and that pain alone, which is considered to be 'the cost' of ending the affair, otherwise justified in terms of the self's emancipation, the self does not necessarily emerge from the love affair as, unqualifiedly, a winner. Exit from a confluent love is by definition unilateral, but entering a confluent love relation takes two – and it is the volume and the quality of resources available to each one that determine the chances of success. The denial of consequentiality – the pretence that a confluent love affair does not seriously mortgage the future – is a two-pronged deception: a duplicitous consolation for the abandoned partner, but a self-illusion for the abandoning one. Non-consequentiality is credible only together with a corollary belief that the pool of alternative 'confluent loves' does not diminish in time; the latter belief is, however, a potentially costly mistake. 'Pure relationship', one with 'no strings attached', no mutual duty and no guarantee of duration, seems to be an offer one sees no reason to refuse as long as the pool of alternatives looks inexhaustible. The richness of the pool is, however, but the reflection of the amplitude of one's own resources; when the resources shrink, as they inevitably do with age, so does the pool. Yet the discovery that this is the case arrives, like Kafka's Messiah, a day after its arrival.

We have found both strategies of escaping love's aporia wanting. Their own ambivalence (measured by the ambivalence of their effects, anticipated or not) is no less intense and vexing than the ambivalence they strove to resolve or at least mitigate. Moreover, each medicine proved to be effective in the treatment of a particular ailment, while showing itself to be lethal to love as a whole. Fixation extends love's life but only in the form of an apparition hovering above the grave; while flotation cancels the irritating bond between

---

[33] Compare, for instance, *The Provocation of Lévinas: Rethinking the Other*, ed. Robert Bernesconi and David Wood (London: Routledge, 1988), p. 163.

stability and unfreedom but only at the expense of barring love from visiting the depths it otherwise joyously, though perilously, fathomed. It seems that love cannot survive the attempts to cure its aporia; that it can last, as love, only together with its ambivalence. With love, as with life itself, it is the same story again: only death is unambiguous, and escape from ambivalence is the temptation of Thanatos.

5

Beyond the Moral Party

*Je ne suis pas faite pour la politique puisque je suis incapable de vouloir
ou d'accepter la mort de l'adversaire.*

Albert Camus, *Carnets*

In the last chapter we visited the 'primal scene' of morality; that
'before being' where 'the better' is yet to create 'the is', and whatever
'being with' is spawned, is but the yield of 'being for'; where the
Other is first encountered, meaning yet no more than my responsibility – responsibility un-spoken, un-codified and therefore unlimited and un-conditional. The 'primal scene' of morality is the
realm of 'face to face', of 'intimate society', of the 'moral party'; this
is the cradle and the home of the moral self. This is where morality
begins; morality has no other beginning, all other claims to paternity
being presumptuous or fraudulent.

For better or worse, morality – with its awesome potential for love
and hatred, for self-sacrifice and domination, care and cruelty, with
ambivalence as its prime mover – may rule the intimate 'society of
two', of I and the Other, uncontested. There, it is self-sufficient. It
does not need reason nor knowledge, argument nor conviction. It
would not understand them anyway; it is 'before' all that (one cannot
even say that the moral impulse is 'ineffable' or 'mute' – ineffability
and dumbness come after language, but moral impulse precedes
speech). It does not need standards either; it is its own standard, it sets its
standards as it goes, it is an act of continuous creation. It does not know
of guilt or innocence; its is the purity of naivety (as Vladimir
Jankélévitch pointed out, 'one cannot be *pure* except under the condition
of not *having* purity, that is to say of not possessing it knowingly').[1]

---

[1]   Vladimir Jankélévitch, 'On Conscience, or on the Pain of Having-Done-
It' (fragment of *Traité des vertus*, 1968), in *Contemporary European Ethics:*

We would better restate previous observations about ambivalence of the moral impulse: the moral drive, the 'being for', is ambivalent *in its consequences*, but is itself not aware of that ambivalence – not 'ambivalent *für sich*'. Only in the presence of law which strives to distil pure good and separate it from pure evil, does that moral self acquire the awareness of its innate ambivalence: but this is the moment when the purity of moral opening to the world is lost. 'Anxiety', wrote Shestov, 'is not the reality of Freedom but the manifestation of the loss of Freedom'; and he proposed to consider the eviction of Adam and Eve from Paradise as the allegory of the ever repeated loss of moral innocence:

> God, the finest being, does not choose between good and evil. And the man whom he had created did not choose either, for there was nothing there to choose . . . Only when man, obeying the suggestion of a force hostile and incomprehensible to us, held forth his hand towards the tree did his mind fall asleep and did he become the feeble being, subject to alien principles, that we now see.[2]

Only when it is gazed upon from outside, does the 'moral party' congeal into a 'couple', a 'pair', a 'they out there' (and by the law of reciprocation which rules outside, the 'they' is expected to be translated by those inside the 'couple' into 'we' with no loss of meaning). The outside gaze 'objectifies' the moral party and thus makes it into a unit, a *thing* that can be *described* 'as it is', '*handled*', *compared with* others 'like it', *assessed* and *evaluated*, *ruled about*. But from the point of view of me as a moral self there is no 'we', no 'couple', no supra-individual entity with its 'needs' and 'rights'. There is just me, with my responsibility, with my care, with the command which commands me and me alone – and the Face, who triggers all that. Whatever is there, flows from what I have done and am doing. My togetherness with the Other has solely me to rest on,

Selected Readings, ed. Joseph J. Kockelmans (New York: Doubleday, 1972), p. 52. 'Regret is the nostalgic melancholia of the irreversible, that is to say of the past that is too much past', says Jankélévitch; but in the face-to-face world of moral relationship, no past is 'too much a past', as a relationship woven out of responsibility is a continuous affair, a perpetual present, a constant search, and a possibility, of pardon. As Paul Ricoeur suggests, the experience of sin (of having sinned) may appear only with the arrival of the finite law, which always jars with the moral demand always infinite: 'the law is a "pedagogue" who helps the penitent to find out that he is a sinner' (*Philosophie de la volonté: Finitude et culpabilité*, vol. 2 (Paris: Aubier Montaigne, 1960), p. 62).
2   *A Shestov Anthology*, ed. Bernard Martin (Athens: Ohio University Press, 1970), pp. 313, 311.

and it will not survive the disappearance or the opting out of myself or the Other. There would be nothing left to 'survive' that disappearance. The togetherness of a 'moral party' is exceedingly vulnerable, more than any other imaginable collective. It is weak, fragile, perpetually endangered, living precariously with a shadow of death never far away – and all this *because* neither I nor the Other in this party is *replaceable*. It is precisely this *irreplaceability* which makes our togetherness moral, and the morality of our togetherness self-sustained and self-sufficient, needing no rules of law. Because *each of us* is irreplaceable there is no way in which actions of any of us could be classified as 'egoistic' or 'altruistic'. Good can be seen only in its opposition to evil – but how can one stay inside a kind of 'society' in which (in a jarring opposition to the 'genuine' society) *no one* is replaceable, that what is good for one may be bad for another? It is inside such a 'moral society', the 'moral party of two', that my responsibility cannot be fathomed or satisfied, and feels unlimited; and it is under this condition that the command needs no argument to gain authority, nor the support of a threat to be a command; it feels like a command, and an unconditional command, all along.

All this changes with the appearance of *the Third*. Now true society appears, and the naive, un-ruled and unruly moral impulse – that both necessary and sufficient condition of the 'moral party' – does not suffice any more.

The earthquake of the Third, or the birth of society

Society *sensu stricto* begins with the Third. Now priority means 'being before', not 'better'. Now the pristine, naive togetherness of I and the Other has stopped being either pristine or naive. There are now a lot of questions which can be, and are, asked about that togetherness. Responsibility desperately seeks its limits, the command is flatly denied being unconditional. Baffled, moral impulse pauses and awaits instructions. Now I live in a world populated by 'All, Some, Many and their companions. Similarly, there is Difference, Number, Knowledge, Now, Limit, Time, Space, also Freedom, Justice and Injustice, and, certainly, Truth and Falsity.' These are main characters of the play called Society, and all of them stay far beyond the reach of my moral (now, '*merely* intuitive') wisdom, apparently immune to whatever I may do, powerful against my powerlessness, immortal against my mortality, pristine against my blunderings, so that my blunders harm me only, not Them. *They* are the characters who act now: as Agnes Heller pointedly put it, 'Reason reasons, Imagination imagines, Will wills, and Language speaks (*die Sprache spricht*). This is how characters become actors in their own right. They come into existence. They live independently from their creators . . .'[3] And all this had been made possible, nay inescapable, since the entry of the Third; that is, once the 'moral party' outgrows its 'natural size' and turns into society.

The Third is also an Other, but not the Other we encountered at the 'primal scene' where the moral play, not knowing of itself as a play, was staged and directed by my responsibility. The otherness of the Third is of an entirely different order. The two 'others' reside in different worlds – two planets each with its own orbit which does not cross with the orbit of the other 'other' – and none would survive the swapping of orbits. The two 'others' do not converse with each other; if one speaks, the other one does not listen; if the other one does listen, he will not understand what he hears. Each can feel at home only if the other one steps aside, or better still stays outside.[4] The other who is the Third can be encountered only when we leave the realm of morality proper, and enter another world, the realm of Social Order ruled by Justice – not morality. To quote Lévinas once more,

> this is the domain of the State, of justice, of politics. Justice differs from charity in that it allows the intervention of some form of equality and measure, a set of social rules established according to the judgement of the State, and thus also of politics. The relationship between me and the other must this time leave room for the third, a sovereign judge who decides between two equals.[5]

[3] Agnes Heller, *A Philosophy of History in Fragments* (Oxford: Blackwell, 1993), p. 85.

[4] In *Modernity and the Holocaust* (Cambridge: Polity Press, 1989), pp. 187–8, I tried to make sense of the amazing, logic-defying separation in the consciousness of most Germans between the images of 'Jew as such' – Jew as a category, universally condemned or treated with cool indifference – and the Jewish neighbour, the Jew next door, whose image stood stubbornly unaffected by the categorial stereotype. I suggested in conclusion that 'the proximity-cum-responsibility context within which personal images are formed surrounds them with a thick moral wall virtually impenetrable to "merely abstract" arguments. Persuasive or insidious intellectual stereotype may be, yet its zone of application stops abruptly where the sphere of personal intercourse begins. "The other" as an *abstract category* simply does not communicate with "the other" I know.'

[5] Roger-Pol Droit, interview with Emmanuel Lévinas, *Le Monde*, 2 June 1992.

What makes the Third so unlike the Other we met in the moral encounter is the *distance* of that Third, so sharply distinct from the moral Other's *proximity*. In his assessment of what he called 'the sociological significance of the third element', Georg Simmel[6] brought the unique and seminal role of the Third down to the fact that 'the third element is at such a distance from the other two that there exist no properly sociological interactions which concern all three elements alike'. The 'third' is constantly left behind, set apart by anything that brings close any of the 'dyad' inside the 'triad'. We may guess that precisely this setting apart, this dis-sembly, this de-coupling of concerns, which may be dubbed 'the loss of proximity', had set the Third in the unique role of the '*disinterested* third party'. 'Disinterestedness' rebounds as 'objectivity'. From the vantage point of the Third, and the Third alone, the 'moral party' congeals into a *group*, an entity endowed with a life of its own, a totality which is 'greater than the sum of its parts'. Thus, simultaneously, the selves (unique and irreplaceable though they are inside the moral party) become comparable, measurable, amenable to be judged by extra-personal, 'statistically average' or 'normative' standards – and the Third is firmly placed in the position of the judge, umpire, he-who-passes-the-verdict. Against the moral selves' non-rational propul-sions, the Third may now set the 'objective criteria' of interests and advantages. Asymmetry of the moral relationship is all but gone, the partners are now equal, and exchangeable, and replaceable. They have to explain what they do, face the arguments, justify themselves by reference to standards which are not their own. The site is cleared for norms, laws, ethical rules and courts of justice.

And the site must be built upon, and urgently. Objectivity, the gift of the Third, has delivered a mortal, and at least potentially terminal, blow to the affection which moved the moral partners. 'A third mediating element deprives conflicting claims of their affective qualities', says Simmel; but it also deprives affection of its force as life-guide. Reason – that enemy of passion – *must* step in, lest there should be disorientation and chaos. Reason is what we call the ex post facto accounts of actions from which passion or naivety has been drained. Reason is what we hope will tell us what to do when passions have faded and no more propel us. We cannot live without reason once the survival of the 'group' is something else than life of the Other and my responsibility that sustains it, once the unique Other has dissolved in the otherness of the Many; it is now the matter

6 All quotations which follow come from *The Sociology of Georg Simmel*, ed. and trans. Kurt H. Wolff (Glencoe: Free Press, 1950), pp. 145–53.

between my life and the life of the many. The survival of the many and my own survival are two different survivals, I might have become an 'individual', but the Other has most certainly forfeited her individuality now dissolved in a categorial stereotype, and thus my being-for has been split into the *task* of self-preservation and the *obligation* toward the preservation of the group.

When the Other dissolves in the Many, the first thing to dissolve is the Face. The Other(s) is (are) now faceless. They are persons (*persona* means the mask that – like masks do – hides, not reveals the face) I am dealing now with masks (classes of mask, stereotypes to which the masks/uniforms send me) not faces. It is the mask which determines who am I dealing with and what my responses ought to be. I have to learn the meanings of each *kind* of mask and memorize the associated responses. But even then I cannot be totally secure. Masks are not as reliable as faces, they may be put on and off, they hide as much as (if not more than) they reveal. The innocent, hopeful confidence of the moral drive has been replaced by the never quelled anxiety of uncertainty. With the advent of the Third, fraud appeared – even more horrifying in its premonition than in its confirmed presence, more paralysing than real dangers out there – for being a non-exorcizable spectre. And I have to live with this anxiety. Whether I like it or not, I must *trust* the masks – there is no other way. Trust is the-way-of-living-with-anxiety, not the way to dispose of anxiety.

Consider two sharply contradictory opinions: Løgstrup's first, and then Shestov's:

> It is a characteristic of human life that we mutually trust each other . . .
> Initially we believe one another's word, initially we trust one another . . .
> To trust, however, is to deliver oneself over into the hands of another . . .
> That trust and self-surrender that goes with it are a fundamental part of human life is seen . . . when trust is violated.
>
> *Homo homini lupus* is one of the most steadfast maxims . . . In each of our neighbours we fear a wolf. 'This fellow is evil-minded, if he is not restrained by law he will ruin us', so we think each time a man gets out of the rut of sanctified tradition.[7]

The two accounts contradict one another, yet they do not exclude each other – spiting logic, they are simultaneously correct: it is our life condition itself that is shot through by contradiction and thus bound to stay incurably ambivalent. We trust, and we do not; we are equally afraid of trusting (that will render us easy prey to any confidence man) and mistrusting (regular mistrust would render our life unbearable). Left to our own devices (what would they be?) we

---

7 Knud E. Løgstrup, *The Ethical Demand*, trans. Theodor I. Jensen (Philadelphia: Fortress Press, 1971), pp. 8–9; *A Shestov Anthology*, p. 70.

are incapable of choosing between trust and mistrust. So we believe others to be trustworthy and suspect at the same time, which casts us in a state of permanent cognitive dissonance. We are lost, confused, vulnerable. We need help.

Society is the name of that help. 'In the ethics of strangers', wrote Stephen Toulmin, 'respect for rules is all, and the opportunities for discretion are few', whereas 'in the ethics of intimacy, discretion is all, and the relevance of strict rules is minimal'.[8] Those who can no more rely on discretion need rules badly. Society is the name of the warehouse where the rules are shelved, stored and from where they are obtained.

It appears, though, that there are two warehouses; one making offers the customers find hard to refuse, another which does not take refusal for an answer. It would appear as well, on occasion, that society supports the moral self much like the rope supports the hanged man – norms being the rope and reason the ropemaker.

Structure and counter-structure

In one of the most underrated among the great works of anthropology (or one of the greatest among the sorely underrated works of anthropology) Victor W. Turner has separated two distinct modes of togetherness according to the fashions in which behaviour of those being (or coming) together is prompted, framed and co-ordinated.

> It is as though there are here two major 'models' for human interrelatedness, juxtaposed and alternating. The first is of society as a structured, differentiated, and often hierarchical system of politico–legal–economic positions with many types of evaluation, separating men in terms of 'more' and 'less'. The second . . . is of society as an unstructured or rudimentarily structured and relatively undifferentiated *communitas*, community, or even communion of equal individuals who submit together to the general authority of the ritual elders.

At first glance, Turner's duality of societal models seems but another version of the hallowed ideal–typical distinction between *Gesellschaft* and *Gemeinschaft*. But unlike Tönnies, Turner intimates not a historical succession and temporal exclusivity of the two forms, but their coexistence, interpenetration and alternation, and a perpetual and regular one at that. To set apart his bipartite model from the conceptual pair banalized in social-scientific folklore, Turner proposes to speak of *societas* and *communitas* – the second putting, in

---

[8] Quoted after Jeffrey Blustein, *Care and Contract: Taking the Personal Point of View* (Oxford University Press, 1991), p. 218.

his view, a regular overt appearance even in a tightly structured society, whenever an individual or a group pass, or are transported, from one site in social structure to another (the gist of Turner's argument, developed from the analysis of the 'rites of passage', is that there is no direct way leading from one socially defined place in social structure to another; travellers must first pass through *communitas*, which in terms of the *societas* is a limbo, a void, a nowhere). Turner sometimes articulated the opposition differently, as one of 'structure versus anti-structure': the condition of *communitas* is dissipation or suspension or temporary cancellation of the structural arrangements which sustain at 'normal times' the life of *societas*.

The conditions of *societas* and *communitas* are mutually opposite in virtually every aspect. Some aspects seem, however, particularly relevant to our theme. If *societas* is characterized by its heterogeneity, inequality, differentiation of statuses, system of nomenclature, *communitas* is marked by homogeneity, equality, absence of status, anonymity. The above cluster of related differences is symbolically reflected in the ostentatious, salient oppositions between, say, status-related distinctive clothing on the one hand and uniform clothing (or nakedness; stripping in public is the most emphatic of 'anti-structural' statements) on the other; or between over- and under-symbolization of sexual distinctions; or between care and disregard for personal appearance. In other words, *communitas* melts what *societas* tries hard to cast and forge. Alternatively, *societas* moulds and shapes and solidifies what inside *communitas* is liquid and lacks form.

The (overt or under-cover) co-presence of the two conditions Turner explains by and large functionally: the brief stopover of status–changers in *communitas* between two stretches of settled residence in *societas* has

> the social significance of rendering them down into some kind of human *primo materia*, divested of specific form and reduced to a condition that, although it is still social, is without or beneath all accepted forms of status. The implication is that for an individual to go higher on the status ladder, he must go lower than the status ladder.[9]

---

[9]   Victor W. Turner, *The Ritual Process: Structure and Anti-structure* (London: Routledge, 1969), pp. 96, 170. True, towards the end of his study Turner considers – without elaborating – the possibility of a 'double conscience' haunting every society, and expressed in implicit references to 'two contrasting social models'. 'In the process of social life, behaviour in accordance with one model tends to "drift away" from behaviour in terms of the other. The ultimate desideratum, however, is to act in terms of *communitas* values even while playing structural roles' (p. 177). However, throughout his discussion

Individuals need to be humbled in order to be elevated; stripped of previously worn status-linked paraphernalia so that they could be clothed in different ones; this need, dictated mostly by the pre-requisites of systemic reproduction, makes the co-presence of two 'states' functionally indispensable. Even if no conscious design is implied, it is still the needs of system-management that are held to be the 'explanation' of duality. Thus, the commanding position of 'structure' over 'anti-structure' is reconfirmed, obliquely, in the logic of explanation: in the explanation, the 'anti-structure' makes its appearance as the handmaiden of 'structure'. What makes functional 'explanations' not much more than narratives of domination – the domination told as a story – is the 'fore-grantedness' of their assumptions, which had allocated the master and servant roles before the effort of explaining took off. The functionality theme needs therefore to be removed from Turner's analysis, lest the topic should be, once more, mistaken for a resource.

There is another aspect of Turner's analysis which needs rethinking and revision as well: the largely subconscious tendency to think of the 'anti-structure' after the pattern of 'structure', to treat it as another structure, structure with a minus sign. Either as another (temporally confined) reality of society or a part of society, or as an analytical model, anti-structure appears as a 'state' of social reality. In its turn, structure (though we know it now to be a process, an ever-going and never totally repetitive activity of self-reproduction) tends to be thought of in terms of its 'objective'; that is, of a steady state, the steadiness of which it strives to attain and perpetuate. This way of thinking has spilled over Turner's otherwise revolutionary discovery of anti-structure, and manifested itself in painting an essentially static picture of the 'non-structural structure'. The precipitate of such structure-induced thinking needs to be also removed from Turner's theoretical vision if it is to be used in the analysis of ways in which human togetherness is attained when and where moral impulses have ceased to suffice as guides for action.

I suggest that it helps to think in terms of two social *processes*, rather than *states* of society; and that, rather than think of one as a 'functional supplement' of the other, it is better to think of each as a phenomenon in its own right and of its own, autotelic significance; and that both processes may be best conceived of as 'brute facts' of the human condition, so that the questions 'Why?' and 'What for?' become redundant while interpretation focuses on the fashion in which each

---

Turner holds the two conditions to be two separate, analytically self-sufficient 'states' of social arrangement, or two equally separate theoretical models.

process works and on the forms it spawns in the course of the work done.

The two processes (both being processes of *structuration* according to Giddens's criteria) are those of *socialization* and *sociality*. Referring to the metaphor of social space (whose imagery stakes the odds from the start in favour of the 'structure', bent on exclusive domination), we can speak of processes that proceed, respectively, 'from the top down' and 'from the bottom up'. Or, alternatively, we can think of the difference between the two processes as one between 'management' and 'spontaneity'. In another way yet, we may express the opposition as that between replacing morality with *discursive rules*, and replacing morality with *aesthetics*. Socialization (at least in modern society) aims at creating an environment of action made of choices amenable to be 'redeemed discursively', which boils down to the rational calculation of gains and losses. Sociality puts uniqueness above regularity and the sublime above the rational, being therefore generally inhospitable to the rules, rendering the discursive redemption of rules problematic, and cancelling the instrumental meaning of action.

The two processes are at cross-purposes and in a state of constant competition, sometimes erupting into overt struggle, though only the first is overtly and self-admittedly in a state of war of attrition against the second. As Sorel remarked, 'there is a tendency for the old ferocity to be replaced by cunning, and many sociologists believe that this is a real progress'.[10] Indeed, throughout the modern era, many (most) sociologists, taking the ideas of the strong for strong ideas, and the sediments of long coercion and indoctrination for laws of history, tended to side with the managers and empathized with their worried concern about the hurdles arising on the road to harmony and order. By virtually unanimous consent, the future belonged to the managers; the future was to be a managed society – and thus anomalies which did not fit the imagery of progress fought in vain for their lawful place inside the sociological vision of the world. If admitted, it could be solely in the *a priori* criminalized capacity.

Out-rationalizing the moral impulse

Socialization is a manageable process (though not always managed by managers one can point to and name), aimed at the reproduction

[10] Georges Sorel, *Reflections on Violence*, trans. T.E. Hulme (New York: Collier, 1967), p. 191.

(perpetuation) of certain arrangements of identities; it consists, in its ideal objective if not in practice, in assigning identities to each and every member of a collectivity. Socialization is the vehicle of classification and differentiation: indeed, one may say that the management of social order consists first and foremost in the activity of classification and differentiation of socially assigned rights and duties which combine into identities carried individually or shared within categories of individuals. In modern society, what was classified and differentiated and assigned in the first place were not explicit identities, but rather varying measures of freedom of movement between identities, or – if one prefers to put it this way – freedom to *choose between identities*. It was that freedom which was unevenly distributed, providing by the same token the major dimension of differentiation (inequality).

A relatively small proportion of the population came close to the pole of Nietzschean 'overmen' – the choosers, the rule-setters, the self-makers, the 'individuals' in the strict sense of the word, that is of self-contained and self-propelled entities. On the other side were the rest, not trusted with choice-making, denied moral capacity and the ability to put freedom, if granted, to an acceptable use. In Stanley Cohen's summary[11] – 'the great project of discipline, normalisation, control, segregation and surveillance described by historians . . . were all projects of classification'. The great majority of the population has been 'classified out' of moral self-sufficiency and self-management. Their aspirations to make choices (if such aspirations made themselves at all felt), their singly or severally made attempts to elide the assigned identities were consequently criminalized as conduct deserving penalty, or requiring intensive treatment, or both.

'The rest' embraced was quite voluminous and entailed categories of varying degree of ethical incapacitation and untrustworthiness. 'Inferior races' – backward, lacking in wisdom and intelligence, both childlike in their inability to think ahead and dangerous in the untamed physical potency which they deployed in short-lived bursts of passion. The poor and indigent – moved by dark impulses rather than reason, greedy yet unable to eke out their welfare through thrift and hard work, easily diverted from duty by sensual pleasures, improvident themselves yet jealous of the fruits of other people's prudence. Women – endowed or burdened with greater admixture of animality than their male counterparts, incapable of following the

---

[11]   Stanley Cohen, *Visions of Social Control: Crime, Punishment and Classification* (Cambridge: Polity Press, 1985), pp. 191–2.

voice of reason consistently since constantly in danger of being diverted and led astray by emotions. What united such sharply distinct classes of people, rendering them objects of choice rather than choosers, and thus a source and the target of ethical-reformatory-punitive concern, was the feature of *moral incapacity* imputed to them all. The assumed absence of capacity for ('proper', 'mature') moral judgement made *a priori* all their choices suspect, in as far as they were autonomous choices, own choices, unsolicited and uncontrived choices. Foucault's surveillance, the 'great incarcerations' of the nineteenth century, were but a practical expression of the guiding principle of socialization-promoted ethics as aimed at the 'morally indolent' classes: the canon that their good conduct can be only heteronomous, enforced, externally induced.

Freedom of choice among the inept and dangerous classes, whenever it made itself manifest in practice or in inspiration, had been by the same token alternatively pathologized (medicalized), or criminalized. Indeed, the boundary between moral incapacity and criminal behaviour was all but effaced: criminals resorted to their heinous ways because of their moral vices – so that taking their freedom of choice away was the sole method of defending them against their own criminal impulses and, eventually, reforming – that is, 'drilling in' obedience to ethical precepts. Clive Emsley vividly summarized the resulting strategy:

> Throughout the period 1750 to 1900 most experts and commentators went out of their way to deny all relationship between low wages, poverty and the bulk of crime. The main causes of crime were given as moral weakness, luxury, idleness, corrupting literature, parental neglect, and lack of education . . .
> [Committed to gaols were] those who were perceived to be on the slippery slope to perdition and therefore in need of correction – the disorderly, the idle, the vagrants, or even some described simply as 'pilvering persons'.[12]

Criminalization and incarceration acted as self-fulfilling prophecies. Individual differences between offenders were levelled down and declared irrelevant; criminals were cast in conditions which were designed to elicit monotonously identical behaviour while at the same time reducing to a minimum the number of occasions for the inmates to act as persons having standards and be guided by them. The facelessness of the mass deemed to generate criminality and the criminals supplied the ground for a difference-effacing, uniform

[12] Clive Emsley, *Crime and Society in England, 1750–1900* (London: Longman, 1987), pp. 49–50, 202.

penal context, which in its own turn could not but visibly corroborate the truth of the initial assumption. As Nils Christie found out in
his study of contemporary penal practice,

> A political decision to eliminate concern for the social background of the
> defendant involves much more than making these characteristics in
> appropriate for decision on pain. By the same token, the offender is to a
> large extent excluded as a person. There is no point in exposing a social
> background, childhood dreams, defeats – perhaps mixed with some
> glimmer from happy days – social life, all those small things which are
> essential to a perception of the other as a full human being. With the
> Sentencing Manual and its prime outcome, the Sentencing Table, crime is
> standardized as Offence Levels, a person's life as Criminal History Points,
> and decisions on the delivery of pain are reduced to finding the points
> where two lines merge.[13]

In classifying, differentiating modern society criminalization
remains of course the treatment of the fringes; the latter are not,
however, just the 'non-fitting' margins, left over after the bulk of
society has been successfully allocated to respective categories and
thus made into orderly totality (though this they are as well).
Criminalization, incarceration and penal practice as such can be rather
seen as embodiments of the 'control technique' of modern society
pushed to its radical extreme, or – better still – coming close to that
ideal horizon which sets its standards and determines the direction of
its progress. By this interpretation, penal practice may serve as a
laboratory where the tendencies attenuated and adulterated elsewhere
can be observed in their pure form; after all, control and order are the
outspoken objectives of the prison system – and objectives overtly
accorded priority over any other considerations and freed from
constraints imposed by other, potentially incompatible, ends. It may
serve as such a laboratory for students of modern society; it certainly
serves as such a laboratory for its practitioners. Stanley Cohen
suggests that the overall trend of penal practice (we may add: also of
medical, psychiatric, industrial, educational and all other practices of
control which in the era of 'great incarceration' began with confining
their objects in a closed, constantly invigilated space) is from
impermeable walls which hide their interior from the unwelcome

[13]   Nils Christie, *Crime Control as Industry: Towards Gulags, Western Style?*
(London: Routledge, 1993), p. 138. The patterns of de-personalization,
facelessness, and grinding down of individualities hover over the modern
prison as constantly strived for, though never fully reached, ideals. The
'progressiveness' of penal installations is measured, at least in the USA, by
closeness to that ideal. Christie quotes, after the *Los Angeles Times* of 1 May

curiosity of those outside, to the 'opening up' of the practices to everybody's interested scrutiny and dedicated use, while dismantling both the walls dividing the 'controlled' and 'free' areas, and the difference between 'inmates' and 'freemen'.[14]

What one can observe in that laboratory is the role assigned to heteronomy of behaviour as the supreme principle of social control. The emphasis is on expertly designing a context where the variety of actions is reduced if not totally eliminated. No random responses which normally follow from freedom of choice; instead, a maximum transparency of the link between external stimulus and bodily movements; maximal predictability of responses achieved by translating uniformity of context into uniformity of conduct. One may say that the ordering practice of modern society follows intuitively behaviourist methodological principles: the most orderly society will be one in which idiosyncrasy of the individual's motivations is deprived of all influence on his or her actions; one in which what the actors think and feel matters no more – since whatever their thoughts and emotions are, the outcome is not affected. If social order is to rest on reasonable expectation that most of its denizens most of the time will follow a uniform ethical code, measures are to be taken first to reduce or eliminate the impact of moral impulses, always – irreparably – so personal, so obstreperous, so unpredictable.

Keeping order means keeping society – that web of social interactions – *structured*.

Ontologically, structure means relative repetitiousness, monotony of events; epistemologically, it means (for this reason) predictability. We call 'structured' a space inside which probabilities are not randomly distributed: in which some events are more likely to happen than others. It is in this sense that 'society' is 'structured' – an island of regularity in the sea of randomness. This precarious regularity may only exist as a continuous, perpetual product of the 'socializing' pressure (the *processual* dimension of what, when frozen in a snapshot, is described as '*social organization*'). All social organization, big or small, global-societal or local and functionally specific, consists in subjecting the conduct of its units to either *instrumental* or

---

1990, the description of the 'state of the art' Pelican Bay prison, which is 'entirely automated and designed so that inmates have virtually no face-to-face contact with guards or other inmates' (p. 86).

[14] 'The way *into* an institution is not clear . . . The way *out* is even less clear . . . nor is it clear what or where *is* the institution' (Cohen, *Visions of Social Control*, p. 57).

procedural criteria of evaluation. More importantly still, it consists in delegalizing and forcing out all other criteria, and first and foremost such standards as elide the legislating authority of the totality, and thus render the behaviour of units resilient to socializing pressures.

Among such standards marked for suppression, pride of place is kept by moral drive – the source of a most conspicuously autonomous (and hence, from the vantage point of the organization, *unpredictable* and inimical to order) behaviour. As we have argued before, the autonomy of moral behaviour is final and irreducible: morality escapes all codification, as it does not serve any purpose outside itself and does not enter a relationship with anything outside itself; that is, no relationship that could be monitored, standardized, codified. Moral behaviour is triggered off by the mere presence of the Other as a *face*: that is, an authority *without* force. The Other demands without *threatening* to punish, or promising reward. The other *cannot* do anything to me, neither punish nor reward; it is precisely that weakness of the Other that lays bare my strength, my ability to act, as responsibility. Moral action is what follows that responsibility. Unlike the action triggered by fear of sanction or promise of reward, it does not bring success or help survival. As purposeless, it escapes all possibility of heteronomous legislation or 'discursive redemption'; it remains deaf to *conatus essendi* – and hence elides the judgement of 'rational interest' and advice of calculated self-preservation, those twin bridges to the world of 'there is', of dependence and heteronomy. The face of the other (so, as we remember, Lévinas insists) is a limit imposed on the effort to exist. It offers, therefore, the ultimate freedom: freedom against the source of all heteronomy, against all dependence: against nature's persistence in being. Confronted with such freedom, 'society' is disarmed; calls to order fall on deaf ears, arguments of reason meet with incomprehensions, threats of punishment cease to frighten.

The organization's answer to such autonomy of moral behaviour is the heteronomy of instrumental and procedural rationalities. Law and interest displace and replace gratuity and the sanctionlessness of moral drive: actors are challenged to justify their conduct by reason as defined either by the approved goal or by the rules of behaviour. Only actions thought of and argued in such a way, or fit to be narrated in such a way, are admitted into the class of genuinely *social* actions; that is, *rational* actions; that is, actions which serve as the defining property of actors as *social* actors. By the same token, actions that fail to meet the criteria of goal–pursuit or procedural discipline are declared non-social, irrational – and *private*. The organization's way of socializing action includes, as its indispensable corollary, the privatization of morality.

All social organization consists therefore in neutralizing the disruptive and deregulating impact of moral impulse. This is achieved through a number of complementary arrangements: (1) assuring that there is a *distance*, not *proximity* between the two poles of action – the 'doing' and the 'suffering' one; by the same token, those on the receiving end of action are held beyond the reach of the actors' moral impulse; (2) exempting some 'others' from the class of potential objects of moral responsibility, of potential 'faces'; (3) dissembling other human objects of action into aggregates of functionally specific traits, and holding such traits separate – so that the occasion for re-assembling the 'face' out of disparate 'items' does not arise, and the task set for each action can be exempt from moral evaluation.

Through these arrangements, the organization does not promote immoral behaviour. It does not sponsor evil, as some of its critics would hasten to charge; yet it does not promote good either, contrary to the scripts composed for its self-promotion. It simply renders social action morally *adiaphoric* (the term *adiaphoron* belongs to the language of *ecclesia*; it meant originally a belief or a custom declared by the Church indifferent – neither merit nor sin – and hence requiring no stand, no official endorsement or prohibition): neither good nor evil, measurable against technical (purpose-oriented or procedural), but not against moral criteria. By the same token, it renders moral responsibility for the Other ineffective in its original role of the limit imposed on 'the effort to exist'. (It is tempting to surmise that the social philosophers, who at the threshold of the modern age first perceived social organization as a matter of design and rational improvement, theorized precisely this quality of organization as the 'immortality of Man' that transcends, and privatizes into social irrelevance, the mortality of individual men and women.)

Let us go one by one through these arrangements that, simultaneously, constitute 'the ethics' of social organization and morally adiaphorize social action.

To start with the removal of the effects of action beyond the reach of moral limits: finding themselves in the 'agentic state',[15] and

---

[15] 'Agentic state' (the term coined by Stanley Milgram, see his *Obedience to Authority: An Experimental View* (London: Tavistock, 1974), p. 133) refers to the situation when responsibility is shifted away from the actor, the actor acting out someone else's wishes. The definition of the situation as an agentic state is from the actor's point of view heteronomous and includes the description of the actor as the authority's agent.

separated from both the intention-conscious sources of the action-chain and the ultimate effects of action by a sequence of mediators,[16] the actors seldom have the chance to consider the intentions which their own contributions are meant to serve, and even less often face point-blank the consequences of their deeds. More importantly still, were they ever to face them, they would hardly conceive of them as, indeed, the consequences of their deeds. All in all, it is unlikely that they will perceive their own job – small and insignificant when compared with all other jobs which added their share to the final results – as *morally* relevant. As each action is both *mediated* and 'merely' *mediating*, the suspicion of causal link is convincingly dismissed through explaining the evidence away as an 'unanticipated', or at any rate 'unintended' product (or, better still, 'by-product' or 'side-effect') of, by itself, a morally neutral act; a fault of reason, rather than ethical failure. The organization may be, in other words, described as a machine to keep moral responsibility afloat. 'Floated' responsibility belongs to no one in particular, as everybody's contribution to the final effect is too minute or partial to be sensibly ascribed a causal function, let alone the role of the decisive cause. Dissection of responsibility and dispersion of what is left results on the structural plane in what Hannah Arendt poignantly described as 'rule by Nobody'; on the individual plane it leaves the actor, as moral subject, speechless and defenceless when faced with the twin powers of the assigned task and the procedural rules.

The important corollary of the agentic state is that though removed now at a safe distance from the ultimate human targets of collective, first fragmented and then secondarily co-ordinated action, the moral capacity of the actors has not been extinguished altogether; it can be now channelled in a convenient direction – turned towards other members of the action-chain, people in a similar agentic state, the 'intermediaries' in the actor's proximity. It is for *their* weal and woe that the actor, as a moral self, is now responsible. Moral capacity of the actor which is now prevented from interfering with the overall *aim* and the *outcome* of collective effort, is deployed in the service of the *efficiency* of this very effort: it renders 'loyalty to the mates', to the 'comrades in arms' the main measure of moral propriety, and thus

---

[16] 'Mediated action' (the term coined by John Lachs, see his *Responsibility and the Individual in Modern Society* (Brighton: Harvester, 1981), pp. 12–13, 57–8) refers to the presence of an indefinite number of 'intermediary men' between the actor and the ultimate effects of action; our ignorance of the true consequences of action of which we are parts (but parts only) 'is largely a measure of the length of the chain of intermediaries between ourselves and

strengthens dedication of all to the task at hand, reinforces discipline and willingness to co-operate, quashing on the way whatever moral scruples about the far-away effects of co-operation might have arisen.

The second arrangement could be best described as 'effacing the face' (a process equivalent to 'de-humanization'). It consists in casting the objects at the 'receiving end' of action in a position at which they are denied the capacity of moral subjects and thus disallowed from mounting a moral challenge against the intentions and effects of the action. In other words, the objects of action are evicted from the class of beings who may potentially confront the actor as 'faces'. The range of means applied to this effect is truly enormous. It stretches from an explicit exemption of the declared enemy from moral protection, through classifying selected groups among the resources of action which can be evaluated solely in terms of their technical, instrumental value – all the way to the removal of the stranger from routine human encounter in which his face might become visible and glare as a moral demand. In each case the limiting impact of moral responsibility for the Other is suspended and rendered ineffective.

The third arrangement destroys the object of action as a (potentially) moral self. The object has been dissembled into traits; the totality of the moral subject has been reduced to the collection of parts or attributes of which no one can conceivably be ascribed moral subjectivity. Actions are then targeted on specific traits of persons rather than persons themselves, by-passing or avoiding altogether the moment of encounter with morally significant effects. The traits are statistically processed 'units of computation', fully detached, in virtue of the methodology of such processing, from the 'total persons' from which they have been originally abstracted. (It had been this reality of social organization, one can guess, that was articulated in the postulate of philosophical reductionism promoted by logical positivism: to demonstrate that entity P can be reduced to entities x, y and z entails the deduction that P is 'nothing but' the assembly of x, y and z. No wonder that 'meaningfulness' of moral statements was among the first victims of logical–positivist reductionist zest.) As it were, the impact of narrowly targeted action on its human objects as total selves is left out of vision, and exempt from moral evaluation for not being a part of the intention. (Again, the only 'whole persons' who appear in the actor's vision are the actor's 'comrades in arms', and it is on them that the actor's moral impulses are focused.)

---

the acts'. As a result, it is extremely difficult for an ordinary actor 'to see how our own actions, through their remote effects, contributed to causing misery'.

Conjointly, the three arangements secure a large degree of emancipation of social organization from the constraints imposed by human moral impulses. (It is by and large this emancipation that sets the organization apart from the 'moral party' and allows it to set purposes a moral party would not be able to fulfil; as a matter of fact, purposeful action as such becomes possible only in the framework of social organization.) They also organize the vast social space extending beyond the reach of moral self-sufficiency. The two-pronged effect of the organization is making the space 'structured': orderly, regular, amenable to calculation, allowing prediction of the results actions may bring. Within this space, it is rational calculation, rather than non-rational, erratic and uncontrolled moral urge, that orients the action.

The overall effect of the above arrangements is also the *heteronomy* of action, though not in every case is this fact self-evident. The heteronomous nature of action is obvious when the action is conducted in the formalized framework of an organization, with its officially endorsed flotation of responsibility and the deployment of command and coercion as the principal determinants (or at least background factors) of action. It is less obvious or not visible at all when the command appears in disguise, in the form of 'advice' given by 'experts' – persons acting in the roles on which have been socially conferred the authority to pronounce binding (true, effective, trustworthy) sentences. Heteronomy is still more difficult to detect when such advice is 'purchased' by the 'customer' from *experts* who have no power to coerce: consumer freedom manifested in commercial transaction, and the subsequent freedom of the client to apply or disregard the purchased instruction, effectively hide the fact that the advice is the product of someone else's definition of the client's situation, someone else's vision of the client's weal, and someone else's criteria of distinguishing right from wrong, proper from improper. Above all, the commercial nature of the transaction hides the fact that it is a social mechanism, of whose workings clients have little knowledge and still less control, that has selected the address to which the client turns for guidance; that it is such a heteronomous mechanism that inspires the very propulsion to seek someone else's briefing, and to seek it at the addresses named in the expertly produced 'Yellow Pages', believed to list the agencies in which the trust may be securely invested. It is true that an employee of an organization is paid money in exchange for his obedience to the bosses' command, while a market customer himself pays money in exchange for the expert's command to which he may then be obedient. Otherwise, however, the advice of the experts does not differ much from the command of the bosses in its impact on emancipating the action from the moral responsibility of the actor and submitting it instead to the heteronomously controlled standards of gain and instrumental effectiveness.

Out-aesthetizing the moral impulse

The other fashion in which moral selves happen to be expropriated of their moral capacity is almost exactly the opposite of the first. If socialization anticipates the state-to-be-achieved before it takes off, and monitors and reinterprets it as it goes – sociality has no direction, nor does it know where it is going. If socialization is plotted in time, always aimed at the time that is not yet – sociality, however long may last the forms it spawns, lives totally in the present. If socialization is a cumulative process, leaning on yesterday's accomplishments to reach the targets of tomorrow – sociality is flat, all at one level, moving without changing place, at every moment starting anew; unlike socialization, sociality has no biography and interrupts, rather than 'makes', history. If socialization cuts down the number of still open options with every step it takes – the living possibilities multiply with the eruption of sociality, and the dead ones are resurrected. While socialization can be analysed, dissembled into stages and constituent acts, into partial performances and complementary functions – sociality is cut as if of one block and remains itself only in its totality. If socialization serves as the paradigm of meaningful, articulated narrative, with the beginning, plot, and dénouement, sociality is vociferous when it erupts but cannot be reported or retold in its original truth. Consciously or when re-scanned retrospectively, socialization is or appears to be a means to an end. Sociality has no objective, is an instrument of nothing but itself; this is, perhaps, why sociality lives only in fits and starts, in spasms and explosions; it reaches its end the moment it erupts.

The most conspicuous difference is that between the purposefulness of socialization and the disinterestedness of sociality. Socialization is meaningless without a purpose other than itself – but that purpose pours substance into every step it takes. It is the presence of purpose – construction or protection of a certain order, reaching a certain state of affairs – that allows socialization to be a calculated process, to compare the relative value of steps to be or not to be taken, to count gains against losses, distinguish between success and failure, compute 'value for money', grade effectiveness of performances. There are, however, no standards with which to measure and evaluate manifestations of sociality, since it sets out to achieve nothing and its costs may be counted only when it is all over, while the gains dissipate once the outburst of sociality runs out of steam. As sociality cannot be thought of in terms of means and ends, it does not – by Weber's standards – belong to the family of rational actions.

Instead, sociality, that counter-structural structuration, is an *aesthetic* phenomenon: disinterested, purposeless and autotelic (that is, its own end). Its only mode of being is the momentary synchronization of sentiments. Feelings are shared, but they are shared *before* having been articulated and *instead* of being spelled out: the *sharing itself* is foremost among the feelings shared – the most overwhelming of feelings, overriding all other feelings, leaving no room or time for the scrutiny of other feelings. The otherwise tortuous road to the co-ordination of affects, endlessly winding through the agonies of self-scrutiny, ineptitudes of expression, lameness of words – is abruptly cut short. Preliminaries are unnecessary: sharing is now, here, right away. It used to be a long way from One to anOther; now the distance is no more, no gaps and no holes are left in the universe of 'we', that 'we' that is but a plural of 'I'; no bridges need to be built.

Proximity? Perhaps, but of a sort very different from the one we met in the '*moral* party of two'. Yes, like moral proximity, this one knows not and hears not of rights, obligations, contracts or legal entitlements. Like moral proximity, it has no space for reasoning and would not understand demands to explain and excuse itself. Like moral proximity, this proximity of emotional meltdown is 'before' being – before knowledge, argument, agreement, consensus. But here the similarity ends. Moral proximity was the nearness of the Face. This one, the aesthetic proximity, is nearness of the crowd, and the meaning of the crowd is facelessness.

The Face is the otherness of the Other, and morality is the responsibility for that otherness. The crowd is the smothering of otherness, abolition of difference, extinction of the otherness in the Other. Moral responsibility feeds on difference. The crowd lives of similarity. The crowd suspends and shoves aside society with its structures, classifications, statuses and roles. But it also puts paid, for a time, to morality. Being in the crowd is not *being for*. It is *being with*. Perhaps not even this: just *being in*.

Overcoming of distance (better still: not allowing the proximity to dissipate into a distance) is an uphill struggle, the never ending ordeal of the moral self. The crowd wipes out distance without effort, and instantly. As Elias Canetti put it – in a single act of *discharge*.

> The most important occurrence within the crowd is the discharge. Before this the crowd does not actually exist; it is the discharge which creates it.

This is the moment when all who belong to the crowd get rid of their
differences and feel equal.

A man stands by himself on a secure and well-defined spot, his every
gesture asserting his right to keep others at a distance . . . All life, so far as
he knows it, is laid out in distances – the house in which he shuts himself
and his property, the positions he holds, the rank he desires – all these serve
to create distances, to confirm and extend them . . . No man can get near
another, nor reach his height . . .

Only together can men free themselves from their burdens of distance;
and this, precisely, is what happens in a crowd . . . and an immense feeling
of relief ensues. It is for the sake of this blessed moment, when no one is
greater or better than another, that people become a crowd.[17]

Instantaneous sociality of the crowd is a counter-structure to
socialization's structure. In one glorious moment of 'discharge' it
annuls years (perhaps centuries) of patient labour. It has no structure
of its own; it ruminates in the debris of the structure it just exploded –
the only structure 'society' knows of. Structure and history come
together and together they vanish, and the crowd has no history –
only 'collectively lived present'.[18] Once it comes together, the crowd
has accomplished everything there was to be attained. The crowd
may intoxicate itself with images of another world, but it does not set
itself that image as a goal, a task, a work to be done (being a crowd, it
is not capable of 'doing work' anyway); it thereby cancels its own
future.

The latter circumstance may add to the crowd's inborn curse: its
innate fragility. On second thought – perhaps not a curse, after all:
without ephemerality, without forgetting the past and shrugging off
the future, without extemporalizing the present moment – the great
simplification, the crowd's main seduction, would not be feasible.
Still, the crowd is brittle and short-lived: its glorious moments are

[17]   Elias Canetti, *Crowds and Power*, trans. Carol Stewart (Harmondsworth:
Penguin, 1973), pp. 18–19. 'Man petrifies and darkens in the distances he has
created', says Canetti. Man lightens up and comes alive the moment (and this
is, literally, a moment) when the distances melt in the heat of 'being with'. In
the Dionysian throng, among the Dionysiac revellers, 'the slave emerges as a
freeman; all the rigid, hostile walls which either necessity or despotism has
erected between men are shattered' (Friedrich Nietzsche, *The Birth of
Tragedy*, trans. Francis Golffing (New York: Doubleday, 1956), p. 23).
[18]   Michel Maffesoli, 'Jeux de Masques: Postmodern Tribalism', trans.
Charles R. Foulkes, in *Design Issues*, vol. 4, nos 1–2 (1988), p. 146. Maffesoli
connects this characteristic with the specifically *postmodern* phenomenon of
'neo-tribalism'. Cancellation of historical time is, however, a universal
feature of the crowd phenomenon; only its prominence can be truly thought
of as 'postmodern'.

fleeting moments. The structure is suspended, not dismantled. The crowd is a leave of absence from structure, but there is nowhere else but structure to return to after that leave is over.

Socialization offered one safe passage to the 'world of the Third', the world outside the moral party. The explosive sociality of the crowd offers another passage, more exciting though much less safe. Socialization made that vast world out there habitable through norms and rules to be memorized and obeyed. In the world, created in a flash by the crowd's sociality there are no norms and no rules to constrain – only the outstretched hand, hoping to grasp other hands nearby. 'We are all in it together.' Norms differentiate; normlessness dissolves the differences. In the crowd, we are all alike. We go about together, we dance together, we punch together, we burn together, we kill together – 'the only important thing being, in the final analysis, that all should bathe in the affectual ambience'.[19] 'What to do' is no more a *problem*. The target is immediately *obvious* – crystal-clear, readable in the eyes, gestures and movements of *everybody* around. Just do what others do. Not because what they do is sensible, useful, beautiful or right, or because they say so, or because you think so – but because they do it. There is a chance to glue together what has been a moment ago so agonizingly separated and estranged – and to do it through just a grimace, a gesture, a yell.

While socialization replaces moral responsibility with the obligation to obey procedural norms, in the crowd the question of responsibility never arises. The crowd brings the comfort of non-decision and non-uncertainty. Everything has been decided upon before anything started. Socialization floats responsibility off the agenda of the decision-maker. Sociality of the crowd disposes of responsibility together with the agenda and the decision-making.

As far as morality is concerned, the two outcomes are much the same. Heteronomy (of rules or crowds) takes the place of the autonomy of the moral self. Neither structure nor counter-structure, neither socialization of society nor the sociality of the crowd, tolerate moral independence. Both enforce and obtain obedience – though one by design, the other by default. Neither reason (at least the one reason that claims the right to this name: reason embodied in the power-assisted laws of society), nor passion, seething in the togetherness of the crowd, help the self to be moral: they only, for better or worse, help the self to survive in the wide, strange world that has no home for morality.

[19]   Michel Maffesoli, 'The Ethics of Aesthetics', trans. Roy Boyne, *Theory, Culture and Society*, vol. 8 (1991), p. 11.

The natural history of structure and counter-structure

Two processes, two principles. They are – or so it seems to you and me, to the modern – at cross-purposes: what one painstakingly builds up and vigilantly protects, the other assaults and tears to pieces. And yet – so it seems again – one can hardly live without the other. Without structure kept alive by incessant effort of socialization, there will be neither daily life nor history: only structures have history, since only they can last longer than lives and deeds of the mortal humans who compose them, fabricate them and are in turn fabricated by them. But structure achieves this remarkable feat at an enormous price of stifling the creative powers of those whose continuous collective history it assures: it has to paralyse so that it can galvanize, to deaden life in order to prolong it. If it had it its way, unchallenged – there would be no history, only endless repetition. Perhaps even the latter would not happen: structures are good at splitting people apart, but unless the fragments cling together even the effort of keeping them apart, each in the little cage of status and function, would run out of steam – commands would sound hollow and calls would fall on the blank wall of incomprehension. The two processes can hardly trust each other and cohabit in peace, but they must stop hostile actions short of the adversary's attrition. They are doomed to accommodate each other, or perish. A *modus vivendi* must be, and has been, found. Or, rather, a number of modes, in succession.

Of the first mode, we learn from Durkheim's remarkable study of the 'elementary forms of religious life'. In that mode, the two processes achieved, it seems, wondrous and exemplary co-operation – and they achieved it by the simple stratagem of temporal and spatial separation: there is time and place for one, and time and place for the other, but the two never meet and thus never clash:

> Sometimes the population is broken up into little groups who wander about independently of one another, in their various occupations; each family lives by itself, hunting and fishing, and in a word, trying to procure its indispensable food by all the means in its power. Sometimes, on the contrary, the population concentrates and gathers at determined points for a length of time varying from several days to several months.

It is difficult to imagine a sharper, more radical opposition between two times and places. In dispersion, life is 'uniform, languishing and dull'. But the very fact of concentration changes it all, locust-style; it acts as an 'exceptionally powerful stimulant'. 'A sort of electricity is formed', men and women are transported to an 'extraordinary degree of exaltation'. An 'avalanche' grows amidst 'violent gestures, cries, veritable howls, and deafening noises of every sort'; 'the effervescence often reaches such a point' and the 'passions released are of such impetuosity' that 'they can be restrained by nothing'.

Nothing exceptionally primitive about all this, to be sure. 'In the midst of an assembly animated by a common passion' do not we all 'become susceptible of acts and sentiments of which we are incapable when reduced to our own forces'? In the time of great revolutionary changes 'men look for each other and assemble together more than ever'. And then,

> the passions moving them are of such an intensity that they cannot be satisfied except by violent and unrestrained actions, actions of superhuman heroism or of bloody barbarism . . . Under the influence of the general exaltation, we see the most mediocre and inoffensive bourgeois become either a hero or a butcher.

What is genuinely peculiar to the 'primitive' societies to which Durkheim turned in search of understanding, is one thing only: mutual isolation and the smooth, peaceful and regular alternation of the two 'heterogeneous and mutually incomparable worlds' – that of quotidianity and carnival, structure and counter-structure, the *profane* and the *sacred*. The separation made wonders: the profane, 'languishing and dull' rhythm of quotidianity could replenish its energy, rejuvenate itself year by year, swilling the water of life from the fount of popular emotions without being threatened in the intervals by the uncontrolled eruption of the crowd's frenzy. This peaceful and profitable cohabitation 'puts clearly into evidence the bond uniting them to one another, but among the peoples called civilized, the relative continuity of the two blurs their relations'[20] – that is, the mutual services they proffer are not as clearly visible behind ostensible clashes as they once were thanks to the ingenuity of Australian aborigines.

This latter point went on worrying Durkheim, as we remember, when he looked desperately for the sources of moral vigour in our own world of strict division of labour and professional separation. It was Durkheim's strong belief that 'moral remaking cannot be achieved except by the means of reunions, assemblies, and meetings where the individuals, being closely united to one another, reaffirm in common their common sentiments'. But we, in our modern society proud of its rationality and good sense, are going through a stage of 'moral mediocrity' – 'we can no longer impassionate ourselves for the principles' of old, but we have not yet warmed up for any new ones.

[20]   Cf. Émile Durkheim, *The Elementary Forms of the Religious Life*, trans. Joseph Ward Swain (London: Allen & Unwin, 1968), pp. 209–20.

'In a word, the old gods are growing old or already dead, and others are not yet born.' The specifically modern form of the intricate relation between the profane and the sacred (structure and counter-structural sociality, in the vocabulary we have been using thus far) Durkheim found wanting. Such a state, he concluded, 'cannot last for ever. A day will come when our societies will know again those hours of creative effervescence.'[21]

What was that modern form, which Durkheim found inadequate and unlikely to survive for long, like? In a nutshell, modern times were prominent for the ruthless assault of the profane against the sacred, reason against passion, norms against spontaneity, structure against counter-structure, socialization against sociality. We seem to know by now why this had to be the case. The new order emerging from among the ruins of the *ancien régime* was state-managed and state-monitored, and so all vestiges of local ('parochial', 'traditional') authority could not but be seen and shunned as disruptive. Indeed, the yet uncertain order felt uneasy and reacted nervously to any manifestation of spontaneity. Cultural crusades of early modernity were aimed at uprooting and destroying the plural, manifold, communally sustained ways, in the name of one, uniform, civilized, enlightened, law-sustained pattern of life. What the crusades set out to extirpate was theorized as the 'old' and 'backward' modes of existence; no wonder that any, however gingerly, manifestation of spontaneity, even the palest copy of those festivals of frenzy lovingly narrated by Durkheim, could not but be seen as hiccups of the not-yet-fully-eradicated 'uncivilized', crude and in the end inhuman past. That is, as long as such festivals of passions were *eruptions* in the world aiming to be orderly, and *spontaneous* in the world wishing to be regular and law-abiding.

In fact, cultural crusades were but one side of the picture. The war against the local, the irregular and the spontaneous was merciless, but the modern state and its educational arm seldom aimed at pouring out the child of the sacred together with the bathwater of local pluralism. Earnest efforts were made throughout the modern era to replace manifold communal gettings-together, in their much needed func-tion of replenishing the reservoirs of sacred unity, with a centrally designed and controlled pantheon and calendar of festivities. As a rule, these were to become the focal points, symbols and the rituals of the new religion: that of nationalism. With the old, inconveniently obstreperous (that is, controlled not by the new powers) modes of reproduction of the sacred safely out of the way, a new friendly

[21] Cf. Durkheim, *The Elementary Forms of the Religious Life*, pp. 427–8.

armistice was hoped to be established, but this time, unambiguously, on the terms set and interpreted by the agencies in charge of the structure and socialization. In George L. Mosse's words, in the modernizing state,

> The general will became a secular religion . . . [The myths] were meant to make the world whole again and to restore a sense of community to the fragmented nation . . . Nationalism, which at its beginnings coincided with romanticism, made symbols the essence of its style of politics.

This was a tendency, gathering in force as the new nation-states searched for the means to sew back together the social and political body, which the civilizing process (the process of the self-assertion of the modern elite) split apart. This tendency gathered force as the consistently undermined, often persecuted, local traditions were losing their hold and their power to set the moral agenda and to supervise its implementation. The tendency reached finally its peak in the era of mass politics (that is, the era in which the gradual dissipation of communities into 'masses' came close to fulfilment), and can be best gleaned in the practice of fascist countries, which tried harder and with more determination what the liberal variants of the modern state struggled to achieve but half-heartedly and with only mixed success:

> [Nazi] rites and liturgies were central, an integral part of a political theory . . . The spontaneity itself was never a fact; all festivals are planned. But the carefully constructed illusion of spontaneity infused them with greater meaning.[22]

The same could be found in profusion in the practice of communist

---

[22]   Cf. George L. Mosse, *The Nationalisation of the Masses: Political Symbolism and Mass Movements in Germany from the Napoleonic Wars through the Third Reich* (New York: Fertig, 1975), pp. 2, 6, 9, 96. The Nazis were acknowledged masters-supreme in constructing the sacred destined to serve the profane, and inventing for this purpose traditions trimmed to the needs of the state and celebrated under close state supervision; what they did, however, was only to bring to near perfection what was undoubtedly the demand, and chance, of the age. Mosse presents, among others, the founder of Jewish nationalism, Theodore Herzl, as one of the modern leaders who intuited the new form which the marriage between the state and the sacred was to take under the auspices of the nation-state: 'When he dreamed about the future Jewish state, he envisaged national festivals with gigantic spectacles and colourful processions. He was going to commission popular hymns, and believed that with the proper flag, "one can lead men whenever one wants to, even into the Promised Land". He termed himself a dramatist and indeed his interest in the theatre was important. But he was equally fascinated with the problem of directing and leading crowds' (p. 97).

states. No wonder intellectuals from far and wide were fascinated; with a mixture of admiration and jaundice they watched the unfolding spectacle of custom-made popular enthusiasm, so painfully missing in their own homes, which by contrast looked much like the last retreat of 'languishing and dull life', the last and already doomed trenches of the 'jaded', 'senile' civilization. (What in that spectacle so strongly enticed the intellectuals who could not but dream of the spiritual leadership of the masses, was no doubt 'the taming of the beast', the apparently successful harnessing of the exuberant popular activism to the chariot of seductive societal vision – with the state firmly in the driver's seat and not for a moment letting the reins out of hand.) Indeed, the quotidianity of the legal-rational state seemed to leave no room, and certainly no respectable place, to the kind of things which the cultural creators were good at dreaming of and being after. Such feelings have been unerringly spotted and vividly recorded by Serge Moscovici:

> As reflection, held at a distance, gains ground, the emotions are repudiated, the bonds between individuals become more impersonal and the behaviour of each human being follows a logical course. The dreariness of the daily chores, of duties mechanically performed, of managing affairs, infects the existence in general of society . . .
>
> [T]he cultures that have preceded our own and which still form the majority, have succeeded in *institutionalizing mania* . . . By contrast, our modern culture tries successfully to *institutionalize melancholy* . . . [S]corning of ceremony and ritual, the struggle waged against the passions on grounds of self-interest, and against collective outbursts of enthusiasm in the name of organization could only end in this way. This condition of active indifference flows logically from a life that becomes egocentric and isolated, and from relationships dominated by laws that are neutral.[23]

Melancholy, ennui, apathy; these were endlessly repeated charges against the legal-rational, unemotional, business-like conduct of politics in a liberal-democratic state. Behind the charges was the feeling that neutral, formal laws are not a soil on which the moral life of the nation can flourish. If observing the letter of the law was to be the beginning and the end of human duty, what should induce the citizen to be concerned with anything but himself, and stop him from caring merely for his own gain, at whatever cost to the others? The injection of moral vigour was something that the state (once it had successfully disempowered the diffuse, local sources of moral authority) had to do *on top of* law-making. Promoting the 'national spirit'

---

[23]   Serge Moscovici, *The Invention of Society: Psychological Explanations for Social Phenomena*, trans. W.D. Halls (Cambridge: Polity Press, 1993), pp. 63–4.

met the bill well. It made the state with its 'neutral laws' not just the common constraint, but common concern as well. The majority – 'the mass' – those who had little use for individual freedom which the neutral laws offered – could still find consolation in the collective glory of the nation. Deprived of access to resources and activities which promised immortality of individual works, they could still bask in the sun of the nation's eternity.

The coercive powers of the modern state, when combined with the state-centred spiritual mobilization, made a poisonous mixture, the oppressive power and the murderous potential of which was unravelled in the practice of the communist and fascist regimes. More than any other forms of modern state those regimes succeeded in the short-circuiting of structure and counter-structure, socialization and sociality. The result was a well-nigh total subordination of morality to politics. 'Conscience collective', that (in Durkheim's view) sole source and guarantee of moral sentiments and morally guided conduct, was condensed, institutionalized, and merged with the legal powers of the political state. Moral capacity was all but expropriated, and whatever resisted the etatization was persecuted with all the might of the Law.

The postmodern divorce

It is one of the most seminal characteristics of the postmodern era that the state has no more capacity, need nor want of spiritual (and this includes the moral) leadership. The state 'lets go', by design or by default, the counter-structural powers of sociality.

First, the *capacity*: its tremendous power of colonization and coercive regulation of daily life the modern state derived from combined sovereignty over all crucial dimensions of individual and collective survival. For the greater part of modern history the state had to be a 'viable' totality – that is, able to contemplate a degree of economic solvency, offer a more or less complete list of cultural services, and defend its borders militarily. There were few nations large enough and resourceful enough to meet these conditions, and thus the number of sovereign nation-states was limited and essentially non-expandable. (A side-effect of that situation was that most states were as a rule ethnically heterogeneous, with an ethnic majority reigning over many minorities – as few nations or would-be nations were resourceful enough to pass the tests set for state sovereignty on their own; under the circumstances, cultural conversion, cultural crusades and concentrated effort of uniformization had to remain foremost preoccupations of the states.) Perched securely on the economic–cultural–military tripod, each nation–state was in a better position than any political unit before or after to take in, enlist, supervise and directly administrate the resources subjected to its power, including the moral resources of the population, and the counter–structural potential of sociality.

This tripod, however, has now fallen apart. The much talked about *globalization* of economy and cultural supplies, together with the defensive insufficiency of any political unit taken alone, spells the end of the modern state 'as we know it'. 'National economy' is today little more than a myth kept alive for electoral convenience; the economic role of most governments boils down on the whole to maintaining hospitable local conditions (docile labour, low taxes, good hotels and entertaining night life) to entice cosmopolitan, stateless and nomadic capital-brokers to visit and stay. 'Cultural sovereignty' is denied even the posthumous existence of the myth, as the culture industry and culture creators have been first to break through the confinement of the state borders. And the global reach and exorbitant costs of weapons put paid to national armies as guarantors of peace and security. In virtually every field, monopoly of power over their respective populations falls from the weakening hands of the state.

Second, the *need*: as old functions, one after another, slip away from the nation–state, taken over by the institutions which escape its political sovereignty, the state can do without mass mobilization of its citizenry. Indeed, a politically inactive, apathetic population best fits the remaining, mainly service-providing, functions of the state. The state lost interest in the sentiments and emotions of its subjects, as long as they did not interfere with 'law and order'. Obedience to the 'laws of the country', and to the growing volume of the stateless laws which the government of the country is obliged to police, can be achieved at a lesser cost with the help of the twin strategies of seduction and repression. (I have discussed these strategies, as well their mutual dependence which renders them effective only when they appear together, in my *Legislators and Interpreters* (Cambridge: Polity Press, 1987). Ideological legitimation of the state's right to determine the national values is required no more. Even less so, when the number of the seduced outgrows the number of the repressed – when the majority of the electorate becomes, in Galbraith's terms, 'contented' with their plight of independent managers of private destinies and thus believe their plight to benefit from the continuous shrinking of the state's interference. The contented majority would repeat after Peter Drucker: 'no more salvation by society'. They are taxpayers first; beneficiaries of state's power and glory only, if at all, a distant second.

This change of circumstance has been all too often glorified in the late-modern political theory. As Quentin Skinner points out, in a sharp opposition to early-modern Italian city-republics, which saw close kinship between freedoms of their citizens and 'civic glory and greatness' of the *polis*, between autonomy and participation,

> [r]ecent liberal theorists of freedom and citizenship have generally been content to assume that the act of voting constitutes a sufficient degree of democratic involvement, and that our civic liberties are best secured not by involving ourselves in politics but rather by erecting around ourselves a cordon of rights beyond which our rulers must not trespass.[24]

Third, the *want*: neither the operators of the state administration, nor the majority of those whom they administer, seem to desire a return to the project of merging 'society' and 'community' under the auspices and daily management of the state. Dislike of the idea comes from many sources. The privatization of self-formation and self-assertion in the case of the contented majority plays a prominent part among them, and is a sufficient reason for the present state of affairs to continue as long as the 'contented' remain in the majority. But there are other reasons to resent the state-management of sociality and to sympathize, if only grudgingly, with Skinner's 'liberal theorists of freedom and citizenship' – the most salient by far being the gruesome experience of only recently dismantled totalitarian systems. None of us, regardless of visions of good society we subscribe to, is sure nowadays whether the marriage between political state and social morality (always in the past leading to the state's drive to dissolve morality in state-administered law) may under any circumstances enhance the chances of moral life; and whether it may be at all insured against acting on its oppressive (and, in its radical extreme, genocidal) potential.

One way or the other, the present divorce between state-centred politics and the moral existence of the citizenry, or more generally between the state-managed institutional socialization and communal sociality, seems far gone and perhaps irreversible. Once more, as during the early years of the 'civilizing process', the field of sociality lies fallow, with no powers-that-be eager to till it.

---

[24]   Quentin Skinner, 'The Italian City-Republics', in *Democracy: The Unfinished Journey 508 BC to AD 1993*, ed. John Dunn (Oxford University Press, 1992), p. 68. Skinner's view is that in the result of the political transformation lauded by 'recent liberal theorists', governments 'impoverished the lives of their citizens' (p. 65).

Exit the nation–state, enter the tribes

It can not, and is not likely to lie fallow for long. The mass, in the fashion Prigogine portrayed in his theory of 'spontaneous structuration', seems to have an inner tendency to assemble (and to dissemble again) local quasi-structures. One may think of such spontaneous structurations as instances of crystal-forming in a satu-rated solution – time and again triggered off, albeit in a place and moment impossible to specify in advance – by the accidental intrusion of however minuscule a speck, or by however slight a disturbance; or, alternatively, one may think of them as whirlpools, forming in the current but retaining their shape for a time thanks to the incessant movement and exchange of contents. The short-lived, restless products of such spontaneous structuration are the neo-tribes. Tribes – because the levelling-down of units, erasure of differences, and militant assertion of collective identity are their mode of existence. 'Neo' – because deprived of the mechanisms of self-perpetuation and self-reproduction. Unlike 'classic' tribes, neo-tribes do not last longer than their units ('members'). Rather than being a collective compensation for individual mortality, they are vehicles of the *deconstruction of immortality*; tools of a kind of life which is a daily rehearsal of death and thus, by the same token, an exercise in 'instant immortality'. (I have discussed deconstruction of immortality, as a defining trait of postmodern culture, in *Mortality, Immortality and Other Life Strategies* (Cambridge: Polity Press, 1992). Michel Maffesoli, who introduced the term 'neo-tribes' to current dicourse, emphasizes that 'once the play has ended, what formed a whole becomes diluted until another mode emerges'. The overall result of such kaleidoscopic 'falling into shape' only to lose shape again, is that 'the succession of "presents" (with no future) is the best character-ization of the atmosphere of the moment'.[25]

Neo-tribes are, undoubtedly, eruptions of sociality – usually unplanned expeditions into the world beyond moral reach, now no more tightly 'structured' by either hereditary communities or legis-lative organs of the political state; brief reconnaissance invasions, boosted by a hope (though not by realistic prospects) of more protracted, even lasting, colonization. In this sense they are akin to the phenomenon of the crowd as briefly discussed above. Yet unlike the case of 'classic' crowds, the physical co-presence in a confined space (the circumstance which Durkheim believed to be the condition

[25]   Michel Maffesoli, ' "Affectual" Post-Modernism and Megapolis', in *Threshold*, vol. 4, p. 42.

of the 'effervescence', high intensity of emotions, frenetic activity typical of the crowd) is not required by the neo-tribes. The latter follow the pattern foretold by Gustave Le Bon a century ago, when he pondered the possibility of the 'psychological crowd', which:

> does not always imply the simultaneous presence of many individuals in the same place. Thousands of separate individuals may at certain moments, under the influence of certain violent emotions, for instance a great national event, assume the characteristics of a psychological crowd.[26]

With the world-wide, efficient network of communication, and illusion of immediacy arising from the mostly visual form which information assumes, it is all too easy for even small-scale, local and one-off events to become 'national', or even world-wide – in their notoriety, if not impact. The media-transmitted patterns for copy-cat imitation have the power to sustain 'crowds' of enormous sizes (though brittle structure) by the expedient of simultaneous 'replay' of action in places located at vast distances from each other. But the fact that the patterns are media-transmitted and have no other means of transmission or sources of credibility[27] determines also the brevity of their existence; media are inclined to vie for public attention, the commodity most scarce in the oversaturated market of information, and the attention-arresting capacity of news dissipates by the day. In spite of all the high-tech tools at their disposal, psychological crowds – exactly like their 'classic', physical ancestors – have an exceedingly short life-expectation. Each single neo-tribe is doomed to an episodic and inconsequential existence. What is neither episodic nor inconsequential is the postmodern condition in which neo-tribes become the dominant mode of counter-structural expression and sociality as such.

'Psychological crowd' is not the most felicitous of terms if one wishes to grasp the character of neo-tribal phenomenon. One would rather speak of *vestigial crowds*, or *rudimentary tribes*. Both terms convey the traits which seem to be most salient and intriguing in the postmodern forms of counter-structural collective sociality. Post-modern crowds and tribes are indeed 'residual': they are, so to

---

[26]   Gustave Le Bon, *Psychologie des foules* (Paris: Alcan, 1907), p. 12.

[27]   Most Germans interviewed during recent racist outrages that spread throughout Germany with the speed of a forest fire in imitation of what had initially been strictly local trouble, said that if it had not been for the vivid television images they would not have known that there were neo-Nazis in Cottbus, and certainly the thought of setting fire to migrants' camps would not have crossed their minds.

speak, 'single-issue' formations, with allegiances wrapped around one topic in public attention, and a comparatively simple topic (reduced to the 'lowest common denominator'), so that it can be absorbed by, excite and boost into action the otherwise disparate and differently 'positioned' or 'embedded' selves. Residual is also the repertoire of crowd behaviour. Seldom, if at all, do all self-appointed 'members' of a neo-tribe appear in one place and act in unison, as a crowd should. Rather, their mode of existence can be thought of as one of a diffuse, thinly spread plasma, which sporadically condenses locally in episodic displays of conduct emulating the pattern which has become the vestigial crowd's trade-mark. If the classic crowd is born and consumed by collective action, the vestigial crowd is better seen as a form of dispersion of the probabilities of action. If classic tribes are polysemic, multi-functional and multi-final, rudimentary tribes are 'specialized' in one issue, one type of action and one set of symbols.

To recapitulate: socialization and counter-structural sociality are two distinct, often opposed, ways in which the social space beyond the reach of moral impulse come to be domesticated and inhabitable: each in its own fashion makes possible the coexistence ('being with') among the multitude which does not constitute, nor is likely to establish, a 'moral party'. Socialization is in principle (though, because it is always linked to a sovereign power short of universality, not in practice) infinitely expandable; sociality, on the contrary, seems to be inherently divisive. Socialization is capable of sedimenting structures much more durable than the notoriously ephemeral and protean products of sociality. On the other hand, while socialization is prominent for its tendency to cool off, suppress and extinguish sentiments of the kind typical of moral drive, sociality gives emotions free rein and brings them to boiling point.

Neither, however (though for different reasons), can be considered as an extension of the 'moral party'. Neither makes social space amenable to moral husbandry: socialization, because of disarming and invalidating moral capacities; counter-cultural sociality, because of confiscating, expropriating, and channelling off the emotions which used to animate moral actions.

The two distinct modes of colonizing social space beyond the reach of the 'moral party' play down or sequestrate *empathy* – which Arne Johan Vetlesen (in his perceptive critique of my earlier formulations of moral theory presented in the last chapter of *Modernity and the Holocaust*) rightly defines as 'the specific cognitive-emotional precondition of moral capacity', an 'emotional faculty' 'that *underlies* and so facilitates the entire series of specific, manifest emotional attitudes and

ties to others, such as love, sympathy, compassion, or care'.[28]
Indeed, for interpersonal empathy no room is left in the social space
formed in the course of and for the duration of either systematic
socialization or combustive sociality. (Obedience to rules specifically
excludes empathy; the crowd-style togetherness plays on emotional
identification with the 'supra-personal' intolerant of personal specificity.) When both have done their job, the social and aesthetic spaces
which they plot out remain, as in the beginning, inhospitable to the
'emotional faculty' of moral selves.

[28]   Arne Johan Vetlesen, 'Why Does Proximity Make a Moral Difference?',
in *Praxis International*, vol. 12 (January 1993), p. 383. Vetlesen objects to the
thesis that a moral stance begins from an impulse oblivious to the prospect of
reciprocity. He insists that responsibility for others '*follows* from and is the
accomplishment of the living with others' experienced as 'a *we*-experience'.

6

Social Spaces: Cognitive, Aesthetic, Moral

Much has been written on the distinction between 'physical' – 'objective' space, 'space as such' – and *social space*. It is commonly agreed that the two stand in a metaphorical relationship with each other. On the one hand, we speak of social space using the terms coined to account for the physical, 'objective' and measurable proximity/distance. On the other hand, however, one can also point out that the idea of such a 'physical space' could be arrived at solely through phenomenological reduction of daily experience to pure quantity, during which distance is 'depopulated' and 'extemporalized' – that is, systematically cleansed of all contingent and transitory traits; only at the end of such reduction the 'objective space', the 'space as such' may be conceived of – as 'pure space', 'empty space', space devoid of any content relative to time and circumstance. On this other view, physical space is an abstraction which cannot be experienced directly: we grasp physical space intellectually with the help of notions which have been coined originally to 'map' the qualitatively diversified relations with other humans.

Social space itself is, however, far from simple and needs further unpacking. In particular, it ought to be seen as a complex interaction of three interwoven, yet distinct processes – those of *cognitive*, *aesthetic* and *moral* 'spacings' – and their respective products. The three varieties of 'non-objective', 'human-made', social space are often talked about in one breath, and the three concepts used as if standing for 'facets' of the same social mapping. And yet though all three spaces deploy the notions of proximity and distance, closeness and openness – the three space-producing mechanisms are different in their pragmatics and in their outcomes. If the cognitive space is constructed intellectually, by acquisition and distribution of knowledge, aesthetic space is plotted affectively, by the attention guided by curiosity and the search for experiential intensity, while moral space is 'constructed' through an uneven distribution of felt/assumed responsibility.

Knowing the Other, knowing of the Other

That to live is to live *with others* (other human beings; other beings *like us*) – is obvious to the point of banality. What is less obvious and not at all banal, is the fact that what we call 'the others' we live with (that is, once we live a sort of life which includes the awareness that we live it *with* others) is what we *know* of them. Each of us 'construes' his or her own assortment of 'others' out of the sedimented, selected and processed memory of past encounters, communications, exchanges, joint ventures or battles.

The basic knowledge from which any construction of the other takes off is so simple and 'matter-of-fact' that we hardly ever give it a thought, unless we are philosophers who make it our vocation to be puzzled by the evident and the familiar. Awareness that 'others like us' exist and that their existence matters one way or the other, is the elementary attitude which Alfred Schütz, following Max Scheler (and opposing Husserl, to whom the existence of others appeared as the most bewildering of challenges facing the philosopher who embarked on the search for certainty) called 'natural' – meaning that it precedes rather than follows the conscious efforts to learn from personal experience or instruction. 'Natural attitude' consists of 'background knowledge', of what we take 'for granted' (that is, what we take as a truth which calls for no tests and requires no proof; a non-reflected-upon truth).

> I simply take it for granted that other men also exist in this my world, and indeed not only in a bodily manner like and among other objects, but rather as endowed with a consciousness that is essentially the same as mine . . .
>
> It is self-evident to me in the natural attitude not only that I can act upon my fellow-men but also that they can act upon me . . . [T]hey, my fellow-men, experience their relations which reciprocally include me in a way that

is similar, for all practical purposes, to the way in which I experience them.[1]

The basic knowledge, 'pre-packaged' in the natural attitude – the 'naive' knowledge, the knowledge we all have without knowing that we 'have' it – is the knowledge of 'being with' other humans; within natural attitude the 'with' stands for a perfectly symmetrical relationship. Everything in this elementary 'with'-relation is *reciprocated*: perceptions of the objects given to the senses, abilities to act upon them, motives of action. The natural attitude assumes what Schütz calls 'reciprocity of perspectives': what I see, you see, the objects of seeing being 'the same' for whoever looks at them (though, as Ludwig Wittgenstein told us, there is no way we can ever find out whether this is indeed the case); what I mean by these words I have uttered – these words also mean for you who hear them; we *understand* each other. Understanding is natural and normal, *mis*-understanding *un*-natural and abnormal. It is the *mis*-understanding that requires explanation, makes us pause and think, sets minds moving, triggers the process of conscious knowledge-building.

The symmetry of natural attitude casts humans as alike; the experience of misunderstanding posits humans as unlike each other. 'Understanding' is always the same, and so it can be thought of only in the singular. 'Misunderstandings' are many, all specific and different, and they can and are thought of in the plural. We start to differentiate between the others from the experience of diverse fashions in which the assumption of symmetry and reciprocity has been flouted. 'The world as world is only revealed to me when things go wrong.'[2] The construction of the social world starts in earnest when naive expectations are frustrated, and thus cease to be naive.

What happens then is what Martin Heidegger described as the transfer of objects from the *zuhanden* to the *vorhanden* mode. In the first mode, the objects are not reflected upon. They are just where we know they are and nowhere else, they are just what we know they are and nothing else – they never give us a surprise, let alone a shock; we do not need to think twice to handle them, and thus we have no opportunity to think of handling them as 'handling'. It is only when

---

[1] Alfred Schütz and Thomas Luckmann, *The Structures of the Life-World*, trans. Richard M. Zaner and H. Tristram Engelhardt Jr. (London: Heinemann, 1974), pp. 4–5.
[2] Arland Ussher, *Journey through Dread* (New York: Devin-Adair, 1955), p. 80.

they behave oddly, in an 'unusual' fashion, that they call for a second thought. In the *zuhanden* mode, they were 'in hand'; in the *vorhanden* mode, where they have moved now, they are 'out there', out of reach: they need to be grasped first before they can be handled. This is the challenge of which knowledge is born. Knowledge picks up from the point of breach, disruption, *mis*-understanding.

One may say that once this happens, objects become *visible* (that is, I am aware of seeing them, I see them as definite objects) – since there is now a *distance* between me and them. At a distance, I may look at them, examine them from various angles, 'form a picture'. Knowledge is the management of that distance. I can see better things that are closer to the eye – but one may say with equal justification that this ratio works the other way as well: what I 'see better' (that is, what I have more knowledge of) I perceive as 'closer'; the scarcer and more perfunctory is my knowledge, the dimmer the objects appear – the 'further away' they are. The statements 'I know better such things as are close' and 'close are the things which I know better' are two equivalent articulations of the inextricable link (indeed, identity) between reflection and distance, knowledge and social space. In the life-world, proximity and remoteness of objects is measured (indeed, made) by the degree of richness or paucity of knowledge.

What applies to objects in general obviously applies as well to such objects as happen to be other human beings (that is, to humans *as* objects). Distance between me and them is also made (or un-made) by my knowledge. To quote from Schütz once more, 'the system of spatial arrangements' 'enters into the differentiation of intimacy and anonymity, of strangeness and familiarity, of *social* proximity and distance' – and all these distinctions refer to the relative volume, durability, intensity of my 'biographical experience' of the person in question, plotted between the poles of intimacy and anonymity.[3]

At the intimacy pole, quite a lot of biography is shared with the Other. No wonder that the accumulated knowledge is vast and multifaceted. I have observed the Other daily, on all sorts of occasions, in all kinds of actions and in all moods and states of mind. There is virtually nothing in the Other identity that I might have missed, or I may think of as something I am ignorant of. One could almost say that at the intimacy pole the Other has been returned from the *vorhanden* to the *zuhanden* mode – but we cannot really say that, since the intimate Other looms large in my life because of the huge volume of knowledge invested, not naively; innocence once lost can be never recovered. However close the Other

[3] Schütz and Luckmann, *The Structures of the Life-World*, pp. 40–1.

might have become to me, she is now construed of knowledge I have acquired and keep acquiring as we go on interacting.

At the anonymity pole, one cannot really speak of social distance at all. A truly anonymous Other is outside or beyond social space. Such another is not truly an object of knowledge – apart, at best, from a subliminal awareness that there is, potentially, a human who could be an object of knowledge. For all practical intents and purposes, she is not human at all, since humans we know of are always 'specific' humans, classified humans, humans endowed with categorial attributes through which they can be identified. The space between the poles of intimacy and anonymity is made precisely of such classes and categories. The humans who inhabit that space do not have identities of their own, no 'personal' identities – they derive identity from the classes to which they 'belong' – or, rather, to which they have been assigned. And the assignment is accomplished in the process of the acquisition of knowledge. These humans we do not know; we know *of* them. We know of them in a roundabout way, through the information we have put together about the categories the specimens of which they are. We know of them, as Schütz would say, through the process of *typification* – as types, not persons. The world of contemporaries, says Schütz, 'is stratified according to levels of anonymity'.[4]

The farther away they are from the intimacy pole, the more other humans become *strangers* (until, at the anonymity extreme, they vanish from view altogether). Of strangers, we know too little to engage in any but a most shallow and perfunctory interaction (the co-presence most palatable in such a case is, in fact, the mutual abstention from interacting). The 'strangeness' of strangers means precisely our feeling of being lost, of not knowing how to act and what to expect, and the resulting unwillingness of engagement. Avoidance of contact is the sole salvation, but even a complete avoidance, were it possible, would not save us from a degree of anxiety and uneasiness caused by a situation always pregnant with the danger of false steps and costly blunders.

Blunders arise from the ignorance of rules, and the strangeness of strangers is, at bottom, our ignorance. 'Types' (classes, categories) are construed of differentially distributed rules of conduct (and, by the same token, differentially distributed anticipations of response); social space is rule-governed, and habitable as far as rule-governed. The more 'strange' the stranger is (the less knowledge I have of her), the less am I confident in my decision to assign her to a type. The

[4]   Schütz and Luckmann, *The Structures of the Life-World*, p. 80.

confidence of my typification wilts and peters out with the growth of distance (i.e. with the paucity of knowledge). There is, however, a yet more powerful source of anxiety, of which we do not hear from Schütz: I may know of the stranger so little that I cannot be even sure that she 'fits' any of the types I am familiar with. There is always the danger of the stranger 'sitting across the barricade', blurring the boundaries which ought to be kept watertight, and thus sapping the securely 'typified' world. The stranger carries a threat of wrong classification, but – more horrifyingly yet – she is a threat to classification as such, to the order of the universe, to the orientation value of social space – to my life-world as such.

However, as we saw at the beginning, social and physical spaces do not overlap; neither is the cognitive assimilation necessarily proportionate to the length of physical distance. Consequently, situations abound where possibility (or, indeed, the imperative) of effective action (thanks to the *physical* proximity) coincide with the absence or ignorance of action-guiding rules (because of the *social* remoteness). This is why social space, so to speak, is constantly under fire and in danger of chaos. An assortment of expedients is called for to defend its integrity.

The alien next door

Through a large part of human history, physical and social proximity did overlap – or were, at least, closely correlated. For the self, the world of the *biologically* human split into two sections kept strictly apart and rarely confused: that of the neighbours and that of the aliens. An alien could enter the radius of physical proximity only in one of three capacities: either as an enemy to be fought and expelled, or as an admittedly temporary guest to be confined to special quarters and rendered harmless by strict observance of the isolating ritual, or as a neighbour-to-be, in which case he had to be made like neighbour, that is made to behave like the neighbours do. In the classic summary of Lewis Mumford, '[t]he unattached person during the Middle Ages was one either condemned to exile or doomed to death; if alive, he immediately sought to attach himself, at least to a band of robbers.'[5]

[5]   Lewis Mumford, *The Culture of Cities* (New York, 1938, p. 29). The advent of the 'untrammelled individual' caused modern times, on the other hand, to be 'a world governed by the ideas of safety and salvation' – since stabilization and equilibrium turned now to be problematic (p. 64).

Familiarity refers solely to a satisfactory volume of knowledge we possess, and so it did not then, as it does not now, necessarily mean friendship. Neither had it to mean trust. Nor readiness for altruistic sacrifice. Nor sentiment of unity, mutual loyalty, brotherhood. Ideology which represents community as a unit held together by the *awareness* of unity, by a fraternal sentiment which makes it family-like without making it a family, as a territory of unqualified co-operation and mutual help – such an ideology came later, as a sure symptom of a neighbourhood already losing, and losing fast, its identity, clear boundary, and hence also its grip over human attitudes and reciprocal relations. The reality of the neighbourhood was more diversified than the latter-day ideology of community would allow or accept. It had room for love as much as for hostility, for solidarity as much as for conflict. And yet the physical neighbourhood stood out from the rest of the social space for the absence of strangers, and hence the satisfying, secure fullness of normative regulation.

What truly distinguished the neighbour from the rest was not therefore sympathy felt toward him, but the fact that he had always been potentially within sight, always leaning towards the intimacy pole, always a prospective partner of intercourse and biography-sharing. Knowledge of the neighbour was ample, typification residual, and whenever applied, rarely revised and hardly for a moment provisional. There were thus rules for every occasion and hardly any occasions under-supplied with rules. And, for once, the assumption of 'reciprocity of perspectives' was more often than not correct and seldom frustrated. Symmetry or complementarity of perceptions was genuine, self-reinforcing and self-reproducing. Societies which offered such a life-world could do without professional teachers of behaviour in public. And without the police.

They could not do without the armies, though. Social space stopped at the neighbourhood's boundary. On the other side of the boundary stretched fallow waste, semantic void, wilderness: the intellectually alien world inhabited by faceless bodies. The bodies could cross the frontier, but the rules of coexistence stayed at home and could not survive the trespassing. Societies which did not need police installed no mercy, compassion, or fellow-feeling for the unknown. They had no rules to deal with the aliens. The aliens were beyond norms and rules. Humans did not divide into neighbours and aliens: either they were humans, or they were aliens. In the stable agricultural societies he investigated, Edmund Leach found a remarkable overlap between topographical and kinship series of categories 'which discriminate areas of social space in terms of distance from Ego (self)': the relations 'self–sister–cousin–neighbour–stranger' paralleled that of 'self–pet–livestock–game–wild animal', and both were isomorphic with the chain 'self–house–farm–field–far(remote)'.[6] The strangers (aliens), wild animals and the remote 'far away' all stood for the same absence of rules of interaction.

A totally new situation emerges when the co-ordination between physical and social/cognitive proximity is broken. Aliens then appear physically inside the confines of the life-world. The strangeness of the strangers ceases to be a temporary breach of the norm and a curable irritant. Strangers stay and *refuse to go away* (though one keeps hoping that they will, in the end) – while, stubbornly, escaping the net of local rules and thus remaining strangers. They are not visitors, those stains of obscurity on the transparent surface of daily reality, which one can bear with, hoping that they will be washed out tomorrow (though one would still be tempted to do the washing right away). They do not wear swords; nor do they seem to hide daggers in their cloaks (though of that one can never be sure). They are not like the aliens, the outright enemies that prompt one to draw out the sword (or at least this is what they say). However, they are not like the neighbours either. True, one cannot avoid being aware of their presence, seeing, hearing and smelling them, even talking to them or being talked to by them on occasion. But the encounters are far too brief and casual to make a firm classificatory decision, and then there are so many of them coming and going.

Simmel considered money, that *Eigenschaftenlos* abstraction of pure and neutral quantity devoid of all substance and qualitative differentiation, as simultaneously the inescapable product, indispensable condition and a most illuminating metaphor of city life:

> The significance of the stranger for the nature of money seems to me to be epitomized in miniature by the advice I once overheard: never have any financial dealings with two kinds of people – friends and enemies. In the first case, the indifferent objectivity of money transactions is in insurmountable conflict with the personal character of the relationship; in the other, the same condition provides a wide scope for hostile intentions which corresponds to the fact that our forms of law in a money economy are never precise enough to rule out wilful malice with certainty. The desirable party for financial transactions – in which, as it has been said quite

---

[6]   Edmund Leach, 'Anthropological Aspects of Language: Animal Categories and Verbal Abuse', in *New Directions in the Study of Language*, ed. Eric H. Lenneberg (University of Chicago Press, 1964), p. 36–7. In particular, Leach suggested the 'friend/enemy ambiguity' which sets the neighbour apart from other items in the series may be seen as semiotic equivalent of 'alternating friendship/hostility' which characterizes postures taken towards 'game' (p. 44).

correctly, business is business – is the person completely indifferent to us, engaged neither for us nor against us.[7]

Money transaction is, indeed, the foremost epitome of the urban-type intercourse (that is, a 'cognitively malnutritioned' intercourse). Its character must be defended not just against hostility and malice, but against friendship and sympathy as well. It can be properly performed only under conditions of emotional neutrality; or, rather, under conditions free of the disturbing impact of affects. The two polar categories of neighbours and aliens into which the pre-modern human world was split, were equally ill-suited and inhospitable to money exchange. Proliferation of the money economy came together with the pushing aside and marginalizing of both sides of the once all-embracing dichotomy, and the filling of the vacated centre by the vast, infinitely expandable area of 'neither/nor' relationships. The intercourse which takes place inside this area cannot be executed in emotionally charged situations. It needs partners as faceless as the monetary signs, guided in their expected and actual behaviour solely by the shared consideration of quantity, rather than by inevitably unique, subject-bound qualitative values. Cut free from its anchor in another person, attention can now be attached to the impersonal rules of the transaction itself.

The arcane art of mismeeting

The most striking and off-putting trait of strangers is that they are *neither* neighbours *nor* aliens. Or, rather – confusingly, disturbingly, terrifyingly – they are (or may be – who knows?) both. Neighbourly aliens. Alien neighbours. In other words, *strangers*. That is, socially distant yet physically close. The aliens within physical reach. Neighbours outside social reach. Inhabitants of no man's land – a space either normless or marked with too few rules to make orientation possible. Agents and objects of an intercourse which for that reason is doomed to remain disconcertingly erratic, hazardous, with no assurance of success. Intercourse with the strangers is always an incongruity. It stands for the paucity or incompatibility of the rules which the non-status or confused status of the stranger invokes. It is best not to meet strangers at all. As one cannot really keep away from the space they occupy or share, the next best solution is a meeting which

[7] Georg Simmel, *The Philosophy of Money*, trans. Tom Bottomore and David Frisby (London: Routledge, 1978), p. 227.

is not quite a meeting, a meeting pretending not be one, a (to borrow Martin Buber's term) *mismeeting* ('*Vergegnung*', as distinct from the meeting, *Begegnung*).

To live with strangers, one needs to master the art of mismeeting. The application of such art is necessary if the strangers, for their sheer number if not for any other reason, cannot be domesticated into neighbours. On the other hand, it is the application of this art that constitutes the other as a stranger and reaffirms him in this capacity.

The art of mismeeting, if mastered, would relegate the other into the background; the other would be no more than a blot on the backcloth against which the action is set. True, shifting the other to the background does not make him disappear. The background is undeniably there. One knows that, were this her wish, she would be able to bring it into focus at any time. And yet one sees no reason to do so. The background bears no impact on the course and the results of action except for providing its physical setting. In the Schützian process of *periodeusis*, that scanning of the world-within-reach which results in the assignment of *topical relevances*, the stranger is assigned none. His is an irrelevant presence, a non-recognized being, a non-admitted existence: a non-being being – an incongruity resonant with his own. By the technique of mismeeting, the stranger is allocated to the sphere of disattention,[8] the sphere within which all conscious contact, and above all a conduct which may be recognized by him as a conscious contact, is studiously avoided. This is the realm of non-engagement, of emotional void, inhospitable to either sympathy or hostility; an uncharted territory, stripped of signposts; a wild reserve inside the life-world. For this reason it must be ignored. Above all, it must be *shown* to be ignored, and to be wished to be ignored, in a way allowing no mistake.

In the set of techniques that combine into the art of mismeeting, the most prominent perhaps is the avoidance of eye contact. It is enough to note the number of furtive glances each pedestrian needs to cast in order to monitor the movements of passers-by and so to avoid

---

[8]   Erving Goffman, *Relations in Public: Microstudies of the Public Order* (London: Allen Lane, 1971), p. 312. Being included in such a sphere, according to Goffman, means to require only *civil inattention* and to respond with a similar 'courtesy'. 'The forms of civil inattention, of persons circumspectly treating one another with polite and glancing concern while each goes about his own separate business, may be maintained, but behind these normal appearances individuals can come to be at the ready, poised to flee or to fight back if necessary.' As long as it is maintained, civil inattention sustains 'the surface character of public order' (pp. 331–2).

collision; or the surreptitious visual scanning of the crowded office or waiting room one enters in order to locate an unobtrusive place for himself – to realize how complex are the skills this technique requires.[9] The point is to see while pretending that one is not looking. To look 'inoffensively', provoking no response, neither inviting nor justifying reciprocation; to attend, while demonstrating disattention. What is required is scrutiny disguised as indifference. A reassuring gaze, informing that nothing will follow the perfunctory glance and no mutual rights or duties are presumed.

But the summary effect of the universal application of *civil indifference* is, as Helmuth Plessner has cogently demonstrated,[10] the *loss of face*: or, rather, a failure to acquire one. The urban crowd is not a collection of individuals. It is rather an indiscriminate, formless aggregate in which individuality dissolves. The crowd is faceless, but so are its units. Units are replaceable and disposable. Neither their entry nor their disappearance makes a difference. It is through their facelessness that the mobile units of urban congestion are defused as the possible sources of social engagement.

The overall effect of deploying the art of mismeeting is 'desocializing' the potentially social space around, or preventing the physical space in which one moves from turning into a social one – a space with rules of engagement and interaction. The techniques of mismeeting all serve to achieve this effect and to inform whoever may watch that the effect has been achieved and indeed intended. To evict from social space the others who are otherwise within reach (that is, physically close), or to deny them admittance, means to abstain from acquiring knowledge about them (and to deny them knowledge of oneself). The evicted others hover in the background of the perceived world, and are prompted to stay there – the featureless, faceless, empty shells of humanity which they are. My subliminal awareness

[9]   The techniques of avoidance necessary for life in a city ('a stranger among strangers'; or, as Benjamin Nelson once put it, the 'universal otherhood') have found a thorough ethnographic description and a strikingly convincing analysis in Lyn H. Lofland, *A World of Strangers: Order and Action in Urban Public Space* (New York: Basic Books, 1973). According to Lofland, the key to urban survival is the 'capacity for the surface, fleeting, restricted relationship' (p. 178); this is the task which the techniques of disattention, in common with other specifically urban skills, serve.

[10]   Cf. 'Über Menschenverachtung', in Helmuth Plessner, *Diesseits der Utopie* (München: Suhrkamp, 1974). Loss of face, Plessner suggests, inevitably follows that looking at each other 'at a distance', which the contemporary world cannot do without regardless of the price of deindividualization it must pay.

of their humanity should not be allowed to surface in the recognition of their subjectivity.

By the same token, it is now my courtesy and good judgement which makes me tolerate their presence – even if it is only their backdrop presence that I tolerate. In doing so, I give tribute to my generosity, not to their rights. I myself set the limits to which I would go. The limits may shift, there is nothing obligatory about them, the stuff of which boundaries are carved has no resilience of its own, no structure to which I must attend with the same care with which I examine my carving tools and calculate their carving powers. De-faced, the formed – or the never-fully-formed – individuals blend in the homogeneous compound in which my life is inserted. Like all other samples of this amalgam, they appear, in Simmel's memorable phrase, 'in an evenly flat and grey tone; no one object deserves preference over any other'. If differing values of objects, and hence the objects themselves *qua* objects, are noted, they 'are experienced as insubstantial'. All things, as it were, 'float with equal specific gravity . . ., lie on the same level and differ from one another only in the size of the area which they cover'.[11]

Simmel insists that this maintenance of a distance at which all faces blur and turn into shapeless and uniformly grey blots, this detachment always tinged with aversion and antipathy (or, rather, with effort to stave off the risk of sympathy), is a natural defence against the dangers inherent in living among strangers. Repulsion and subdued hostility, controlled most of the time yet never fully eradicated and always ready to condense into hatred, make such living technically possible and psychologically bearable. They sustain the dissociation which is the only form of socialization under the circumstances: living next to each other (though not together). They are now the natural, and the only available, means of self-defence.

Unlike real encounters, mismeetings are events without prehistory (no one anticipates that strangers will be there) and lived in a way that deprives them of the aftermath. They are *episodes*; and an episode, as Milan Kundera wrote, 'is not an unavoidable consequence of preceding action, not the cause of what is to follow; it is outside the causal chain of events which is the story. It is merely a sterile accident which can be left out without making the story lose its intelligible continuity, and is incapable of making a permanent mark upon the life of the characters.' An episode is not part of the story; it is cast

[11]   Georg Simmel, 'The Metropolis and Mental Life', in *Classic Essays on the Culture of Cities*, ed. Richard Sennett (New York: Appleton-Century-Crofts, 1969), p. 52.

beyond that realm of the conscious in which knowledge is earnestly gathered and – successfully or not – stored. The episode, one may say, is an interval, a break in the game of typifying, categorizing and mapping. Mismeeting, like all episodes, does not depend on past achievements of social cartography; neither does it improve on the current state of cartographic art – it leaves, in principle, everything as it was . . .

Or so it is hoped; though all too often in vain. Before the encounter is over and the partners find themselves again, like before it started, beyond each other's reach, there is no way of telling whether their evanescent face-to-face has indeed tapered off to the point of a mismeeting. But even after the apparent end of the encounter – long after – its consequences unforeseen at the time may suddenly surface, thus belying its supposed episodic nature (to avail ourselves once more of the great story-teller's wisdom: 'nobody can guarantee that some totally episodic event may not contain within itself a power that some day would unexpectedly turn it into a cause of further events'.)[12] No matter how hard one tries to prevent the chance encounter from breaking through the tight frame of mismeeting, a residue of anxiety cannot be wiped out. One knows, or feels without knowing, that there may yet be a sequel to what seems now a non-event, and that there is no telling which of the possibilities is going to be the case, and that the time of telling this will probably never arrive. Defence of social space is never foolproof. Boundaries cannot be hermetically sealed. There is no really infallible cure against strangers, let alone against the dread they arouse.

The city is a place of mismeetings. Urban physical space is so organized that meetings which are not actively sought may be avoided; if unavoidable, they may still remain inconsequential. Richard Sennett gave us a perceptive, thoughtful description of some of the foremost achievements of modern urban architecture (Lever House in New York, Brunswick Centre in London, Defence Office in Paris) as 'vast areas of empty space', areas 'to pass through, not to use', 'to move through, not to be in'. The spatial organization of the city as a whole, with its thoroughfares and urban motorways, underground trains and air-conditioned and tightly sealed cars, may be conceived of as a facility for making 'a journey from place A to

---

[12]   Milan Kundera, *Immortality*, trans. Peter Kussi (London: Faber & Faber, 1991), pp. 338–9. No episode, sums up Kundera, 'is *a priori* condemned to remain an episode for ever, for every event, no matter how trivial, conceals within itself the possibility of sooner or later becoming the cause of other events and thus changing into a story or an adventure'.

place B',[13] for breaking the continuity between places, isolating homely spots from the wilderness in between. In addition, the organization of urban space is prominent for its pronounced tendency to segregate classes, ethnic groups, sometimes genders or generations – so that the techniques of mismeeting could be applied more concertedly and with greater trust in their effect; yet, more importantly, segregation spawns vast areas within the city (and these are the areas where one tends to visit most often) where the visitor may disarm, or at least put weapons aside for a moment, since the threat attached to unsolicited intercourse with the kind of strangers likely to be present there feels less oppressive than elsewhere; indeed, meeting strangers feels for a change like an exciting opportunity rather than a danger.

If cognitive space could be projected upon the city map, or upon the map of a country or the modern world as a whole, it would take the shape of an archipelago, rather than a circle or any other compact and continuous figure. For every resident of the modern world, social space is spattered over a vast sea of meaninglessness in the form of numerous larger and smaller blots of knowledge: oases of meaning and relevance amidst a featureless desert. Much of daily business is spent in travelling through semiotically empty spaces – moving physically from one island to another. Islands are not contiguous, but neither they are exchangeable; each harbours different knowledge, meanings, relevance. To preserve their respective identities, measures need to be taken to fortify the coastline, to stem the flood. In other words – to keep the strangers confined to their places. Defence of social space boils down to the struggle for the right to mobility for oneself and for the limitation of such rights of others. The regular police was a modern, urban invention, and its original brief was the defence of urban public space against intruders whose annoying curiosity deprived the others of the protection of anonymity.[14] 'Loitering' has been a typically urban offence – conceived as a punishable crime only because it clashed with the conception of the public space as an 'area to move through, not to be in'. The never-

[13]   Richard Sennett, *The Fall of Public Man* (Cambridge University Press, 1974), pp. 12–14.
[14]   The instruction given to the police force freshly set up in Derby in 1835, also spelling out the main reason for instituting a professional order-protecting force, offers a good illustration: 'Persons standing or loitering on the footway without sufficient cause, so as to prevent the free passage of such a footway . . . may be apprehended and taken before a magistrate' (quoted after Anthony Delves, 'Popular Recreations and Social Conflict in Derby,

reached, always aimed-at ideal of the urban space would be perhaps a set of little walled off and well-guarded fortresses linked by a spaghetti-like maze of freeways, thoroughfares and urban motor-ways.

In the process of development of the urban organization of space as a setting for mismeetings, and of the habits of civil inattention, the cause and effect reinforced each other to the point of becoming difficult to separate. In the end, one is unthinkable without the other.

The stranger's aporia

The massive entry of strangers into the living space has rendered the pre-modern mechanisms of social spacing obsolete – but, above all, woefully inadequate. The sheer volume of the phenomenon pre-cludes their application. Instantaneous polarization of the strangers 'within reach' into neighbours and aliens has lost whatever chances it might have had of a success. Even if attempted, it would have brought but doubtful, contested and precarious results. Once a temporary irritant, the strangehood has become a permanent con-dition. The problem of modern society is not how to eliminate strangers, but how to live in their constant company – that is, under the condition of cognitive paucity, indetermination and uncertainty. Which does not mean that the attempts to cleanse the life-world from strangers have ground to a halt. The contrary is true, if anything: the endemic uncertainty which the presence of strangers cannot but keep galvanizing finds its outlet in the continuous efforts to gain control over social spacing – that is, to confine and regiment freedom of the strangers and altogether 'keep them where they belong'.

On the other hand, as has been cogently demonstrated by Simmel's exposition of the unbreakable link between strangehood, money economy and intellect – modern life in the form it has historically acquired cannot do without strangers. The ban on emotional engage-ment, indifference to qualitative difference, prising the encounter free from past constraints and the considerations of the future – all these remarkable features which contacts with strangers and only those contacts possess – are indispensable in the modern business of life. Strangehood, so to speak, must be preserved and cultivated if modern life is to go on. None of the essential institutions of modern

1800–1850', in *Popular Culture and Class Conflict, 1590–1914: Explorations in the History of Labour and Leisure*, ed. Eileen and Stephen Yeo (Brighton: Harvester, 1981), p. 95).

society would survive a miraculous triumph of 'communal togetherness' were it ever to happen; nor would they survive a colonization of
the field of mismeetings and civil inattention by personal, emotionally charged relations. Were there no strangers, one may say, they
would need to be invented . . . And they are – daily, and on massive
scale.

Hence the deep ambivalence of the position and role of the stranger
in social space. Strangers are continuously spawned in the course of
the selfsame daily life which strives to eliminate strangehood (physically, by separation and confinement; or psychologically, by inattention). Strangers are products of the same social spacing which aims at
assimilating and domesticating the life-world. Expectedly, the ambivalence of existential status is semiotically commuted (mirrored) in
the ambivalence of attitude. The baffling mixture of authorship and
receivership, experienced as a simultaneity of need and threat,
rebounds in the perception of strangehood as, simultaneously, the
anchor and the bane of existence. The 'solution' of ambivalence, that
condition admittedly without solution, is then desperately sought
through projecting its inner incongruity upon a selected social target
(that is, focusing the ambivalence which saturates the whole of social
space on a selected sector of that space), and ongoing efforts to 'burn
out' the germ of ambivalence in that effigy. The efforts are bound to
be interminable, being, as they are, as much inescapable as they are
inconclusive.

Commenting upon the research conducted by his student John
Scotson in a Leicester suburb, where a new estate populated by a
mixed bunch of newcomers was erected in the vicinity of a long
settled residential area, Norbert Elias coined the conceptual pair of
'established' and 'outsiders'. The pair was meant to capture a kind of
social figuration in which two groups are sedimented, set against each
other in a continuous warfare of boundary drawing and boundary
defence, yet locked together through the services each one renders to
the other group's search for identity. The original initiative which set
in motion the processes of mutual separation and stereotyping, Elias
ascribed to the 'established' group. (It was, in fact, one trait which in
two groups relating to each other in an otherwise strikingly similar
way, allowed the distinguishing of one group as 'established' and the
other as 'outsiders'.) It was the repulsion of newcomers by the
established population, resentful of the challenge to their own,
previously uncontested, right to 'social spacing', and their flat
rejection of the newcomers' good-willed search for acceptance,
which set off the processes of segregation. The old group had
obviously the power to do so; and doing so was the material

substance of their power. The superiority of their power was embodied in the fact that their version of social spacing prevailed over the counter-mapping by the newcomers. The split into 'established' and 'outsiders' was born of, and reinforced by, the asymmetry of power as entailed in the administration of the social spacing – in the effort to cut social space according to the cognitive map promoted by the administrators. And as it was the powerful who first declared the need of keeping the distance impassable, it is reasonable to suppose that the roots of division should be sought in the problems haunting those in charge of social spacing (that is, in problems involved in the incurably aporetic process of social spacing itself).

Modern living means living with strangers, and living with strangers is at all times a precarious, unnerving and testing life. The chance to carve out the residents of the new estate as eponymous 'outsiders', as the incarnation of anything foreign and alien and the ultimate source of pollution, came handy. True, it did not cure the modern condition from its congenital blemish – but at least it dangled an illusory solution to a fate without solution. It focused the dispersed anxiety, it condensed the fears (all the more frightening for their diffuseness) into a concrete, tangible danger one could fight and – who knows? – conquer. At least one knew where the danger lay, and so one could feel somewhat less disoriented, and helpless, than before. Now, it was the residents of the new estate who were *the* danger. And the deeper was the fright, the feeling of 'being threatened', the less certain the 'established' felt about the security of their own establishment – the more blood-curdling and fear-arousing proclivities tended to be squeezed into the stereotype of the 'outsiders' which came now to embody all the inner demons of the frightened. In Scotson/Elias's findings, the stereotype coined by the established was 'a highly simplified representation of social realities. It created a black and white design which left no room for the diversities to be found among the Estate people. It corresponded to the "minority of the worst".' On the whole, 'the more threatened they [the 'established' group of any kind] feel, the more likely is it that internal pressure . . . will drive common beliefs towards extremes of illusion and doctrinaire rigidity'.[15] In an apt commentary by Stephen Mennell,

> [t]his process of stigmatization is a very common element in domination within such highly unequal power balances, and it is remarkable how

[15] Norbert Elias and John L. Scotson, *The Established and the Outsiders: A Sociological Inquiry into Community Problems* (London: Frank Cass, 1965), pp. 81, 95.

across many varied cases the content of the stigmatization remains the same. The outsiders are always dirty, morally unreliable and lazy, among other things. That was how in the nineteenth century industrial workers were frequently seen: they were often spoken of as the 'Great Unwashed'. That was, and is, how whites often perceive blacks.[16]

I propose that what unites the variegated characteristics imputed to the category cut out from the social/cognitive space as 'outsiders' is the feature of ambivalence. All traits ascribed to the outsiders signify ambivalence. Dirt is, as we know, a thing out of place, something which ought to stay elsewhere, lest it should blur the divisions which ground the order of things. Unreliability means erratic behaviour which defies probabilities and makes calculation based on the knowledge of rules useless. Laziness stands for defying universality of routine and, by proxy, the very determined nature of the world. A similar semantic load is carried by other most common elements of the outsiders' stereotype: they are morally lax, sexually promiscuous, dishonest in business deals, overemotional and incapable of sober judgement – and altogether irregular and unpredictable in their reactions. In other words, the outsiders are the gathering point for the risks and fears which accompany cognitive spacing. They epitomize the chaos which all social spacing aims staunchly yet vainly to replace with order, and the unreliability of the rules in which the hopes of replacement have been invested. If only they could be confined to the outer fringes of social space, perhaps the outsiders could take all the rest of ambivalence, scattered all over the place, with them . . .

Whoever keeps the hard-won right to draw the charts of social space binding on the others (this right, we may say, is the hard core of all domination and oppression; it is also the coveted prize of the fight against present oppression and a ticket for the future one), would tend to defuse the aporia through selecting among the strangers of whom one cannot rid oneself, one category of 'absolute strangers' one can, allegedly, do without; the category which carries the sins of the strangers without sharing in their uses, and thus can be (so one hopes) disposed of without undermining the business of life. All designation is, of course, a palliative, coming nowhere near the genuine 'problem'. Yet as long as it retains its mobilizing power, thus sustaining the cognitive spacing as a going concern and daily task, it purveys a considerable, perhaps crucial, contribution to making the world of strangers livable.

[16] Stephen Mennell, *Norbert Elias: Civilization and the Human Self-Image* (Oxford: Blackwell, 1989), p. 122.

In *Tristes tropiques*,[17] one of the most hauntingly beautiful and thoughtful works of anthropology ever written, Claude Lévi-Strauss suggested that 'primitive' societies deal with their danger-carrying strangers with the help of a strategy different (though not necessarily inferior) from the one which we practise and consider normal and 'civilized'. Theirs is the *anthropophagic* strategy: they eat up, devour and digest (*biologically* incorporate and assimilate) such strangers as master powerful, mysterious forces, perhaps hoping in this way to avail themselves of those forces, absorb them, make them their own. Ours is an *anthropoemic* strategy (from Greek εμειν 'to vomit'). We throw the carriers of danger up – and away from where the orderly life is conducted; we keep them off society's bounds – either in exile or in guarded enclaves where they can be safely incarcerated without hope of escaping.

Thus far Lévi-Strauss. I propose, though, that the strategic alternative he describes is endemic to every society, including our own, rather than marking the distinction between historically successive types of societies. *Phagic* and *emic* strategies are applied in parallel, in each society and on every level of social organization. They are both indispensable mechanisms of social spacing, but they are effective precisely because of their co-presence, only as a pair. Alone, each strategy would spawn too much waste to be able to secure a more or less stable social space. Together, however, the two strategies, disposing of each other's waste, may make their respective costs and inadequacies somewhat less prohibitive or more bearable.

The phagic strategy is 'inclusivist', the emic strategy is 'exclusivist'. The first 'assimilates' the strangers to the neighbours, the second merges them with the aliens. Together, they polarize the strangers and attempt to clear up the most vexing and disturbing middle-ground between the neighbourhood and alienness poles. To the strangers for whom they define the life condition and its choices, they posit a genuine 'either/or': conform or be damned, be like us or do not overstay your visit, play the game by our rules or be prepared to be kicked out from the game altogether. Only as such an 'either/or' do the two strategies offer a serious chance of controlling the social space. They are therefore included in the toolbag of every domination.

Rules of admission are effective only in as far as they are

---

[17] Claude Lévi-Strauss, *Tristes tropiques* (Paris: Plon, 1955), esp. ch. 38; English trans. John Russell published under the title *A World on the Wane* (London: Hutchinson, 1961).

complemented by the sanctions of expulsion, banishment, cashiering, blackballing, sending down – but the latter series may nudge its objects towards conformity only as long as the hope of admission is kept alive. Uniform education is supplemented by 'corrective institutions' for the failures and the recalcitrant; cultural ostracism and denigration of 'alien customs' are supplemented by the allure of cultural assimilation, nationalistic proselytism is supplemented by the prospect of 'repatriation' and 'ethnic cleansing', legally proclaimed equality of citizenship is supplemented by immigration control and deportation rules. The meaning of domination, of control over social spacing, is to be able to alternate the phagic and the emic strategies and to decide the criteria by which one or the other is set in operation – as well as to adjudicate which of the strategies is 'appropriate' for the case in question.

In the modern world strangers are ubiquitous and irremovable; simultaneously an indispensable condition of life (for modern life to be possible, the majority of human beings in whose company it is lived must be cast as strangers, allowing for no more than 'mismeetings' in the mode of civil inattention) and the most painful of that life's congenital ailments. The two strategies are in no way 'solutions' to the 'problem' of strangers – nor to the anxiety they generate or to the endemic ambivalence of their status and role; they are but ways of 'controlling' the 'problem'. Whoever is in control (in charge of social spacing), re-forges the aporetic phenomenon of strangehood into social domination: level and scale of domination reflect the level and the scale of control.

The confused, ambivalent sentiments aroused by the presence of strangers – those under-defined, under-determined others, neither neighbours nor aliens, yet potentially (incongruously) both – I propose to describe as *proteophobia*. The term refers to the apprehension aroused by the presence of multiform, allotropic phenomena which stubbornly defy clarity-addicted knowledge, elide assignment and sap the familiar classificatory grids. This apprehension is akin to the anxiety of misunderstanding, which – after Wittgenstein – can be explicated as 'not knowing how to go on'. Proteophobia refers therefore to the dislike of situations in which one feels lost, confused, disempowered. Obviously, such situations are the productive waste of cognitive spacing: we *do not know* how to go on in certain situations because the rules of conduct which define for us the meaning of '*knowing* how to go on' do not cover them. We set apart such anxiety-arousing situations, therefore, precisely because there has already been some cognitive spacing done, and so we have mastered some rules which regiment conduct within the ordered space – and yet in some cases it is not clear which of these rules apply. Encounter with strangers is by far the most blatant and harrowing (though also the most common) of such cases. From the point of view of those in charge of order, strangers are solid leftovers of the productive process called 'social spacing'; they posit perennial problems of recycling and waste-disposal. Only the domination-induced and sponsored myopia casts, however, the last two activities on a different level from the 'positive' effects of social/cognitive spacing.

The administration of social space does not eliminate proteo-phobia; neither is it meant to. It uses proteophobia as its main resource, and willingly or inadvertently, but constantly, replenishes its stocks. To control the processes of social spacing means to shift the foci of proteophobia, to select the objects on which proteophobic sentiments are targeted and then to expose such objects to the alternation of phagic and emic strategies.

Moral spacing: dismantling the cognitive space

In the construction and maintenance of social space as, essentially, a cognitive process, sentiments are either suppressed or – when they show – reduced to a servant role. Trials and tribulations of spacing are of primarily cognitive nature: the most common and pertinent of its endemic afflictions is cognitive bafflement: imprecision of rules, rebounding as the lack of knowledge of how to go on.

Moral spacing takes no notice of the rules that define the social/cognitive space. It is oblivious to the social definitions of proximity and distance. It relies on no previous knowledge; neither does it involve production of new knowledge. All in all, it engages no human intellectual capacities – such as examination, comparison, calculation, evaluation. By the intellectual standards proper to cognitive spacing, it looks abominably 'primitive': a cottage industry compared to a scientifically managed factory.

The objects of cognitive spacing are the others we live *with*. The objects of moral spacing are the others we live *for*. These others are resistant to all typification. As residents of moral space, they remain forever specific and irreplaceable; they are not specimens of categories, and most certainly do not enter the moral space in virtue of being members of a category which *entitles* them to be objects of moral concern. They become objects of a moral stance solely by virtue of having been targeted directly, as those concrete others out there, by moral concern. Moral responsibility is apportioned while remaining deaf and blind to the voice and the signposts of reason presiding over the social space.

It may so happen that moral proximity would overlap with the cognitive one; that moral concern would reach its highest intensity where knowledge of the other is at its richest and most intimate, and that it would thin out as knowledge tapers off and intimacy is gradually transformed into estrangement. This, indeed, may happen; but in no way is the overlap inevitable – it is not even necessarily the privileged possibility. The two spacings are guided by different, and mutually autonomous factors, and the spectre of clash and mutual destruction hovers continuously over their uneasy coexistence.

Whoever administers the activity of social/cognitive spacing must be wary of moral spacing, which cannot but appear un-reasonable, wayward and erratic. (Moral spacing is negligent of reasons, refers to no communicable knowledge and is unable to mount an argued self-defence, let alone convince those in doubt to accept its results.)[18] This hardly applies in reverse, as moral spacing involves little thought and thus cannot be 'wary' of anything: it just ignores the precepts of cognitive space (or, rather, proceeds *as if* it has ignored them). If the sediments of cognitive spacing cannot be made secure without more or less conscious attempts to ward off moral spacing or undo its effects, moral spacing simply snubs the accomplishments of cognitive spacing – a vice that adds further to its ignominy. The intellectual resources of social/cognitive spacing are abominably ineffective in the face of moral responsibility, the sole resource founding the moral space.

Since one can never be sure that moral responsibility has been extinguished once for all and cannot be resurrected – the most that cognitively based social spacing may aim at is to confine moral responsibility, if it comes alive again, within boundaries roughly corresponding to the distinction between the intimacy of social proximity and the estrangement of social distance: to carve out, by means at its disposal, the permissible 'universe of social obligations',

---

[18]   In *Modernity and the Holocaust* (Cambridge: Polity Press, 1989) I analysed the findings of research conducted among 'the righteous' – the individuals who in Nazi-occupied Europe rescued the victims of Nazi genocide in express defiance of the powers-that-be as well as, more often than not, of the pressures of majority opinion. The most remarkable message these findings convey is the absence of any correlation between the assumption of supreme moral responsibility and all the 'objective' or objectifiable factors which are believed to be the 'social determinants' of behaviour. This means that by all

beyond which moral responsibility would not reach, and thus would not interfere with the managerial decisions of those in charge of the social space. This would be tantamount to exempting certain cat-egories of humans, earmarked for banishment from social space (be it criminals, 'enemies of the people', enemies of the nation, party or any other cause, or 'alien' – and hostile – 'races') from the class of potential objects of moral responsibility; in other words, to the *de-humanizing* of such categories of people.

Efforts of such a kind are hardly ever fully effective; a weakness which haunts in equal measure the opposite efforts – of stretching the boundaries of moral responsibility to include more potential objects. Moral space seems to be reluctant to all intellectual argument, whatever its substance; as if there were no communication line between cognitive and moral spacing, reason and sentiment, calcu-lation and human impulse. Thus we hear that many thousands of residents of Heidelberg, the university town proud of its humanist tradition, took to the streets demanding concern and care for 1,300 asylum-seekers settled temporarily in the vicinity. At the same time, several hundred residents of the area close to the University signed a petition demanding immediate expulsion of 100 of the newcomers, destined to be settled in their immediate neighbourhood.[19] It was not clear to what extent the ranks of demonstrators and of the signatories of the petition overlapped. It may be that to a large extent they did, as well they might, since one area where co-ordination is least likely to occur is that between the intellectual, social spacing, and the affective, moral one. Commitment to an 'all men are brothers' type of ideology does not seem to ward off intolerance of such men as might have taken the brotherhood rights too literally, while hostility to the stereotype of the alien does not seem to preclude the heroic defence of an alien who happened to get into trouble when crossing one's street.

In the cognitively mapped social space, the stranger is someone of whom one knows little and desires to know even less. In moral space, the stranger is someone of whom one cares little and is prompted to care even less. The two sets of strangers may, or may not, overlap. So in all likelihood we will go on committing both irrational and

standards deployed and deployable by the powers-that-be, morally induced conduct appears to be totally unpredictable, and thus – more worryingly yet – uncontrollable.

[19] Cf. 'Hostel Plan Tests Liberal Conscience', in *The Guardian*, 2 December 1992, p. 7. 'A Heidelberg refugee project has caused a "not in my backyard" response', commented the author of the report, David Gow. On the other

immoral deeds – as well as deeds which are irrational while moral, and such as are rational yet immoral.

The aesthetic space

One may say that if proteophobia is the driving force of cognitive spacing – *proteophilia* prompts the efforts of aesthetic spacing.

The techniques of mismeeting and civil inattention are the tools of social/cognitive spacing. They produce the Other primarily as the stranger which best melts into the meaningless physical space: the unavoidable nuisance one would prefer to live without, yet one cannot. Under the circumstances, the sole knowledge one seeks of the strangers is how to keep them in their status of strangers.

The physical space of the city is, however, also the territory of aesthetic spacing: the uneven distribution of interest, curiosity, capacity to arouse amusement and enjoyment. The outcomes of cognitive and aesthetic spacings do not coincide. The stranger of the social/cognitive space may be the object of intense curiosity as the source of entertaining experience. The technology of cognitive spacing would demand that one averted one's gaze when in the company of strangers. The technology of aesthetic spacing makes the eye into the primary aperture through which the pleasures the crowded space has to offer can be taken in. The strangers, with their unknown, unpredictable ways, with their kaleidoscopic variety of appearances and actions, with their capacity to surprise, are a particularly rich source of spectators' pleasure. Aesthetically, the city space is a spectacle in which the amusement value overrides all other considerations.

Though cognitive and aesthetic spacing produce different charts of the city, in no way are the two processes unrelated. The theatre needs its usherettes and, indeed, some kind of security guards, though preferably plain-clothed and unobtrusive, effective mostly through the comfortable subliminal awareness of their presence 'if need be'. Strangers can be enjoyed only if their strangehood has been already assured, if the spectators intuit it and are confident that complacency

---

hand, remember Schleicher's difficulty with making the repulsiveness of the 'abstract Jew' stick to the 'Jew next door' – or, indeed, Himmler's complaint that loyal SS men ready to exterminate the Jews as a race each knew a familiar 'good Jew' who deserved to be spared (see Bauman, *Modernity and the Holocaust*).

holds no danger. Aesthetic spacing may redraw the charts drawn in the course of cognitive spacing – yet there would be nothing to redraw, nor would there be the will or capacity for redrawing, did not the social/cognitive spacing effort already produce secure results. Only in the well-administered and policed space can the aesthetic enjoyment of the city take off. Only there can the spectators 'be in control' – in the aesthetic sense of the word.

The beauty of 'aesthetic control' – the unclouded beauty, beauty unspoiled by the fear of danger, guilty conscience or apprehension of shame – is its inconsequentiality. This control will not intrude into the realities of the controlled. It will not limit *their* options. It puts the spectator into the director's chair – with the actors unaware of who is sitting there, of the chair itself, even of being potential objects of the director's attention. Aesthetic control, unlike that other, gruesome and sinister social control which it playfully emulates, allows to thrive that contingency of life which social spacing strove to confine or stifle. Inconsequentiality of aesthetic control is what makes its pleasure unclouded. I see that man there meeting that woman. They stop, they talk. I do not know wherefrom they came. I do not know what they are talking about. I do not know where they will go when they finish talking. Because I do not know all that and much more, I may make them into whatever I wish, all the more so that whatever I make them into will have no effect on what they are or will become. I am in charge; I invest their encounter with meaning. I may make him into a philanderer, her into a wife seeking escape from the grinding monotony of marriage. I may send them to bed right from where they stand at the moment, or to their respective rooms, where they will sulk the missed chance. The power of my fantasy is the only limit the reality I imagine has, and the only one it needs. Life as bagful of episodes none of which is definite, unequivocal, irreversible; life as a play.

The joy of strolling in the city (in a well-policed city, a city with the job of social spacing properly done) is the joy of playing. 'Wandering without aim, stopping once in a while to look around' (this is how the activity of the *flâneur* – the character made into the epitome of the modern urbanite by Baudelaire and his most famous interpreter, Walter Benjamin – is described) is, one may say, the ultimate play.

Togetherness as playground

The great Dutch thinker, Johan Huizinga, preferred the name *homo ludens* – he who plays – to *homo sapiens* or *homo faber*, more popular but in his view less distinctive names given to Man in order to set Him apart from the rest of living creatures.[20] Play, wrote Huizinga, is older than culture; indeed, it is the very stuff of which culture, that human mode of being-in-the-world, has been and goes on being moulded. A being which is at play is a being that goes beyond the task of self-preservation and self-reproduction; that has not got the perpetuation of itself as its only goal.

From the point of view of all solemn, 'serious', no-joking-matter pastimes with which life aimed at survival is punctuated, play is *gratuitous*. It serves no 'sensible' purpose. It may bring riches, but this is not why it has been embarked on in the first place. It may make us more healthy, but more often than not its impact is the very opposite of what medical men would describe as health. Play is not about survival (if anything, it is what makes survival worth dreaming about and pursuing). When called to justify itself in terms of the function it serves, play reveals its utter and irremediable *redundancy*.

Play is *free*. It vanishes together with freedom. There is no such thing as obligatory play, play on command. One can be coerced to obey the rules of the game, but not to play. (Just as one can bring the horse to water, but not force him to drink . . .) This is perhaps why play remains so stubbornly non-functional. Were it to serve a purpose, were I to play 'in order to' bring about or protect certain things I or the others like or want me to like, there would be little freedom left in my act of playing. The act is truly and fully free only when truly and fully gratuitous.

Being gratuitous and being free is what sets play apart from the 'normal', 'ordinary', 'proper', 'real' life. Play may be serious, and often it is, and it is at its best when it is; but even then it is '*not for real*'; it is enacted 'as if' it were real, this 'as-ifness' quality being precisely what sets it apart from 'real reality'. One plays when knowing that the assumptions are what they are: assumptions, which have been freely accepted and may be freely dropped. We speak of reality when we do not have such knowledge, or do not dare to believe it, or suspect it to be untrue. There is nothing gratuitous and not much that is free about reality.

Besides, if reality is oozy, ubiquitous, straggly, spattered all over the place – play is securely protected behind its temporal and spatial walls. Play has its beginning and its end, both well marked – with a

[20]   Johan Huizinga, *Homo Ludens: Proeve eener bepaling van het spelement der cultur* (1938); I have used the Polish translation by Maria Kurecka and Witold Wirpsza (Warsaw: Czytelnik, 1967).

bell, a whistle, a starter shot, a finishing line, the rise and the fall of the curtain. It does not begin before it begins and it does not go on after it ended. Play has its place – the race course, tennis court, dance hall, sports stadium, discothèque, church, chessboard – all well marked: by stage frame, fence, guarded entries. Play does not spill over, contaminate, reach the parts one would wish to or has to keep clean; it can be isolated, confined in limits so that it does not affect or disturb what it should not; it could be even kept secret. And thanks to the clarity (and conventionality) of borders, one may enter and leave the play, a feat which cannot be accomplished in 'reality'. Now I play, now I don't. I can detach myself if I wish from the play, its assumptions, its 'as-ifness'. It is precisely my ability to detach myself, to opt out, that makes the play the 'as-if' action that it is.

Play may be restarted and *repeated*; even its end is 'as if', not really real. No defeat (no victory either) is final and irrevocable. The chance of revenge sweetens the most bitter of failures. One can always try again, and the roles may still be reversed. Because it can be repeated, played again, because its end just clears the site for another beginning, makes new beginning possible – to play is to rehearse eternity: in play, time runs to its appointed end only to start running again. Time has a 'direction' only *inside* the play, but the repeatability of playing cancels that direction, indeed the *flow of time* itself. Playing is *not cumulative*. Nothing accrues (except the skills of the player, or his fatigue, or his enthusiasm, or his boredom), nothing 'builds up'. Each new play is an *absolute beginning* – the result of the last one does not affect its result, as wide open as the last play was when it started. One may say that play, unlike 'real reality', is a Markov *process*, not a Markov *chain*: the probability of reaching some future state depends solely on the present state, not on the past events that led to it. In a single play, as in reality, past moves confine the freedom of choice of the player – but in the infinitely extendable series of plays freedom recovers its fullness with the start of each new play and is once more unlimited, whatever the player has done in the past. Play has no lasting effects; it does not 'stick'; it does not spawn obligations, does not leave behind bounds and duties.

Each play sets its rules. Play *is* the rules: play has no other existence but a number of players observing rules. Rules have the advantage of being spelled out, so that it is clear, or can be made clear in each instance, what belongs and what does not belong to the game. The clarity of the rules precludes rebellion: 'one cannot be sceptical regarding the rules of the game', says Huizinga; 'It makes no sense to "transgress" a game's rules', says Baudrillard. 'Within a cycle's recurrence, there is no line one can jump (instead, one simply leaves the game).'[21] As it relies on the serious treatment of the rules for its existence, exposing the rule as 'just a convention' amounts to the dismissal of a game as 'just a game' – and this, as we have seen before, is the one occasion no play can survive. The threat which the play fortifies itself against is the *spoilsport*, not a law-breaker.

Out of the yarn of rules the play weaves its own order; a homely order, a cosy order, an order which never hangs above the heads of the players as the laws of society or nature do, but one which is born ever anew, together with the players' willingness to obey it, and evaporates without sediment once that willingness peters out. This is what all order ought to be like; this is what few, if any, 'real' orders are, or seem to be. However meticulously the rule-made order might be observed, the discipline is never lived as oppression. It does not humiliate nor enslave. A dream order, of a kind all orders promise to be but of which few keep the promise: an order that *enables*, empowers, comes complete with that 'knowledge of how to go on', which Wittgenstein saw as the substance of all understanding. Indeed, the order conjured up by play is so attractive, that no order is amiss to steal some of its seductive power: all orders like to speak of obligations as role-playing, of enforced moves as acting, even of its coercive laws as rules of the game . . .

We are all players. The urban *flâneur* is the *travelling player*. He carries his playing with him, wherever he goes. His game is a *solitaire*; so he can squeeze all the allurements of the game to the last drop, unrestricted by the selfish or jealous team-mates and the forever watchful, forever cavilling umpire. His play is to make others play, to see others as players, to make the world a play. And in this play which he makes the world to be, he is in full control. He may disregard other players' moves, that potential limit to his own choice. In the dramas he imagines as he wanders, he is the sole mover, script-writer, director, discerning viewer and critic. To *flâner* means to play the game of playing; a meta-play of sorts. This play is conscious of itself as play. Its enjoyment is mature and pure.

It is pure because the aesthetic proximity does not interfere with social distance; the city stroller can go on drawing the strangers around into his private theatre without fear that those drawn inside will claim the rights of the insiders. Social/cognitive spacing has created distances which aesthetic spacing can transgress only play-fully, only in imagination, only inconsequentially. The stranger who

[21] Jean Baudrillard, *Seduction*, trans. Brian Singer (London: Macmillan, 1990), p. 146.

appears in the *flâneur*'s play is but the *sight* of the stranger; he is what the *flâneur* sees, and no more than that – an eye impression, detached from the body, the identity, the biography of the person who 'gave' that impression. As Henning Bech insightfully observed,

> In the crowds of the city, human beings become *surfaces* to one another – for the simple reason that this is the only thing a person can notice in the urban space of lots of strangers. The others turn into surfaces for one's gaze, and one self becomes a surface for theirs, which one cannot escape being aware of. Thus, the surface becomes the object of the form of evaluation which can be performed by gaze – i.e. an aesthetic evaluation, according to criteria such as beautiful or disgusting, boring or fascinating.[22]

The actors in the play of which the *flâneur* is the sole director are but surfaces (hence the comforting inconsequentiality of the play, pleasing contingency of the direction). The reduction of players to surfaces, the 'detachability' of surfaces, is, however, an accomplishment of social spacing – a feat which aesthetic powers cannot perform on their own. There must be places in the city where strangers are at their most secure, where all transgressions of strangehood are by common agreement presumed to be inconsequential, temporary, gratuitous, playful. Places in which everyone (but for a few intruders 'in breach of public order', soon to be disposed of by the guardians of the rules) is prepared to appear as simply a surface of oneself and expects all the others to do the same.

There have been in all cities, from the start, the custom-made stages on which to play. The Arcades, lovingly described by Benjamin, were the foremost among them. Spaces designed to offer the visitors the pleasure of looking; to attract the seekers of pleasure. From the start, there was money to be made out of the *flâneur*'s affliction. Wittingly and premeditatedly, these spaces *sold* pleasurable views to look at. In order to attract the customers, though, the designers and the owners of those spaces had to *buy* them first. The right to look gratuitously was to be the *flâneur*'s, tomorrow's *customer*'s, reward. Pleasurable display, fascinating view, the enticing game of shapes and colours. Customers bought through the seduction of the *flâneur*; the *flâneur*, through seduction, was transformed into the consumer. In the process, the miraculous avatar of the commodity into the shopper is accomplished. At the end of the day,

---

[22]   Henning Bech, 'Living together in the (Post) Modern World', paper presented at the session on 'Changing Family Structures and New Forms of Living Together' at the European Conference of Sociology, Vienna, 26–8 August 1992; quoted from the photocopied text.

the dividing line has been blurred. It is no more clear what (who) is the object of consumption, who (what) is the consumer.

In her recent eye-opening study[23] Griselda Pollock pointed out that such a 'merging' of commodity and consumer, of shopping and being the object of shopping, was first the plight and experience of women – long before the pattern practised upon them had been abstracted from its original context and elaborated upon to draw in the rest of us. In the case of middle-class women shoppers, looking and being looked at intermingled from the start, while shopping was self-consciously part of the process of self-selling. 'Women shopped better to make themselves perform their spectacular role in the modern city . . . displaying someone else's wealth' – the function noticed first and so sharply portrayed by Thorstein Veblen. We may add that the custom-made (shopping) spaces for the play of *flâneurisme* offered the would-be female *flâneuses* a safe haven not to be found elsewhere. The *flâneur* could pick and choose where to play his game: to the *flâneuse*, however, most of the *flâneur*'s favourite haunts were out of bounds. The historic link between the playfulness of the *flâneur* and modern/postmodern consumerism, between look- ing and making the looker into an object of looking, between buying and being bought, had been, one may say, originally forged through the social construction of women as consumer and object of con- sumption. The rest of *flâneurisme*'s modern/postmodern history may, with just a little stretching, be told as one of the *feminization* of the *flâneur*'s ways . . .

The managed playground

To weave his tissue of fantasies, to carry unbroken the crucible of fervid imagination, the *flâneur* needs to preserve the elbow-room of the 'man of leisure' while sunk in the crowd; he must see without being seen; it is the untiring curiosity of the spectator that conjures up both – the crowd as a theatre and the freedom of the stroller as the blend of the script-writer and director. In the *flâneur*, 'the joy of watching is triumphant'; the *flâneur* does not 'stagnate in the gaper' (*badaud*): he is 'an amateur detective'.[24] The labour of the *flâneur* is pleasurable, but it is not easy. And it cannot be performed just

---

[23]   Griselda Pollock, 'The View from "Elsewhere": A Politics of Feminist Spectatorship – Reading around Manet's *Bar at the Folies-Bergère*' (MS).
[24]   Walter Benjamin, *Charles Baudelaire: A Lyric Poet in the Era of High Capitalism*, trans. Harry Zohn (London: Verso, 1983), p. 69.

everywhere. The society that set off the *flâneur* on his perpetual voyage of discovery, which made him into the player expecting the world to be a play, had to supply him with the world fit for the play of discovery. Such a world was, originally, the street of the modern metropolis. The rhythm of the *flâneur*'s life is resonant, as Benjamin observed, with the pace of the big city. The *flâneur* 'catches things in flight'. In the crowded streets of the metropolis, things *are* in flight.

Not all streets are, however, the proper grazing ground for the *flâneur*'s imagination. First, the pavements must be wide enough so that 'hanging around', 'stopping once in a while to look around', be physically possible. Second, there must be enough interest in the street and houses that flank it to allure those who have the time and urge to hang around. Like Baudelaire, who served him as a time capsule filled with sights captured and stilled on the film of poetic sensibility, Benjamin found the Arcades of Paris (those 'glass-covered, marble-panelled passageways', 'lined with most elegant shops, so that such an arcade is a city, even a world, in miniature') the archetype of the type of big city street fit to become 'a dwelling for the *flâneur*'.[25] To the arcades, people came to linger and mill around. Arcades were spaces to *be in*, not just *pass through*. In the arcades, the *flâneur* was *chez soi*, at home: a *flâneur* among *flâneurs*, joined in tacit conspiracy to keep the shared secret secure, sworn not to frown at, and still less to interfere with, each other's work, collectively determined to do their jobs as they should be done – singly, in crowded solitude. And there was enough to do for each one: arcades were spaces 'where the action was' – or at least this was the expectation, rarely frustrated, which the Arcades inspired. And the right kind of action, too: an action certain never to become a burden, never to spoil the game for the would-be 'gentlemen of leisure'. Action that commanded no more price than allowing oneself to be watched and fantasized about, mulled over in the heated imagination of the cool stroller. Action with all the charms of open possibility, yet free from the tedium of fulfilment, with all the excitement of a chance yet-uncaught, and free from the triteness of the caught one. Sand-castles of the chance, washed away before being completed. Action offered together with the guarantee against frustration – since the chance missed, unlike the chance grasped, never ages and wrinkles. 'Lightning . . . then darkness!' remembered Baudelaire the beautiful passer-by, all the more beautiful for the beautifying work that free-roaming fantasy could perform uncurbed on the ephemeral, lightning-brief testimony of the eyes: 'Lovely fugitive/whose glance

[25] Benjamin, *Charles Baudelaire*, pp. 36–7.

has brought me back to life! . . . Of me you know nothing, I nothing of you – you/whom I might have loved and who knew that too!'[26]

The Arcades are no more. Where they can be found still, they appear as preserved by the heritage industry in their pristine, yet now functionless splendour: a tourist attraction, perhaps a nostalgic retreat for those few still remembering something they can be nostalgic about; tucked away from the beaten track (now a synonym for thoroughfares, freeways and expressways), where today's action is. Today's action is, after all, different: it is, mostly, about *passing* from here to there, as fast as one can manage, preferably without stopping, better still without looking around. Beautiful passers-by are no more to be seen; they hide inside cars with tinted windows. Those still on the pavement are waiters and sellers at best, but more often *dangerous people* pure and simple: layabouts, beggars, homeless conscience-soilers, drug-pushers, pickpockets, muggers, child molesters and rapists waiting for prey. To the innocent who has to leave for a moment the wheeled-up security of cars, or those others (still thinking of themselves as innocent) who cannot afford that security at all, the street is more a jungle than the theatre. One goes there only if one *must*. A site fraught with risks, not chances; not meant for the gentlemen of leisure, and certainly not for the faint-hearted among them. The street is the wilderness 'out there' from which one hides, at home or inside the car, behind security locks and burglar alarms.

'The street level is dead space . . . It is only a means of passage to the interior', summed up Richard Sennett, two decades ago, his analysis of the most impressive and spectacular urban developments of his time, ushering in the new era of the postmodern metropolis.[27] 'Here there are a few shops and vast areas of empty space. Here is an area to pass through, not to use.' The public space of the 'new and improved' kind has been well marked as definitely *not* 'just the street' – and shielded from the latter, that frightening, uncontrolled space, that favourite location of nowadays Gothic stories, by immense ramps and fences. Everything around oozes the message: 'The public space is an arena to move through, not be in'; the ground, in the urban planner's patois, is 'the traffic-flow-support-nexus for the vertical whole'.

[26]   Charles Baudelaire, 'In Passing', in *Les Fleurs du Mal*, trans. Richard Howard (London: Pan Books, 1982), p. 98.
[27]   Richard Sennett, *The Fall of Public Man* (Cambridge University Press, 1977), pp. 12–15.

Places that want the visitors to stay, to stop and look around, bar themselves with steel and with gun-carrying or electronic guards from the public space of the street, just as their visitors do in their homes. (At long last, the Englishman's home has turned truly into his castle – with burglar alarms and triple locks, the contemporary high-tech equivalents of moats, turrets, and rifles.) Buildings have turned their backs to the street; gates and gateways, once ostentatiously inviting, the proud advertisement of the inside's promises, have now shrunk and become hidden in the least conspicuous corners, as if dreaming to cancel themselves altogether and thus allow the inside to sail away once for all from the treacherous mire of the outside. As if locked up in a perverse conspiracy, tightly entwined in Bateson's 'schismogenetic chain', the shopping-mall affluence and street squalor join efforts in reinforcing and restocking the seductiveness of one and repulsiveness of the other. Definitely, the street is no more the *flâneur*'s hunting ground. The 'outside' is but a traffic-flow-support-nexus. But what about the inside, if you finally get there?

The inside is, indeed, fabulous. And spectacular. And pleasurable. Just a place to 'wander aimlessly while stopping once in a while to look around' – a *flâneur*'s paradise, if ever there was one. Or, rather, so it seems. In fact, the new in-walls haunts are the places of the *flâneur*'s ultimate defeat. The most cherished of *flâneurisme* seductions – the right to write the script and to direct the play of surfaces – has been expropriated by the designers and the managers and the profit-makers of the shopping malls. The scripts are now ready-made and expert-made, discreet yet precise, and leaving little to the imagination and less still to the spectator's freedom. Direction is constant and ubiquitous, though carefully disguised as (managed) spontaneity. These are places of the *second-level play*, of the meta-play: play is here, openly and unashamedly, the name of the game, those lured inside are playing in playing: actors of a meticulously staged spectacle who act out the characters of script-writers and directors.

Such 'guaranteed enjoyment' of ready-made scripts and expert direction, however, can now also be taken home (with video-libraries as the take-away shops). And it is taken home – on a massive scale. (Presumably on a scale likely to become more massive still as the comforts of 'teleshopping' and computer games vie with shopping malls and shopping-mall spectacles, cutting out the displeasures of commuting, which mar the beauty of the first, and the limitations imposed by the second, by means of the joys of the 'interactive' side of the play.) Through these *flâneur*-wares take-aways, the city as the haunting ground of the *flâneur* turns into the *telecity* (another felicitous term coined by Henning Bech). The strangers (the surfaces of strangers) whom the televiewer confronts are 'telemediated'. There is, comfortingly, a glass screen to which their lives are confined: the reduction of their existential mode to pure *surface* is now, at long last, tangibly obvious, indubitable, technologically guaranteed.

Strangers may now be gazed at openly, without fear – much as lions in the zoo; all the chills and creeps of the roaring beast without the fangs ever coming anywhere near the skin. Strangers may be watched robbing, maiming, shooting and garrotting each other (something one would expect strangers, being strangers, to do) in the endless replay of TV crime and police dramas. Or they can be gleefully gazed at in the full flight of their animal passions. Or, better still, they can be moved around, play the scenario, or be put out of action by the slightest move of the joystick. They are infinitely close as objects; but doomed to remain, happily, infinitely remote as subjects of action. In the telecity, strangers are sanitized and safe, like sex with condoms: someone in the know, an expert, a trustworthy expert, an expert trusted all the more for his/her invisibility, has seen to it that they need be feared no more – a pure silver lining without a cloud attached – and thus enjoyment need not be spoiled by fore- or after-thought, care may be forgotten, no thought of consequences needs to stir the conscience or poison the pleasure.

Telecity is the ultimate *aesthetic space*. In the telecity, the others appear solely as objects of enjoyment, no strings attached (they can be zapped out of the screen – and so out of the world – when they cease to amuse). Offering amusement is their only right to exist – and a right which it is up to them to confirm ever anew, with each successive 'switching on'.

Life in aesthetic space is, essentially, a *solitaire*. Whatever sharing there seems to be is incidental and purely superficial, just like the surfaces which populate the world in which that life is lived; or like the *flâneurs* themselves – many but single, shoulder to shoulder in the crowded street yet each weaving silently his or her own narratives out of the space they share, each casting the other as one more prop on the stage s/he sets for the scenario. In the aesthetic space, togetherness is casual and fortuitous – a closeness of monads, enclosed in the invisible, yet impregnable bubbles of their respective virtual realities. The family gathering in front of a TV screen has all the 'sharing' and 'togetherness' of an amusement arcade. But even that form of family gathering is fast receding into the past in which joint family reading, talking and singing have been cast and buried before. There are few occasions for them in multiple-TV houses, equipped with personal stereos, portable disc-players and game consoles for each member of the household. There is no reason now why the *flâneurs* should suspend their peregrinations when under the family roof. The other household members would indeed need to try harder, and harder still, to match (let alone outplay) the allurements of the ubiquitous telecity as objects of amusement and pleasure.

And this is exactly what they are, once subjected to aesthetic spacing: objects of amusement and pleasure. Only in that capacity can they acquire individual, attention-drawing, reckonable-with existence. The alternative is the function of the grey background against which pleasurable objects are set, if not of the malfunction of the 'noise' that disturbs the harmony of the stereo track. Attractions of the telecity set the standard for the whole of the aesthetically spaced world. In that world, proximity depends on the volume of fun and entertainment the other is capable of purveying. The inner circle of proximity is the area of merriment, 'having a good time', 'having fun'. One does not stalk through the aesthetically spaced world – one goes there 'on a spree', on an escapade; one frolics and rollicks, one revels – one *plays*, one *plays in playing*.

The others who enter the aesthetically spaced world must apply for admission displaying their fun-making value. Tickets, if issued, are for one entry only, and the length of stay is not determined in advance. Fun-value must be kept fresh and replenished constantly, in ever more attractive forms, as it needs to fight inevitable devaluation through familiarity and boredom; only such others can count on a longer stay who develop addictive quality – but in this field drugs and skilfully designed high-tech contraptions with the endless supply of ever new games have a decisive edge over mere humans. The landlord of the aesthetic space has the right to refuse service to unwelcome customers at his sole discretion. No negotiation here, no contract, only mutual pleasure – as long as it lasts. While social spacing aims at (without necessarily achieving it) 'structuring', clarity of divisions, stability of categories, monotony and repetitiveness, predictability, foolproof guarantees that the expectations will be fulfilled – aesthetic spacing seeks fuzziness and movable partitions, the shocking value of novelty, of the surprising and the unexpected, expectations that always move faster and stay ahead of fulfilment.

I propose that the falling out of fashion of marriage, the growing trend to replace the more stable, orthodox models of the family with various forms of 'living together' (all programmatically episodic, without strings attached, until further notice), the zest for experimental, fragmentary and episodic togetherness and other manifestations of proteophilia, are all side-effects of the erosion of the social by the aesthetic space, and of the gradual replacement of the criteria and mechanisms of the social by those of the aesthetic spacing.

Moral spacing: dismantling the aesthetic space

Neither the cognitively nor the aesthetically spaced worlds are hospitable to moral spacing. In both, moral urges are alien bodies and pathological growths. In the social/cognitive space – because they sap the lofty and indifferent impersonality of rules and soil the purity of reason with unwashable stains of affection. In the social/aesthetic space – because they tend to fix and arrest and immobilize things which draw their seductive powers solely from being on the move and ready to disappear once commanded.

The aesthetic space is mapped by various shades of amusement intensity. Quantities of knowledge remain in inverse proportion to aesthetic distance, as the objects least known and least knowable carry the highest fun value. The novel and surprising (the mysterious, simultaneously dazzling and vaguely frightening – the *sublime*) is drawn into the aesthetic proximity; it drifts away, to the aesthetically 'far away' and remote, as novelty turns into familiarity and excitement into boredom. Trials and tribulations characteristic of aesthetic space stem from the annoying propensity of novelty to fade and mystery to wane just as the objects are drawn close to be enjoyed. Aesthetic spacing, in contradistinction to the cognitive one, cannot – must not – hold objects in place. Immobility is its mortal sin, solidity and longevity of charts its mortal danger.

Aesthetic space is, one may say, totally consumed in the process of spacing in the course of which it is produced; it dissolves its potential sediments before they had time to precipitate and solidify. For this reason it resents all perpetuity, all time-arresting, and anything that may lead to it. Moral attachment is its anathema: it suspends free roaming of attention – and attention fixed to one place soon runs out of steam and collapses. The moral stance, with its noxious proclivity to forge its own fetters in the form of responsibility for the other (which turns the Other from an object of satisfaction into a demanding Face), is a sworn enemy of drift – that essence of aesthetic spacing. Moral stance ties attention to its object for longer than it would have stayed on its own were it free from constraints: it renders the attention itself a source of responsibility, and the responsibility entails keeping attention in place as long as the Face may need it. In other words, responsibility is a lasting sediment, the consequence of attention; but attention has the capacity for aesthetic spacing only as long as it wanders freely and scans the canvas of possibilities unworried by the consequences of its past stop-overs.

Amusement value is in principle an enemy of moral responsibility – and vice versa. The enemies may, however, live occasionally in peace, or even co-operate, assist and reinvigorate each other. The model of 'successful love' is the foremost example of such co-operation: the respect for the mystery in the beloved, cultivation of difference, suppression of possessive urges, refusal to smother the autonomy of the beloved with the bulldozer of domination – preserve and replenish the sublime, the unknown, the recondite, the tremendous in the partner, thus keeping alive both the moral and the aesthetic value of the partnership. To accomplish such a feat, the seeker of aesthetic satisfaction must be, however, also a moral person. S/he must accept the limits and constraints which aesthetic spacing is bent on sweeping away. Only then the feverish bustle of aesthetic *spacing* may result in an aesthetic *space*; this will be, however, a moral space at the same time. Success may only come as the outcome of co-operation, which may be achieved solely at the price of surrender.

No man's land, but one's own

Says Alan Wolfe, towards the end of his highly original assessment of social sources of moral behaviour and their competitive claims: 'Given the paradoxes of modernity, there is little wrong, and perhaps a great deal right, with being ambivalent – especially when there is so much to be ambivalent about.'[28] Ambivalence in which the moral agent moves and has to live and act is compounded; we have already visited and examined many of its levels and dimensions.

The moral act itself is endemically ambivalent, forever threading precariously the thin lines dividing care from domination and tolerance from indifference.

In the complex network of mutual dependencies, the consequences of any act are bound to be ambivalent – no act, no matter how noble and unselfish and beneficial for some, can be truly insured against hurting those who may find themselves, inadvertently, on its receiving end.

Ambivalence is constantly generated and replenished by the cross-pressures of socialization and sociality, of the norms guarding social space and moral drives which spawn the moral space.

Societally endorsed adiaphorization collides with moral impulse, making a moot issue even of the boundaries of moral concern and duty.

[28]   Alan Wolfe, *Whose Keeper? Social Science and Moral Obligation* (University of California Press, 1989), p. 211.

Following the official signposts is as doubtful a guarantee of being morally in the right as ignoring them and choosing one's own path through the wilderness. The abyss of immorality awaits the unwary at both extremes of obedience to societally recommended and enforced rules of cohabitation.

Always and everywhere, the search for aesthetic satisfaction defies the pressures of moral responsibility, yet unless constantly rejuvenated by aesthetic satisfaction responsibility may flounder, lose its moral identity, ossify into the empty shell of rule-sponsored duty.

No one-sided solution to any of these problems is foolproof. The moral person cannot beat ambivalence; s/he may only learn to live with it. The art of morality (if one is forgiven for using such a blatantly oxymoronic expression) may be only the art of living with ambivalence – and taking upon oneself the responsibility for that life and its consequences.

The context of life, constantly under the pressure of unhinged and uncoordinated motives and forces, is messy – confused and confusing. It is not easy to be a moral person – and this statement itself is bad news for morality, since such a statement may be articulated only in the wake of moral failure that has already occured, as confession or apology. No wonder new offers are made over and over again to release the subject from the burden of moral responsibility, and no wonder that many find the offers irresistibly seductive.

Wolfe discusses two most popular of such offers: the market and the State, both conspiring to expropriate moral authority belonging to what Wolfe calls 'civil society' (that much abused term, one may guess, standing in this case for whatever remains of social context once economic aspects administered by the market and political ones managed by the state have been removed): 'The problems that arise from relying on markets and states are compounded because both forces view the moral agent as a rule-follower, not a rule-maker.'[29]

The market promotes the view (obviously attractive for the tormented moral subject) that consumer choice is the sole choice which counts, as it is only such choice that is likely to increase the sum total of human happiness; 'value for money' is perhaps not the best standard imaginable, but surely the best there is, to tell the right

---

[29]   Wolfe, *Whose Keeper?*, p. 22. The 'paradox of modernity', in Wolfe's view, is that 'the more modern we become, the more likely we are to rely on markets and states for our moral codes . . . Yet the weaker civil society becomes, the harder it is to be modern, for it becomes more difficult to find practical ways of balancing obligations in the near and distant spheres of society' (p. 246).

act from the wrong one; 'we cannot afford more than we can afford'
is the surest way of circumscribing the outer limits of moral duty.
('The Good Samaritan would not have been able to do what he did if
he did not have money', proclaimed, famously, Margaret Thatcher
on the day she assumed charge of the nation's values.) If only each of
us serves well our own interest, the invisible hand will serve us all,
serving the interest we all share. With invisible hand on the twenty-
four-hours-a-day beat, the visible moral agents can sleep undisturbed.

The state has a similar soporific effect on moral conscience. True,
its awesome powers allow the bringing of succour to distant sufferers
which could not be helped by a less resourceful assistance. But
bringing succour is now the *state's* reponsibility, and so are the
decisions about relative importance of needs and the needy. Once
more, the moral subject is put to sleep. He is saved now from moral
agony, but his moral vigilance, and moral competence, get rustier by
the day. They will not be of much use if (or when) the state decides to
put its now uncontested moral authority to immoral uses.

Paradoxically, the modern state and the modern market 'de-
modernize' those exposed to their impact: they both dwarf the most
modern of the modern person's qualities: the ability to choose
autonomously, and to choose where it really counts. Both cloud the
reality of modern moral condition – both belie the fact that at the end
of the day all the substitutes for moral conscience only dull moral
responsibility and render moral action all that more difficult, while
changing nothing or next to nothing in the incurable solitude of the
moral person, face to face with the aporia and ambivalence of her or
his moral condition. No amount of mediators and no 'agentic state'
can change the truth of the matter – that, in the last resort, it is – as it
has always been – a question of being able to act as one's own moral
agent.

If the market's and the state's solutions to moral ambivalence are
illusory, or deceptive, or both – where should the moral subjects look
to reclaim their moral autonomy? Obviously, not to the agencies that
promise to take over their moral responsibilities and carry them out
instead – but to a setting which enables them to face up to moral
responsibilities themselves and act upon them. But where can such a
setting be found?

Wolfe vests his hopes with 'civil society' – conceived of as a setting
for a 'practice negotiated between learning agents capable of growth
on the one hand and a culture capable to change on the other'.
Negotiation implies an ongoing process, but also a process without a
direction guaranteed beforehand, nor one whose outcomes can be

securely anticipated. In such a setting, the triumph of morality is in no way assured in advance; it is touch and go all the way. Neither solemn preaching nor stern legal rules will do much to make the fate of morality less precarious. It is the realization that this is the case, that all and any promises to stop this being the case are – must be – naive or fraudulent, that is morality's best chance. It is also its only hope.

The chance is not completely delusory, the hope is not totally specious. Given the mind-boggling number of little movements of muscles, sinews and bones which need to be co-ordinated and synchronized in the act of riding a bicycle, one could well be excused for proclaiming bicycle-riding both theoretically and practically impossible; but people do ride bicycles (though time and again they lose their muscular balance, and on occasion they fall). And people do act as moral agents and follow the urge of moral responsibility (though time and again they lose their moral balance and on occasion they fall).

'People have a lot of practices for supporting their friends and choosing their friends and abandoning their friends', ascertains Hubert Dreyfus.[30] These are, however, *non-rationalized* (one may go a step further: *non-rationalizable*) practices. They do not serve any purpose other than being mysteriously satisfying in themselves; they are abominably short of standards which would help one to estimate their 'efficiency'. ('As soon as you have friends for your health or your career', says Dreyfus, 'you've got some new kind of friendship which is of a technological-rational kind.' We may add: as soon as you have friends for your fun and amusement you've got some new kind of friendship as well – a friendship in which it is the friends who are for you, instead of you being for them.) For this reason these practices are virtually incapable of defending themselves discursively; once the practitioners attempt to do so, they betray the nature of their practices and step beyond the area where their skills are sufficient to generate and sustain them. Discursive redemption destroys the very moral reality it purports to redeem: 'You want to legislate the quality of life and you get this funny problem that the receptive, spontaneous aspects of the quality of life would be lost if you legislated it.'

Perhaps this news is not good. Perhaps it would be better (it would be certainly less disturbing, more comfortable) if we could, after all,

---

[30]   Cf. Bent Flyvbjerg, 'Sustaining Non-rationalized Practices: Body–Mind Power and Situational Ethics: An Interview with Hubert and Stuart Dreyfus', in *Praxis International*, vol. 11, no. 1 (1991), pp. 93–113. See also Hubert and Stuart Dreyfus, 'What is Morality: A Phenomenological

represent our non-rationalizable and discursively non-redeemable moral practices as following some hard and fast and steady and universalizable principles; or perhaps the gain in that case would at least outweigh the losses. This cannot be done, though, and there is very little one can do about it, however strongly the modern, logical mind, or the postmodern, aesthetic spirit, may rebel. The ambivalence of the moral condition and insecurity of the moral probing that follow are here to stay. This is, perhaps, the curse of the moral person – but it is certainly the moral person's greatest chance.

One could do worse than to repeat after Arne Johan Vetlesen that 'responsibility for others, also a capacity, *follows* from and is the accomplishment of the living with others' experienced 'as *we-experience*'.[31] It is, indeed, an accomplishment – and accomplishments, as we know, are what they are because they may be accomplished or they may *not*. Though, ethically speaking, *being for* precedes *being with*, and the moment the self enters interaction with the other it is already responsible for the other's weal and woe, the only space where the moral act can be performed is the social space of 'being with', continually buffeted by the criss-crossing pressures of cognitive, aesthetic and moral spacings. In this space, the possibility to act on the promptings of moral responsibility must be *salvaged*, or *recovered*, or *made anew*; against odds – sometimes overwhelming odds – the responsibility must exchange its now invalidated or forgotten priority for the superiority over technical-instrumental calculations; a superiority grounded, as Vetlesen suggests, in the ongoing 'we-experience'. If it happens, it will happen only as an accomplishment. There is not and there will never be any guarantee that it will indeed happen. But it does happen, daily, and repeatedly – each time that people care, love, and bring succour to those who need it.

Account of the Development of Ethical Expertise', in *Universalism versus Communitarianism*, ed. David Rasmussen (Cambridge, Mass.: MIT Press, 1990).

[31] Cf. Arne Johan Vetlesen, 'Why Does Proximity Make a Moral Difference?' in *Praxis International*, vol. 12 (January 1993), pp. 371–86.

7

Private Morals, Public Risks

I do not agree with the engineers and technologists who believe that the problems facing us are to be solved by the so-called technological fix . . . I happen to think that the problems raised by technological advance are probably insolvable.

Max Black

The 'technological fix' to which Max Black objects in the above quotation refers to the notion keenly promoted by engineers, technologists and scientists, and widely and uncritically believed by the lay public, that 'If you encounter a technical difficulty you can always expect to solve it by inventing another technological gadget'.[1] It refers to the twin axiom that this is what you *can* do, and this is also what you *should* do.

In our age, technology has become a closed system: it posits the rest of the world as 'environment' – a source of food, raw matter for technological treatment, or the dumping ground for the (hopefully recyclable) waste of that treatment; and it defines its own misadventures or misdeeds as effects of its own insufficiency, and the resulting 'problems' as demand for more of itself: the more 'problems' technology spawns, the more technology is needed. Only technology can 'improve on' technology, curing yesterday's maladies with today's wonder-drugs, before their own side-effects set in tomorrow and call for new and improved drugs. This is, probably, the one problem 'raised by technological advance' which is fully and truly 'unsolvable': from the closed system, there is no exit. It is not so much the question of problems which call for more technology, but of the very presence of technological capacities that cannot but 'problematize' aspects of the world which would not otherwise be seen as 'problems' (that is, as 'wrong' states of affairs calling to be,

[1] Max Black, 'Nothing New', in *Ethics in an Age of Pervasive Technology*, ed. Melvin Kranzberg (Boulder, Col.; Westview Press, 1980), p. 26–7.

forcefully, altered 'for the better'). Neither those who have been taught to expect bliss at the end of the road, nor those who expect nothing but doom, can do other than run in the treadmill that keeps technology going.

At first approximation, what is closed here seems to be a system of self-corroborating *beliefs*: technology setting the vocabulary of the world's narrative in a way that allows nothing but technological action and that expresses any worry and trouble as a demand for a 'technological fix'. As far as the need for legitimation is concerned, that closed system is truly self-propagating and self-perpetuating; it generates its own justification. No one exposed this remarkable quality with more poignancy than Jacques Ellul. Technology, Ellul insists, does not need legitimation any more; or, rather, it has become its own legitimation. The very *availability* of usable yet under-employed technological resources ('We can do something'; 'We have the means and the know-how'; 'We can fix it') calls for their *application*; technological resources, so to speak, sufficiently legitimize their consequences and thus make their use imperative – whatever the results.

> Technology never advances towards anything but *because* it is pushed from behind. The technician does not know why he is working, and generally he does not much care. He works *because* he has instruments allowing him to perform a certain task, to succeed in a new operation . . .
> There is no call towards a goal; there is constraint by an engine placed in the back and not tolerating any halt for the machine . . .
> The interdependence of technological elements makes possible a very large number of 'solutions' for which there are no problems . . .
> Given that we can fly to the moon, what can we do *on it* and *with it*? . . . When technicians came to a certain degree of technicity in radio, fuels, metals, electronics, cybernetics etc., all these things combined and made it obvious that we could fly into the cosmos, etc. It was done because it could be done. That is all.[2]

---

[2] Jacques Ellul, 'The Power of Technique and the Ethics of Non-Power', in *The Myths of Information: Technology and Postindustrial Culture*, ed. Kathleen Woodward (London: Routledge, 1980), pp. 272–3, 280. As Herber Schädelbach points out, 'it is not true that political decisions are made before technologists are ordered to worry about means . . . [P]olitical ends are very often determined by technological information concerning the technical feasibility of realizing these ends' ('Is Technology Ethically Neutral?', in *Ethics in an Age of Pervasive Technology*, p. 30). Jacques Ellul openly opposes most commonly accepted definitions of technology which all agree that technology has something to do with 'reaching the goals'; it is not true, says Ellul, that 'a technique assures a result known in advance'; 'technique is

We may say that 'technological fix' refers not so much to the assembly of available means and resources of action – ingenious gadgets and the skills to use them – as to the unconditionality of the commandment 'to do something', whatever the 'something' which can be done or, as the case may be, not done. If something can be done, it should and will. It is the means which justify the end – any end which the means can produce: the outcomes are worthy because the know-how is there. At the threshold of the modern technological revolution Auguste Comte expressed the spirit of the age with great acumen and perspicacity in his famous definition of progress: 'Savoir pour prévoir, prévoir pour pouvoir'. *Pouvoir* – being able, being capable of – as the ultimate, final purpose, as the 'pure' purpose that is not a means to something else than itself and thus needs not to excuse itself by reference to that something. It does not matter *quoi on peut faire* as long as *on le peut faire*. The destination of modern progress ('modern progress' is a pleonasm; only modernity thinks of itself as of progressive movement) is not to do this or that, things one can specify in advance, but to increase the capacity of doing whatever 'man' may yet happen to wish to be done. ('Man' cannot wish something he does not yet know that he may get.) The 'technological fix' is, in the penultimate account, the declaration of independence of means from ends; in the last account, the announcement of sovereignty of means over ends. 'Have car, can travel'. Destination is

---

nothing more than *means* and the *ensemble of means*' (*The Technological Society*, trans. John Wilkinson (New York: Random House, 1964), pp. 14, 19).

Four years after the dismantling of the Berlin Wall a renewed pressure was recorded in the USA, and particularly in Britain, to resume the testing of nuclear weapons – originally developed 'in order to' keep away and subdue the communist enemy now no more in existence. According to *The Guardian*, 18 May 1993, p. 1, 'The British military establishment has three reasons for continued testing. First, it may yet need to test a new warhead for the RAF's proposed tactical stand-off nuclear missile (Tasm), although the chance of that £3 billion programme ever being funded look increasingly remote. Second, it might want to introduce new safety features into weapons. Third, it wants to maintain a decent level of expertise among scientists at the Aldermaston Atomic Weapons Establishment.' Clearly, reference to the purpose the huge investment of public resources and piling up of increasingly deadly weapons are supposed to serve is no longer required. New weapons have to be produced and tested (possibly never to be used), just to keep the Atomic Weapons Establishment busy and to do something with the new features the busy boffins have contrived. And that this is the case is accepted as obvious and 'natural': the reporter feels no urge to question the reasoning as preposterous or ask about the unknown ends of 'really existing' means . . .

nothing, it is having the car that matters. It is to be in a position to treat all places as destinations that counts – and the only thing that counts.

In Hesiod's original version of the Promethean myth, Prometheus is punished by the gods for cheating them in the division of sacrificial meat; he suffers for his arrogant attempt to change the pre-established order of things, for his ignominious cheek in tinkering with what no human being was allowed to dabble in. Hesiod's poem was composed for an audience who lived their lives as a continuous defence against the fall from the pattern-setting past, from the age which was 'golden' because knowing no threat of fall. For that audience, the past was security and the future dangerous; suffering was the side-effect of the breach of tradition, and itself a departure from what things are and ought to remain by behest of the superhuman will of the Gods. It was only in the later rendition of Aeschylus that the myth was reversed: Aeschylus' Prometheus suffered his cruel punishment for bringing men 'the arts not only of healing, mathematics, medicine, navigation and divination, but also of mining and working metals'.[3] The gods are no more the guardians of order that protects humans from fall. They are now jealous misers clinging to the 'traditional ways' that mean, first and foremost, their privilege. Gods try to pull men back, while men themselves surge forward. Prometheus is no more a justly chastised cheat and a criminal, but a persecuted hero. He had turned into a hero once Athens – alone among ancient civilizations – came to the brink of the modern, defiant and reckless thrust into the great unknown, paved and signposted solely by human capacity to move. 'Mining and working metals' more than anything else made humans capable of moving and setting destinations as they moved. They allowed them to be free from the most awesome of fetters: those of the set, predetermined ends of life. 'Technique', says Ellul, 'advocates the entire remaking of life and its framework because they have been badly made.' But 'badly made' means nothing other than made in a way different from the way it could have been made were the available technical means applied; the reasoning is blatantly tautological, and for that reason invulnerable.

[3] Cf. G. S. Kirk, *The Nature of Greek Myths* (Harmondsworth: Penguin, 1974), pp. 138–41. Kirk comments: 'No doubt his recovery of fire was part of the same conception, but in all probability this extension of his functions is not much older than the sixth century BC, when interest in the evolution of men from a crude and savage state – an idea that directly contradicts the mythical scheme of a decline from the Golden Age – first became prominent' (p. 140).

Technology is defined by the 'complete separation of the goal from the mechanism, the limitation of the problem to the means, and the refusal to interfere in any way with efficiency . . .'[4]

Means unbound

The liberation of means from ends (now recast as constraints) lies at the heart of the modern revolution. To be liberated, means must be 'in excess' of ends; the doers must be able to do more than the ends, as they have known them thus far, have made imperative. It is this excess that infuses the modern world with its unique and unprecedented feeling of freedom. It is this excess which makes modernity into a a continuous transgression, an uninterrupted succession of 'new beginnings'. It is this excess which tears off from the face of reality the masks of sacred providence or dour inevitability. It is this excess which condemns the past and its residue – tradition – to ignominy and, ultimately, to the 'rubbish heap of history'.

In a classic account of the 'industrial revolution' (the code-name under which the etiological narratives, symptomatically, kept hiding the fateful shift from ends to means as the prime mover of human concerns and action) Phyllis Deane singled out the shortage of wood and power as the 'most crucial and general bottlenecks limiting the expansion of the British economy'.[5] Wood, to be sure, was not just a principal bulding material, but also a primary source of energy – whatever energy there was available beyond the limited, unexpandable muscle-power. No excess was feasible as the naturally renewing supplies of wood for burning remained stable. To set the means free, one needed to harness new and above all expandable (at least for a time) sources of power. This achievement ushered into the modern era the epoch of excessive means, liberated from ends (only, as it proved to be, to make a prisoner of their former jailer). The Industrial Revolution, says Carlo M. Cipolla, 'can be defined as the process by

---

[4] Ellul, *The Technological Society*, pp. 142–3, 133.
[5] Phyllis Deane, *The First Industrial Revolution* (Cambridge University Press, 1969), p. 129. On the impact of those 'bottlenecks' (hardly perceived by contemporaries as 'bottlenecks') on public consciousness Deane has the following to say: 'It is fair to say that before the second half of the eighteenth century people had no reason to *expect* growth . . . Population, prices and productivity could, they judged, fluctuate upwards as readily as downwards and there was no reason to expect them to go in one direction rather than the other' (p. 11).

which a society acquired control over vast sources of inanimate energy'.[6]

In pre-industrial (that is, pre-modern) times power available to animate human endeavours was either animate itself, or strictly dependent on the kindness or inclemency of *nature* (that is, on forces by definition beyond human reach): the muscle-power of humans or animals, the power of rivers or winds. Their supply was limited, though endlessly renewable in the case of muscle-power (renewable, that is, as long as it was allowed to remain limited; as any horse- or ox-driver would know, one could squeeze spasmodically more power from an animal but only at the cost of mortgaging the future power-supply), and limited and erratic in the case of water- or wind-power. What united the pre-industrial sources of energy was the sentiment of dependency and confinement they all instilled. It is only a different kind of power, a power that can be used without the joy of use being poisoned by the worry of its future replenishment – power which looks as if one could 'use it up' with each use – that feeds the modern, exhilarating, ebullient, 'everything is possible', 'absolute beginning' sense of freedom.

Deane calls the conversion of the economy from a 'wood-and-water' basis to a 'coal-and-iron' basis 'the most important achievement of the industrial revolution'. In saying so, he merely reiterates the self-eulogy of the 'technical fix' civilization: indeed, mining the riches of the earth never to be replenished in human history is in the self-awareness of modernity an achievement, and 'the most important' one at that. It was not the industrial plant, but the mine that was the beginning of the modern spirit and the most poignant symbol of modern practice. Mining, I suggest, is the metaphor for the whole of modern civilization; or, to put it the other way – the totality of modern postures and strategies can be best understood as metaphors for prospecting.

[6] Carlo M. Cipolla, *Before the Industrial Revolution: European Society and Economy, 1000–1700* (London: Methuen, 1976), pp. 229, 166, 274. It was the harnessing of inanimate (and non-renewable, and thus not confined in its usable volume by the 'natural' capacity of reproduction and replenishment) energy that 'did the trick': 'A basic fundamental continuity characterized the pre-industrial world, even through grandiose changes, such as the rise and fall of Rome, the triumph and decline of Islam, the Chinese dynastic cycles . . . This continuity was broken between 1780 and 1850' (p. 275). Norbert Wiener, the founder of cybernetics, considered the replacement of human muscle as a source of energy to be the only 'industrial revolution' there was (the next to be the replacement of the human brain – see *The Human Use of Human Beings* (Boston: Houghton Mifflin, 1950)).

The eruption of mining practices in the eighteenth and the nineteenth centuries was, as Lewis Mumford suggested, a total cultural revolution:

> Agriculture creates a balance between wild nature and man's social needs. It restores deliberately what man subtracts from the earth; while the plowed field, the trim orchard, the serried vineyard, the vegetables, the grains, the flowers, are all examples of disciplined purpose, orderly growth, and beautiful form. The process of mining, on the other hand, is destructive: The immediate product of the mine is disorganized and inorganic; and what is once taken out of the quarry or the pithead cannot be replaced. Add to this the fact that continued occupation in agriculture brings cumulative improvement to the landscape and a finer adaptation of it to human needs; while mines as a rule pass quickly from riches to exhaustion, from exhaustion to desertion, often within a few generations. Mining thus presents the very image of human discontinuity, here today and gone tomorrow, now feverish with gain, now depleted and vacant.[7]

The practice which threw open the store of the unheard-of supplies of energy was, simultaneously, the epitome of a thoroughly new human order. The new technique which mining practice exemplified was a total affair, as was the 'technological stance toward the world' which made it feasible. Jacques Ellul insists that 'the revolution resulted not from the exploitation of coal but rather from a change of attitude on the part of a whole civilization'. The change involved, as one of the most fateful departures, the new 'plasticity of the social milieu' – resulting from the dissolution of 'natural' groups (that is, paradoxically, refusal to treat those groups as 'natural') and the 'social taboos' which they reproduced and enforced. The immediate effect of the dissolution of groups and breaking up of their protective mental shields was atomization of the social compound into isolated individuals – underdetermined, unbound and free moving: the atomization

> conferred on society the greatest possible plasticity – a decisive condition for technique. The breakup of social groups engendered the enormous displacement of people at the beginning of the nineteenth century and resulted in the concentration of population demanded by modern technique.

Again, it was not the massive movement and territorial rearrangement of men and women that made the world of things and humans (and human things – humans made into things) amenable to technological treatment – but the manipulability of the individuals now 'liberated' from prior assignments and definitions. Such individuals

[7]   Lewis Mumford, *The City in History: Its Origins, its Transformations, and its Prospects* (New York, 1961), pp. 450–1. The reader will note that the

could be, had to be, and indeed were subjected to the processes of 'systematization, unification and clarification'[8] on which technique thrives and for which it is prominent. Not just whole individuals, to be sure: having been detached from 'natural groups' which made them into wholes, the individuals were now amenable to further dissection into aspects, factors, functions – each setting in motion a different technique, each to be 'handled' separately while other aspects were kept out of the field of vision, 'bracketed off' for the duration. (I suggest that the 'individual' – in-dividual, non-divisible unit – as the name of the product of modern dissolution of collectivities, is a misnomer; in fact, that alleged 'in-dividual' has been prominent mostly for its astonishing divisibility, indeed its fissiparousness, unthinkable in the case of its ancestors, in whose lives roles and actions, however diverse, were closely co-ordinated, intertwined and inseparable.) There was more than a coincidental link between the two processes. Making humans fit for technological treatment was an effect of the total 'technological revolution' in positing and handling 'nature', but the latter would not be possible were not 'human resources' liberated first for use in the massive-scale, concentrated efforts to churn out the excess of resources, tools and instruments feverishly searching for ends they may serve.

As Max Weber told us, the world as conjured up by technology is a 'dis-enchanted' world: a world without meaning of its own, because without 'intent', 'purpose', 'destination'. In such a world, 'natural necessity' is an abomination and an offence, *lèse-majesté* to high and mighty humanity – and all resistance of 'dead matter' is but a constraint to be broken. On the other hand, wants (if only backed by technical resources) become human rights which nothing could question or argue away – even the wants of other humans (if not backed by such resources). In modernity, says Louis Dumont,

> there is no humanly significant world order . . . [T]his world devoid of values, to which values are superadded by human choice, is a subhuman world, a world of objects, of things . . . It is a world without man, a world from which man has deliberately removed himself and on which he is thus able to impose his will.[9]

---

bucolic description of the benign effects of agriculture does not reckon with the awesome potential of revolutionary fertilisers, mono-cultural rationalizations and other similar 'scientific improvements'. There is nothing to stop agriculture from being conducted in the likeness of mining; modern sentiments would not allow it to be stopped anyway.

8 Cf. Ellul, *The Technological Society*, pp. 44, 49, 51, 43.

9 Louis Dumont, *Essays on Individualism: Modern Ideology in Anthropological Perspective* (University of Chicago Press, 1986), p. 262.

Because meaning is always round the corner, always in-waiting and not-yet, the 'what is' has no authority over 'what ought to be'. (Modern science, in tune with the spirit of technological revolution, promptly produced the operative definition of being which forbade the use of value-related terms, and so rendered the precept 'values cannot be deduced from reality' tautologically true.) Under the circumstances, the right to set the goals can be freely ceded to the current capacity of making things happen; if something can be done, there is no authority on earth or in heaven which has the right to forbid its happening (unless, that is, that authority has at its disposal an even greater capacity for making things happen of its choice). This makes the world construed by technology exquisitely flexible, fluid, bursting with opportunities and resilient to all fixation. It also makes it pliable, vulnerable, indefensible: a docile prey to technological ingenuity and know-how; a grazing ground for insatiable appetites; 'the other' whose treatment cancels the distinction between the love-relation and rape.

The ideological rationale of technological society is the quest for improvement: originally it was the vision of an orderly, sensibly organized and closely monitored habitat replacing the erratic messiness of nature. Messiness, though, has long been prised off its natural roots; it is almost totally man-made now: the sediment, or waste, of past technological bustle. Technology's miraculous powers are intimately related to the stratagem of close focusing: a 'problem', to become a 'task', is first cut out from the tangle of its multiple connections with other realities, while the realities with which it is connected are left out of account and melt into the indifferent 'backdrop' of action. It is thanks to this deliberate condensation of effort and voluntary forgetting about the rest that technological action is so wondrously effective each time it is undertaken; if it tried to spread its attention more widely, take account of all the multifarious entanglements of the 'task at hand' – it would not be technology 'as we know it'. Technique aimed at 'totality' is a contradiction in terms. ('Totality' is, anyway, sensibly defined only as something which 'sticks beyond' the field on which attention is momentarily focused and thus is deemed responsible for the 'unanticipated consequences' of action; from the vantage point of technological action, totality is, as a rule, what 'has *not* been taken into account'.) True, technological action always substitutes an order for what (when confronted with the model of that order) is perceived as dis-order; but it is always a *local* order that is produced at the far end of technological action; with technology always viewing the world as a collection of fragments (fragments never larger than what can be plausibly handled by the presently available means and the actor's resources) and always selecting one fragment at a time for close focusing, the overall result of local ordering can be none other that global disorder. Local orders are thrown out of balance with the rest; local improvement seldom outweighs the side-effects of the new imbalance.

Technological dissembly of the moral self

The above remark applies to big and small totalities alike; to the planet as a whole as much as to the totality called 'personality', 'human self', or (misleadingly as we have seen) 'individual'. As Harry Redner observed, 'Men have devised a way of systematically dominating, controlling, and disposing of all things, which in the first place was directed against Nature but which they now find is also turning on themselves . . .'[10] It could hardly be otherwise. The sole totality technology systematically constructs, reproduces and renders invulnerable is the totality of technology itself – technology as a *closed system*, which tolerates no alien bodies inside and zealously devours and assimilates everything that comes within its grazing ground. Technology is the sole genuine in-dividual. Its sovereignty can be only indivisible and exceptionless. Humans, most certainly, are not excepted.

Like anything else, modern humans are technological objects. Like anything else, they have been analysed (split into fragments) and then synthesized in novel ways (as arrangements, or just collections, of fragments). And this was not a one-off accomplishment of technology: dissembly and re-assembly go on continuously and have long become self-propelling, as the synthesis which is nothing but another rearrangement of fragments cannot but be a constant invitation (indeed, an all-powerful pressure) to new and improved analyses. 'Every human technique', says Ellul, 'has its circumscribed sphere of action, and none of them covers the whole man.'[11] Techniques may be aimed at the liver, and then whatever happens to

---

[10]   Harry Redner, *In the Beginning was the Deed: Reflections on the Passage of Faust* (University of California Press, 1982), p. 5. 'The story is well known', says Redner, 'how we Europeans launched ourselves on an unparalleled drive for power . . . All the natural and human resources were put at our disposal to be transformed in accordance with our sovereign will.' And yet, 'the more power that Deed unleashes, the harder it becomes for men to control it and the more it begins impersonally to control them' (pp. 13, 15).
[11]   Ellul, *The Technological Society*, p. 388.

the kidneys will be but a side-effect. Or they may be aimed at eliciting more self-assertion, and then whatever happens to the dispensation of parental duties is the side-effect. In technology's lenses, humans appear always as a conjunction of a 'problem' in sharp focus and a vast yet dim area of sprawling side-effects out of focus.

The product of dividing/splitting/fragmenting/atomizing urge and capacity of technology is the division of expertise. Technological know-how and briefings appear to single humans in the form of experts or expert-written DIY manuals. Overtly, each encounter does not much more than to convey the specific advice how to deal with the 'problem' in focus. Covertly yet insidiously, it conveys the wider and more seminal message – about the world subdivided into 'problems', and the advisability of dealing with 'one problem at a time' and 'crossing each bridge as one comes to it'. Each technological instruction promotes itself, *and* the world in which instruction is given in a fashion specific to technology – as a fragment in question and the *principle* of fragmentation. Anthony Giddens wrote of the 'reskilling', even 'empowerment' of modern men and women obtainable through 're-appropriation' of expert knowledge: 'the individual has the possibility of a partial or more full-blown reskilling in respect of specific decisions or contemplated course of action . . . Empowerment is routinely available to laypeople as part of the reflexivity of modernity.'[12] This is undoubtedly correct, yet what is missing here is the recognition that the skills obtained in the result of the reskilling or re-appropriation are not of the same kind as the skills first sequestrated by technological expertise; and that – more seminally still – the reskilling process is a package deal, coming together with the tacit or overt acceptance of the collective authority of expertise and of the conception of the world as a collection of fragments – the conception which *all* experts, the diversity of their opinions notwithstanding, unanimously endorse and promote. What is missing in addition is the recognition that there is an outer limit to the 'modern reflexivity', the limit which no reskilled individual, precisely for being reskilled in this fashion, is given the chance of transgressing: that limit is set by

---

[12] Anthony Giddens, *Modernity and Self-identity: Self and Society in the Late Modern Age* (Cambridge: Polity Press, 1991), pp. 139, 141. Symptomatically – Giddens selects 'back trouble' as an illustration of his thesis, pointing out the individual's (already defined by the *experts* as a patient, and as a patient whose 'problem' consists in back pains) capacity of choosing between conflicting *expert* counsels of osteopathy, physiotherapy, massage, acupuncture, exercise therapy, drugs, diets, hands-on healings etc.

the status of the world, first fragmented and then reassembled by technology, as a collection of fragments. In the process of expertly guided reskilling, the denizens of modernity internalize such a world complete with the fragmenting powers of the experts who are that world's joint builders, administrators and spokesmen at the same time. What the reskilled lose in the process of reskilling is the ability to conceive of themselves as individuals, as totalities 'greater than collections of fragments'.

To quote Ellul once more: if every technique taken separately can truthfully 'assert its innocence' (that is, deny that it is 'working on man as a whole' and remind adamantly that it deals with this problem here and now and nothing else), it is the totality of techniques that counts, as well as the fact that the whole field has been divided by and between them without residue. What counts is 'the convergence on man of a plurality, not of techniques, but of systems or complexes of techniques. The result is operational totalitarianism; no longer is any part of man free and independent of these techniques.'[13] There is no part of the self left free of technological processing which could serve as the 'Archimedean point' for turning the process around, or a bridgehead from which to start the restoration of the self's integrity. One can contest an expert counsel; one can play one expert against another; one can steal the expertise and play with it, boldly, oneself; what one is least likely to do is to put up such a challenge to technology as would not be technological itself and would not lead to more technology and to further reinforcement of technological rule.

And technology means fragmentation – of life into a succession of problems, of self into a set of problem-generating facets, each calling for separate techniques and separate bodies of expertise. When the job of fragmentation is done, what is left are diverse wants, each to be quelled by requisition of specific goods or services; and diverse internal or external constraints, each to be overcome in turn, one-constraint-at-a-time – so that this or that unhappiness now and then can be toned down or removed. In a benign regime sworn to the pursuit of universal happiness and professing legitimacy of all desires, wants may be turned into rights and constraints proclaimed manifestations of injustice. No regime though, however benign, humane,

---

[13] Ellul, *The Technological Society*, pp. 389, 391. Because no single technique 'attacks' totality, a situation hardly ever arises when the person affected is prompted to object to the assault on his or her sovereignty. The absorption of technology's rule takes place gradually and imperceptibly – as a long-term precipitate of many small-scale decisions and acts, none of which ever confronted the issue in its full dimension.

permissive or liberal, would permit a challenge to the sacrosant reality of the fragmented self.

The moral self is the most evident and the most prominent among technology's victims. The moral self can not and does not survive fragmentation. In the world mapped by wants and pockmarked by hurdles to their speedy gratification, there is ample room left for *homo ludens, homo oeconomicus* and *homo sentimentalis*; for gambler, entrepreneur, or hedonist – but none for the moral subject. In the universe of technology, the moral self with its negligence of rational calculation, disdain of practical uses and indifference to pleasure feels and is an unwelcome alien.

On no occasion does the subject confront the totality – of the world, or of the other human. Life is a sequence of many disparate approaches, each one being partial and hence, like the techniques themselves, entitled and prone to claim moral innocence. Fragmentarity of the subject and fragmentarity of the world beckon to each other and lavish mutual assurances upon each other. The subject never acts as a 'total person', only as a momentary carrier of one of the many 'problems' that punctuate her life; neither does she act upon the Other as person, or upon the world as totality. If the effect of the subject's action reached beyond the fragment cast momentarily in focus, this would be promptly and confidently explained away as 'misadventure', 'unanticipated consequence', an unhappy coincidence no one wished to happen – an event casting no shadow on the actor's moral integrity. Out of the partial interests and focused obligations, no overwhelming responsibility for the Other, or the world, is likely to be patched up. The task-oriented action does not allow for an orientation point outside the union between the task at hand and the actor bent on that task.

This does not exclude the possibility that the fragmented selves would commit themselves to collective causes; indeed, such a commitment is likely – as wants gain in intensity when voiced in company, and interests are served better when shared. But the causes, like the tasks and the actors who pursue them, would be similarly fragmented. Collectivization would only collectivize the fragmentation and reinforce the centrifugal powers that keep the self in its dissembled state. This is, typically, the feature of the now prevalent form of collectivization – of the so-called 'social movements'. Contemporary social movements, like all organizations in the technologically structured society, are as a rule dedicated to the pursuit of a single task (undertaking such auxiliary tasks only as may be reasonably hoped to strengthen the chances of the main one); they are, more often than not, 'single-issue' movements. By the very fact of being single-issue, they confirm the principle of singularity and the assumption of autonomy or the self-containment of issues. Obliquely and inadvertently, they corroborate the image of the world as composed of issues that can be pursued and resolved in separation – one at a time, and one independently of the other. Willy-nilly, they co-operate in keeping the *totality* of the actor and of the world out of focus, and consequently also in the substitution of efficiency standards for ethical norms, and technical procedure for moral responsibility.

I propose that the technology-induced fragmentarity, which at one pole results in the concealment of the systemic nature of the human habitat, and on the other in the dissembly of the moral self, is a major, arguably the principal, cause of what Ulrich Beck, and after him a fast lengthening string of analysts, dubbed *Risikogesellschaft* (Risk Society). The problem-focused quest for efficiency, admittedly technology's most powerful and most vaunted asset, rebounds in uncoordinated maximization drives. Even if each drive is effective in resolving the task at hand (or, rather, *because* it is so effective) the global result is the constantly increasing volume and intensity of systemic imbalances. The strategy that gained its laurels from its spectacular success in the construction of local orders, is itself a major factor of the fast growing global disorder.

'Risk Society': technology's last stand

In the course of modernization, says Ulrich Beck, hazards and dangers presented by man-made powers of technology grew continually, until we have passed from the 'industrial society' to the 'risk society' stage of modernity, in which the logic of wealth-production is gradually displaced by the logic of risk-avoidance and risk management – the main question being now, 'How can the risks and hazards systematically produced as part of modernization be prevented, minimized, dramatized, or challenged?' The gravest of problems mankind confronts today and technology has to cope with are those 'resulting from techno-economic development itself'.[14]

---

[14]   Ulrich Beck, *Risk Society: Towards a New Modernity*, trans. Mark Ritter (London: Sage, 1992), pp. 19, 20. '*Risk* may be defined', says Beck, 'as a *systematic way of dealing with hazards and insecurities induced and introduced by modernization itself*' (p. 21) – thereby including in the very definition the idea that what makes the hazards 'risks' is that they are problems *for* technology, not merely problems *of* technology. In the concept of 'risk society', 'risks'

This, according to Beck, brings about seminal changes in the nature of modernity.

First, unlike the old dangers modernization set about eliminating or defusing, the new ones, produced by modernization itself, are invisible to the naked eye and not immediately recognizable as such; above all, they cannot be discovered, let alone coped with, by lay people – the prospective victims of such dangers. The new hazards 'require the "sensory organs" of science – *theories, experiments, measuring instruments – in order to become visible or interpretable as hazards at all'*. Thanks to science, however, dangers are (or at least may be) discovered in advance, so that something can be done about them: 'as the risks of modernization are scientized, their latency is eliminated'. Science is, as before, a major vehicle of progress, but in a novel way: *'the publicly transmitted criticism of the previous development becomes the motor of expansion'*.[15] Science, so to speak, promotes progress through revealing and criticizing the unwholesome nature of its past accomplishments. What this would mean, however, were a long view taken, is that science is busy producing, or encouraging production, of the objects of its future indignation; it reproduces its own indispensability through piling up blunders and threats of disasters, according to the principle 'We have made this mess; we will clean it up'; and, more pointedly yet, 'This is a kind of mess only we know how to clean' . . .

---

enter the stage already appropriated and managed by science and technology – as their unquestionable domain.

Mary Douglas recently suggested that in public discourse 'the idea of risk is transcribed simply as unacceptable danger' and 'has become a decorative flourish for the word "danger"' (see 'Risk and Danger', in *Risk and Blame: Essays in Cultural Theory* (London: Routledge, 1992)). One can point out against this statement that the shift in vocabulary is itself semiotically loaded. Unlike 'danger', 'risk' belongs to the discourse of *gambling*, that is, to a kind of discourse which does not sustain clear-cut opposition between success and failure, safety and danger; one which recognizes their co-presence in every situation, thereby straddling the barricade which separates them in the discourse of 'order' which the term 'danger' comes from and represents. 'Risk' signals that moves are not unambiguously safe or dangerous (or at least that what is the case is not known in advance) – that they differ only in the proportion in which safety and danger are mixed. 'Risk' is also referred to what the gambler does, not to what is done to him (it is the gambler who 'is taking risks'). 'Risk', therefore, more than the 'danger' it allegedly 'simply transcribed', is resonant with the postmodern view of the world as game, and the being-in-the-world as play.

[15]   Beck, *Risk Society*, pp. 27, 154, 161.

Second, 'risk determinations are *based* on mathematical *possibilities*'.[16] Risk may be *determined*; that is, measured *objectively* (this is exactly what science claims to be doing, and doing well) – by computing the statistical probability that disaster will strike, as well as the probable size of the disaster. We may again observe that if the threat of disaster is horrifying, its calculability is – in defiance of logic – consoling. Statistics is the next best thing to certainty, and if one cannot be sure of one's safety, one can at least quell anxiety a bit when at least the probability that one is indeed safe is stated in non-uncertain terms. Probability makes the fate of the prospective victim neither foolproof nor doomed (it is of obvious and undeniable practical use solely to insurance companies – it indeed allows the justification of the selective increases in insurance premiums; one may even dare to guess that dealing with dangers as 'risks', that is computing their statistical probabilities, is truly at home in the world 'as seen by the insurers') – but it brings a degree of psychical comfort through the *illusion* of control over destiny. The risks notwithstanding, one can go on calculating, choosing, playing the game of rationality. Reason rules OK. Business as usual. The 'risk society' is still a legitimate mode of familiar modernity and there is no need to question modernity's foundational creed: that by application of reason we may, jointly, bend realities to our will and make our sojourn in the world more pleasurable.

Third, the 'risk society' is a *reflexive* stage of modernity. Reflexivity 'means scepticism', but scepticism is not a late arrival in the house of modernity and thus reflexivity 'means not less but more modernity'.[17] There is a tacit, but pervasive implication in the description of the 'risk society' as a territory marked primarily by watchtowers and Geiger counters, that 'reflecting' makes the world safer and that knowing what is going on means knowing how to go on and being able to go on.

This otherwise tacit implication is spelled out by Anthony Giddens: the outcome of reflexivity – the risk assessment – is 'fundamental to colonizing the future', and so 'the monitoring of risk' is 'a key aspect of modernity's reflexivity'. Having surveyed in great detail the impact of the medical statistics of mortality upon avoidance of health risks, Giddens offers it as a pattern for what the new sensitivity to risk, computation of probabilities and reflexivity in general may do

---

[16] Beck, *Risk Society*, p. 29.
[17] Beck, *Risk Society*, p. 14.

for the individual denizen of the late-modern world. Monitoring of health risks, says Giddens,

> provides an excellent example, not just of routine reflexivity in relation to extrinsic risks, but of the interaction between expert systems and lay behaviour in relation to risk. Medical specialists and other researchers produce the materials from which risk profiling is carried out. Yet risk profiles do not remain the special preserve of the experts. The general population is aware of them, even if it is often in a rough and ready way, and indeed the medical profession and other agencies are concerned to make their findings widely available to laypeople. The lifestyles followed by the population at large are influenced by the reception of those findings . . .[18]

There is, in Giddens's rendition, a constant 'trickle-down' effect of the sciences' preoccupation with computation of probabilities: individuals may now take safer routes, abstain from doing things which have been pointed out by experts as carrying higher than average dangers, and altogether put more substance in the perennial modern dream of 'colonizing the future'. Against this benign narrative, Scott Lash raised the worrying prospect of the 'limits to reflexivity', which refer primarily to the lack of identity, and even co-ordination, between the subjective capacity to reflect and the immunity of the world to the practical measures which reflection may suggest.[19] Indeed, one may easily point out quite a few factors which devalue the assets offered by scientifically approved 'risk statistics' to individuals bent on 'colonizing' their individual futures; one can in addition suspect that in a non-negligible number of cases risk-information may actually diminish the individual capacity for controlling individual fate.

To start with, risk information aimed at the lay public and passed over to members of the public in the form of 'DIY survival kits' has an overall effect of a counterfactual *privatization* of risks: the way the risk information works, the collectively produced dangers are 'dumped' into the privatized worlds of individual victims and translated as realities one confronts individually and struggles with through individual efforts. Risks are pre-selected and pre-processed in such a way that the awareness of dangers comes together with the intimation of the individual's blame for continuing risk-exposure and individual responsibility for risk-avoidance. The example of medical statistics is, from this point of view, well chosen: it implies – without

[18]   Giddens, *Modernity and Self-identity*, pp. 111, 114, 120–1.
[19]   Cf. Scott Lash, 'Asthetische Dimensionen reflexiver Modernisierung', in *Soziale Welt*, vol. 3 (1992), pp. 261–77. If the 'risk' is a crucial category of

the need for further argument and without offering a chance of sensible objection – that virtually everything one can do to minimize health hazards rests in the hands of the health–conscious person herself. Its covert message contradicts, therefore, the theoretical wisdom of 'risk society' being reproduced by massive processes mostly beyond control of their victims; in their immediate pragmatic impact, and still more in their long–term 'teaching' effects, that message conceals the fact that, as Scott Lash and Brian Wynne insist in their preface to the English edition of Beck,

> the primary risk, even for the most technically intensive activities (indeed perhaps most especially for them), is . . . that of social dependency upon institutions and actors who may well be – and arguably are increasingly – alien, obscure and inaccessible to most people affected by the risks in question.

Lash and Wynne conclude that the 'public awareness' of dangers is so shaped that the shaken credibility of institutions may be repaired 'without fundamentally questioning the forms of power or social control involved'. Having analysed a characteristic case of risk assessment proffered by the toxicologists in the scientifically reputable Pesticides Advisory Committee, Lash and Wynne bring in their verdict: 'The idealized model of the risk system, reflected in the scientists' exclusive focus on the laboratory knowledge, contained not only questionable physical assumptions but a naive model of that part of society.'[20] I would suggest that whatever naivety there was in the deployed model was not a regrettable yet repairable error; it was deliberate, or at least unavoidable. The model of 'risk society' cannot absorb Lash's crucial concept of the 'limits to reflexivity' without changing itself beyond recognition; without being transformed from technology's last ideological rampart (the last attempt to defend technology rule under conditions of postmodern disenchantment with the liberating potential of modernity's original 'disenchantment of the world') into the battering ram aimed at the very rationale and foundation of society guided by technological values.

The type of reflexivity in which the public is trained by risk-assessments offered for popular knowledge and use, fends off and deflects the blows which otherwise would, perhaps, stand a better chance of aiming at the true causes of present dangers; all in all, it helps the technologically inspired strategies of efficiency-

---

the subjective dimension, the objective amenability to reflexive correction is best grasped, as Lash suggests, with the help of categories like 'difference', 'complexity', 'contingency'.

[20]   Beck, *Risk Society*, pp. 4, 5.

maximization and problem-orientation to survive their unprepossessing consequences, and so to emerge from trials with their danger-producing capacity intact. This happens even in such cases when risk-tracking leads willy-nilly to the doorstep of this or that concrete culprit; say, a 'big corporation' which has produced damage 'traceable to the source' on a scale evidently transcending individual ability to repair (or, better still, a corporation rich enough to be blackmailed into paying for its individual share of collective sin). As in the previously discussed case of the explicit privatization of risk-avoidance and risk management, the requirement of individualized explanation and individual blame has been met, and the promise that the dangers would be done away with if only individual vigilance and self-censoring were maintained has been salvaged. In other words, reflexivity may well increase, rather than diminish, the suicidal tendency of technological rule. This may well be the genuine (though not necessarily intended) meaning of Beck's proposition that reflexivity means 'more, not less modernity'.

Another 'truth of the matter' which the alleged short-cut between reflexivity and risk-defusion by-passes, is the powerful interests which in a market-guided consumer society must arise around every anxiety, panic or fear fit to be deployed as 'selling points' in the ongoing effort to merchandise commodities meant for individual consumption. The potential commercial value of risk-fright is infinite. One can go to any length (that is, to any sale volume) playing on ingeniously fomented fears of health-hazards. (Millions of dollars have been made of the real or putative dangers of obesity, or the fear of the asthmogenic carpet mites, or the 'dirt you can see and the dirt you can not' in the more concealed parts of kitchen sinks.) Risk-fighting is now a big and highly profitable business – and we keep learning time and again that it is also, expectedly, self-perpetuating: cures offered to dangers we see (or are shown, or are prompted to imagine) create as a rule dangers we do not see (or have not been shown, or have been prevented from imagining) – yet. As it has been presently institutionalized, the fashion in which 'risks' are 'fought' may help an appropriately flexible producer of risk-fighting gadgets to defeat once in a while a specific – real or imaginary – threat, and so to establish their credentials and store public trust for the benefit of future products; but a total disappearance of man-made dangers, were it to pass, would spell a commercial disaster (fortunately, it is not on the cards). To keep the wheels of the consumer market well-lubricated, a constant supply of new well-publicized dangers is needed. And the dangers needed must be fit to be translated into consumer demand: such dangers as are 'made to measure' for privatized risk-fighting. One may conclude that the way risk management has been institutionalized in consumer society allows the deployment of the reflexivity not so much as an instrument of individual freedom, fate-control, or 'colonization of the future' – as a device to re-forge public anxiety into corporate profits and, on the way, to further deflect public concerns away from the danger-perpetuating mechanism itself.

The prospects for arresting the mass production of dangers are dimmer still since the majority of prospective victims, as well as most of those who are tormented by the prospect of sharing their fate, have long become, knowingly or not, part of the danger-producing mechanism. We have all developed vested interests in the perpetu-ation of that mechanism, and though many of us may wish – theoretically – the total demise of its products, there are always some of us who will react with horror or anger to the dismantling of any particular part of it, while virtually all of us would deeply resent any blow to the mechanism itself. We are profoundly worried when what we call 'economic growth' slows down or reverts into recession, and governments of all political shades are – in our name and with our support – sworn to prevent this from happening.

We would not take gladly the suggestion that the manufactured products which saturate our daily life, and which we have grown to consider indispensable to a life both decent and agreeable, should be withdrawn from production, or supplied in lesser quantities – just to limit the exhaustion of natural resources or the damage done to fresh air and water supplies. We all bewail the pollution and inconvenience caused by the privatization of 'transport problems' through car business, but most of us would hotly resist the abolition of private cars, while every seventh person among us derives his or her living, directly or obliquely, from the car business's prosperity. So that any slow-down in car production is widely interpreted as national disaster. We are all up in arms against the cumulation of toxic waste, but most of us try to assuage our fears by demanding that waste should be dumped in other (and distant) people's backyards. Declara-tion of war against cholesterol sends dairy farmers to the streets in defence of milk-and-butter markets. Raising popular awareness of the dangers of smoking spells disaster not just for the tobacco companies (who can easily diversify their capital), but to millions of poor farmers for whom tobacco-growing is the only source of livelihood. We want more and faster cars to drive us to the Alpine forest, only to find upon arrival that the forests are no more, eaten up by petrol fumes. We may deeply mistrust the danger-churning industrial system as a whole, but each and every fragment of it will easily find in its managers and employees its most gallant and staunch defenders, ready to take up arms to prolong its existence. We shudder at the thought of killing fields, but much less at the thought of devices which make the killing feasible; owners, workers, local shopkeepers and local MPs will readily join forces to protect arms factories, navy dockyards, or factories that produce potentially murderous chemicals (providing, of course, that the factories themselves are 'environmentally safe' for the MP's constituency). New arms orders are greeted with joy, their cancellation is a cause for mourning. Once the 'evil empire' with its immense research-and-development military institutes designing 'new and improved' weaponry collapsed, so that we have no more reason to write off every few years our stocks of unused weapons on account of the genuine or suspected enemy's 'progress', new targets are actively sought – with our support – to unload the contents of overflowing army warehouses and make room for new and continuous supplies. While we dream of the world as a safer and more peaceful place, the favours of big and small dictators are curried by arms sellers, government-subsidized or not – merchandising their wares as not just weapons, but the poor man's power and glory. Last but not least: we are deeply worried by what we call the 'population explosion' – but we all – naturally, rightfully and credibly – applaud as 'progress' the advances made in prolonging individual lives – and, obviously, each of us is eager to partake personally of its achievements. It is not just that some people's poison may be other people's meat; more disconcertingly still for the anti-risk united front, substances poisonous when in large quantities, in small doses prove to be the daily food most people cannot, or would not, do without. However we may construe the image of 'common interest' – the local interests, the interests which truly count and truly prompt people into action, by and large militate against their defence. This is, perhaps, the most trusty among technology's insurances and built-in protective devices.

A hope has often been expressed that the dangers churned up by the 'risk society', admittedly not being 'class-specific', may – unlike the ills generated by industrial society in its classic form, now left behind – prompt the unification of sufferers into an harmoniously acting force of opposition. Though he admits that even if it is true that the distribution of risks differs from that of wealth, this circumstance 'does not exclude risks from often being distributed in a stratified or class-specific way', Ulrich Beck emphasizes nevertheless that *objectively* 'risks display an equalizing effect'; everyone is now threatened and everyone is objectively predisposed to join the self-defence battalions. 'In class positions', says Beck, 'being determines consciousness, while in risk positions, conversely, *consciousness (knowledge) determines being*'[21] – what is needed for people to join in the fight is but knowledge of the risks and, particularly, of the universality of the dangers they entail. Since, as we remember, it is science which creates and distributes that knowledge of risks which is needed, one may surmise that, in Beck's model, it is science which has been assigned the major role in the forthcoming political mobilization against risks.

Science in the forefront of a war of attrition against risks seems, however, a highly improbable prospect, on the strength of the arguments advanced above: risk-detection and risk management having been declared the most indispensable and precious of science's and technology's social functions, both science and technology feed, perversely, on the resilience and vitality of the selfsame disease they are appointed (or self-appointed) to disarm and shackle.[22] *Objectively* and *subjectively*, they are a major force in perpetuating, rather than arresting, the risk-generating propensity of the social system. The war against risks is science's and technology's last stand; and no generals cherish the thought of a return to civil life, let alone the uncertainties of post-war demobilization.

Science's 'double-agent' role apart, there are still more substantive reasons to doubt the opposition-uniting capacity of the new heightened sensitivity to the risks born of technological developments. First, dangers differ from each other in their potential scope and spread, so that not all affected need worry equally and at the same time. Second, from many a danger one can buy oneself off privately, if only the price-tag does not exceed one's means. (Or at least this is what one can be made to believe; during the Cold War the thriving nuclear-

---

[21]   Beck, *Risk Society*, pp. 35, 36, 53.
[22]   A recently launched journal dedicated to risk management (*Journal of Contingencies and Crisis Management*) specifically meant, as the publicity leaflet announces, 'for chief executive officers, policy makers, policy analysts, management consultants and academic researchers', promises to supply instructions for 'recovery and turnaround management', and advocates in its articles 'the need for disciplined advisory capacities'. A thick layer of new expert professions rapidly wraps around the present recognition of the endemic character of risks and the appreciation of contingency permanently ingrained in the action settings. Risk expertise fast becomes an important branch of the professional world, and itself turns into big business.

shelter industry offered a wide range of secure, more secure and yet more secure private refuges from the holocaust, each at an appropriate price, whose main function was to translate levels of wealth into levels of security.) From some other dangers a collective buy-off seems feasible, and much of the risk-inspired political effort goes into designing locally protective policies which have the increase of dangers threatening other places as their inevitable side-effect. There is therefore no direct line leading from availability and even the acquisition of knowledge to knowledge-specific political actions. The range of possible reactions is wide, yet most of them are undamaging to the risk-producing agencies, and certainly unharmful to the risk-generating technological system as a whole.

One may guess that the 'theorem of the median voter', popular among political scientists, applies also to the public political responses to risks. (According to that theorem, only such policies stand a chance of electoral success as can reach in their appeal as far as the interests of the median voter – which excludes from the pool of viable policies such as overtly represent minority interests only, and offer to the majority merely prospects of 'paying the price of other people's troubles', that is of increased privations.) If applied to the political remedy to risks, the theorem would imply that only such dangers from which the majority would see no non-political escape (that is, no chance of redistributing the risks to the weaker agents' households, or of purchasing risk-exemptions singly or severally) have a good chance to be universally noted by political actors and give birth to a truly unified and effective political action. Most likely, voices of protest will be particularly loud when objecting to the 'selfish' laxity or recklessness of other people's actions, but much softer when it comes to censoring one's own rationalities which other people may find lax or reckless. Which does not spell much hope for the political expression of the alleged or genuine 'equalizing effects' of risks.

These are the political hurdles which need to be leaped over or kicked out of the way if the cumulation of risks is to be contained. But can it be contained, in the unlikely case that the practical political difficulties are overcome?

Believers in the politically unifying effects of properly advertised risks, and most of their sceptical objectors alike, agree on the view that *in principle* modern organization of life may be rendered harmless without forfeiting any of its most cherished benefits; that there is, so to speak, a way of eating a cake and having it – a way still to be found, but bound to be found if the effort and the good will persist and match the enormity of the task. According to this view, the notoriously meagre results of the efforts so far have been the results of selfish myopia, wrong policies or too lukewarm a resolve; numerous as the failed efforts and dashed hopes have been, they do not signal the unworkability of the intention, let alone prove the non-feasibility of purpose.

I propose, however, that this tacit axiom of the current debate should not be itself exempt from reflexive scrutiny, even if (or rather because) virtually all political, economic and intellectual forces and interests seem – by design or by default – to favour and support such an exemption.

The snake chewing at its tail

The Accumulation of Capital, published by Rosa Luxemburg in 1913, was not only a thorough study of the world-wide spread of the capitalist order and the global demise of pre-capitalist (natural, peasant, artisan) economies; not only one of the first reassessments and systematic corrections of Marx's economic theory undertaken by an insider; not only, even, a particularly elaborate prophecy of the imminent collapse of the capitalist economy. It was also (and this is perhaps its main and lasting significance) a pattern-setting exercise: it proposed and explored a model of a system whose way of reproducing itself and keeping alive is itself the primary cause of its expiration. A model of a system which cannot propagate itself without absorbing and assimilating ever new parts of the world, yet the more successful it is in aborbing them the less is left of the resources needed for the system's self-propagation. A model, in other words, of a system that ultimately destroys itself as a result of its own victories; a system that dies of hunger amidst the opulence it has created. Whatever one may say today about the specific analyses of the book, maimed as they were by the not necessarily felicitous choice of the labour theory of value and the conceptual framework of surplus value, the model itself can be shown to outgrow and outlive its limitations. In retrospect, its deployment appears not just pioneering, but presageful and premonitory.

The most seminal issue in the book are the *limits* to accumulation. As if a victim of Lewis Carroll's curse ('Here, you see, it takes all the running you can do, to keep in the same place'), capitalism must expand just to keep its life-functions. It can expand, however, only at the expense of those parts of the world which have not yet been remade into its own likeness: 'The immediate and vital condition for capital and its accumulation is the existence of non-capitalist buyers of the surplus value . . . [T]he accumulation of capital, as an historical process, depends in every respect upon non-capitalist social strata and forms of social organization' – that is, natural economies, peasants and small producers. The trouble is, however, that in order to become instrumental in that 'realization of surplus value' on which accumulation depends ('Capital requires to buy the products of, and sell its commodities to, all non-capitalist strata and societies'), those non-capitalist elements must be first made into 'buyers' – and this means that the non-capitalist ways of gaining livelihood must be sapped and replaced by the capitalist ones. This in its turn means, however, that though capitalism 'needs non-capitalist social organ-izations as the setting for its development', 'it proceeds by assimilat-ing the very condition which alone can ensure its own existence'.

> Non-capitalist organisations provide a fertile soil for capitalism; more strictly: capital feeds on the ruins of such organisations, and although this non-capitalist *milieu* is indispensable for accumulation, the latter proceeds at the cost of this medium nevertheless, by eating it up.[23]

One may say that, according to Rosa Luxemburg's vision, the doom was written into the logic of capitalism from the beginning of its history. Capitalism, in this narrative, is a parasitic suicidal system which gradually emaciates and kills the organism which feeds it and dies together with its host/victim. Luxemburg, to be sure, does not allow for the possibility that the dying system may draw human society into its grave; she believes that well before the chime of the hour of doom the proletariat, the primary and most painfully hit victim of capitalist mismanagement, will rebel; the cancerous growth will be removed, and sanity will be restored by a new socialist organization of society. As we know now, though, this was no more than an expression of hope; but even at the time it was offered only as an expression of hope. Nowhere did Luxemburg explain how socialist economy will do without accumulation; or – if it does accumulate – how socialist accumulation will avoid the moribund logic of the capitalist one. In the event, society run under the auspices of socialism proved to be prone to the same ill fate Luxemburg predicted for capitalist society – with one crucial weakness added,

[23] Rosa Luxemburg, *The Accumulation of Capital*, trans. Agnes Schwarz-schild (London: Routledge, 1951), pp. 366, 387, 416.

though: as the societies that called themselves socialist, being totalitarian societies, systematically destroyed the spiritual or political forces which could, conceivably, slow down or arrest, let alone reverse, the downward slide – it encountered virtually no resistance in its unstoppable drive toward the exhaustion of all sources from which it drew its life juices. Whether the capitalist economy which socialism tried hard to 'catch up with and overtake' will or will not follow it into the grave, Luxemburg's remedy perished before the disease it was hoped to cure.

With, however, the troubles of the dominant, market-centred economy showing no sign of abating, with that economy tumbling from one depressed and depressing state into another, and with all contemplated remedies reduced to the spasmodic fits of crisis-management frenzy – one may be forgiven for suspecting that there is more to Rosa Luxemburg's model than met the eye at the time. Its true – and formidable – foreboding power may be revealed once the outer wrappings of surplus value and labour value theory are peeled off the model, and the self-deceptions of the industrial/market economy are pierced through – so that the stuff really processed by the mechanisms the model portrayed become visible.

That stuff remains very much the same whether its processing takes a 'capitalist', or a 'socialist' form. It is the same for all variants of the social organization known as modernity. As we have seen above, the modern era took off with the harnessing of inanimate sources of energy – that seminal act which allowed the disentangling of action from culturally (traditionally) determined ends and set the means free; the domination of means over ends (grounded in the permanent excess of means over extant ends) meant a fateful switch from action motivated by *what needed to be done* to an action guided increasingly by *what could be done*. Throughout the modern era the excessive potential of action was deployed in the incessant effort to 'improve' on the existing order (or, rather, to substitute artificially designed orders for the 'natural' ones vanquished and dismantled in the process). In the historical perspective, modernity appears to be a continuous yet ultimately inconclusive drive towards rational order free from contingency, accidents, things that can get 'out of hand'. It is to maintain such an artificial order, forever precarious and always stopping short of its ideal, that modernity needed enormous quantities of energy the animate sources could not possibly supply – and ever growing quantities with that: the construction of every next order necessarily included the task of cleaning up the mess and waste left by the abortive efforts to fix the previous one.

As Alf Hornborg of Gothenburg University has pointed out in his eye-opening, revolutionary study,[24] structures

> do not really consume 'energy', which can neither be created nor destroyed, but rather the *order* they can derive from it. Exergy is a quality of energy, indicating the degree of order, or information, it contains. This order in energy can be 'embodied' in the order of material structures, or reconverted into radiation, but always with a resulting loss in total order.

We may say that – contrary to ideologically saturated common sense – the 'production of order' (and each productive act is an act of ordering or reordering) is, in its essence, a destructive event: it produces locally less order than it appropriated for the purpose from the overall supply; to deploy the vocabulary of thermodynamics, we may say that each 'order-making act' increases entropy – that is, detracts from the 'total order'. What follows is that the localized efforts of ordering result in global chaos not just because of the (rectifiable) error of insufficient co-ordination, but because of the inexorable law of thermodynamics, law that cannot be altered and whose consequences cannot be in the long run rectified: exempting for a time a given locality from the entropic tendency may be only achieved by increasing entropy elsewhere. In more practical terms, this means that modernity bent on the construction of rational order at home could only reach a measure of local success through a highly unequal redistribution of the world's energetic resources; that is, by robbing other parts of the world of their 'capacities for order' – their supplies of exergy. As William Leiss pointed out in his recent study, referring to the privileged islands of 'high modernity',

> very little in our system is self-reviewing save the wants that drive it on, and thus we must search in ever more remote places with escalating costs and more esoteric technologies for materials and energy to feed it . . .

[24] Cf. Alf Hornborg, 'Machine Fetishism, Value, and the Image of Unlimited Good: Towards a Thermodynamics of Imperialism', in *Man*, vol. 1 (1992), and 'Codifying Complexity: Towards an Economy of Incommensurable Values', mimeographed text of a paper delivered at the second meeting of the International Society for Ecological Economics at Stockholm, 3–6 August 1992. Just how revolutionary Hornborg's own insights are is demonstrated by the sheer impossibility of locating other studies of 'related interest' and anything like theoretical affinity. Hornborg himself points out, as his intellectual ancestry, the little-noted study by N. Georgescu-Roegen (*The Entropy Law and the Economic Process* (Cambridge, Mass.: Harvard University Press, 1971)); and as the only remotely similar contemporary research, an even more obscure study published by H.T. Odum and J.E. Arding ('Energy Analysis of Shrimp Mariculture in Equador', Coastal Resources Centre, University of Rhode Island, 1991).

The continuing deprivations suffered by so many of the earth's inhabitants elsewhere are considered remediable by further application of the same
industrial technology that brought prosperity to the fortunate minority
. . . [But] the practical obstacles to fulfilment of this promise are enormous. How to deliver the tenfold increase in available resources and
energy required to bring the world's population up to North American
consumption levels?[25]

As long as they are based on certain kinds of pastoralism and
agriculture – says Hornborg – societies 'could theoretically live in
balance with the environments (i.e. in 'a steady state') for as long as
the sun shines on earth'. Modern society, on the other hand, is based
on industrial production, which together with trade is a form of
'energy appropriation' and can be perpetuated only as long as it
indeed secures the purchase of new resources with an exergy content
higher than the exergy used up in past products (in order to
compensate for heat emission, refuse and pollution – the unavoidable
loss of the order-producing capacity). From the point of view of the
entropic process which economic theory of modern societies systematically neglects or deliberately flaunts, all such 'exchange' is unequal
and must remain unequal – since 'merely to manage maintenance,
industry must be paid *more* for its products than it spends on raw
materials, even though it has achieved a *decrease* in the overall sum of
order'. Counterfactually, the modern economic system is grounded
in the pretence that value is *generated* in the process of production. But
the 'value' which is paid for in exchange is in fact the *consumption* of
energy – and for this fiction to be sustained the overall sum of order
must go on deteriorating. 'Only from a *local* perspective' can the
industrial production, that continuous 'sucking in' of negentropy,
appear 'productive' or 'efficient'.

> This perennial predicament is the motor behind (a) the imperative,
> continuous expansion of production ('growth'), primarily through
> increased mechanization ('technological development'), (b) the Western
> expansion in pursuit of new markets (imperialism), and (c) the pervasive
> process of inflation, stemming from the struggle to keep the sum of sales
> always one step ahead of the sum of the costs.

Growth, imperialism and inflation are all ultimately suicidal in
their long-term consequences, and only the enjoyment of local (and

---

[25]　William Leiss, *Under Technology's Thumb* (Montreal: McGill-Queens
University Press, 1990), pp. 94, 81. Following Barry Commoner, Leiss
suggests that about 85 per cent of energy consumed in constructing the
modern type of order is wasted: 'Prodigious waste of those resources seems
to be a necessary function of this accelerating turnover, this impermanence of
wants and products' (p. 94).

temporary) increase of order, misleadingly presented as the spearhead of 'global progress', may conceal for a time their true nature. They are also ineradicable traits of the socio-economic loop (which, again, only locally deflects, and disguises, the overall linearity of entropic growth) set in motion by the departure from the 'balanced exchange' – the watershed hailed as the 'modernizing process'. However far and wide it spreads, the emancipation which modernity brought in its wake (liberation from nature, friability of traditional constraints, infinity of human potential, possibility of an order dictated solely by reason), has been from the start and will remain forever an ultimately local phenomenon, a privilege achieved by some at somebody else's expense; it can only be sustained, for a time, on the condition of *unequal exchange* with other sectors of global society. What we came to call 'economic growth' is the process of *expropriation* of order, not of its global increase. That 'economic growth' represents the insatiable hunger of industry for new and larger profits – but profits (that is, the surplus of money at the end of the productive cycle) are but claims on new sources of energy to be burned in the next cycle. To quote from Hornborg once more:

> Any economic system focused on industrial production must underpay raw materials, for it must see to it that price and 'exergy' content are inversely related. A market economy is the most elegant way of giving such discrepancies free reign. The notion of a 'correct' price conceals the implications of the fact that what is being exchanged is *intact* 'exergy' for *spent* 'exergy'. Finished products and raw materials are incommensurable values because, from a thermodynamic point of view, products are *deteriorated* materials. How can we ever say what a fresh apple is worth in apple cores?

How long can the game continue? For some time yet, probably. As long as new sources of 'exergy' can be made accessible to exploitation, and so new territories and new populations may be transformed into suppliers of 'exergy', or allowed to fade out and vanish if a meaningful place in the unequal exchange cannot be found for them. The limits of inequality have not been reached yet (that is, limits of inequality which those whose opinion counts, and those capable of making their opinions reckoned with, are prepared to consider 'tolerable', or better still not consider at all). Unequal exchange is self-perpetuating; it precipitates the imbalances of economic and military power which stretch the 'tolerability limits' of inequality and allow the privileged side of the exchange to break ever new barriers to expropriation. The 'good press' which inequality enjoys at present in all the islands of privilege, the climate of opinion in which it is in good taste to frown upon 'egalitarian utopias', to call on the poor and the miserable to 'help themselves', to consider the 'welfare state' a failure and all societally managed redistribution of income counter-productive, to proclaim mass starving and mass unemployment an acceptable price of freedom – are sure signs that another, ethical barrier is in the process of being broken (or, rather, that the pretence of respecting it needs to be shaken off as the ground begins to tremble under the feet of the 'advanced societies' which are now finding the 'advancement' increasingly difficult to sustain, and as the throat-cutting replaces the civilizing mission). The immense trade deficits run openly by the growing number of 'advanced countries' unmask the expropriatory nature of 'free trade', though the 'advanced' debtors do their best to drown the revelation in the noise about the sky-rocketing debts of the disprivileged. The lie of the century – baptizing the drained off parts of the globe as 'developing' – still helps to attenuate the dissent and resistance against expropri-ation, brandishing the mirage of 'catching up' with the rich before the eyes of the poor, while selective military interventions may still be counted on to prevent the jaundice-eyed dissent from crystallizing into viable opposition. The limits are tenuous, and may be stretched if pushed hard enough and if no one on the other side has the strength and the determination to resist the pushing. There is no clear point when one can say with confidence that the eating of the tail has ended and the eating of the snake begun. The snake itself would, alas, never have the chance to learn that the point had been passed.

From the above argument, one message comes through loud and clear: contrary to the widely shared view of modernity as the first universal civilization, this is a civilization singularly unfit for uni-versalization. It is by nature an insular form of life, one that reproduces itself solely through *deepening* the difference between itself and the rest of the world by a self-assertion that 'disenchants', disempowers and demeans that rest now transformed into the grazing ground. Such a self-assertion is not a reparable blunder of political thick-headedness or unalloyed greed; not a temporary myopia that can be forced or negotiated out of existence through the imposition of a stronger will or through political consensus reached by reasonable actors. Modernity cannot survive the advent of equality. Endemically and organically, modernity is a parasitic form of social arrangement which may stop its parasitic action only when the host organism is sucked dry of its life juices.

The chances of arresting the damage before it becomes terminal are made slimmer still by the awesome propensity of the modern way of life to deflect all opposition raised against its privilege away from the principle of privilege itself, and re-forge it into the thrust for more privilege (through swelling the numbers of the privileged). It is this catastrophic propensity that is perversely conveyed in the consensual belief that 'more modernity' is needed to heal the wounds modernity afflicts. The propensity in question may be seen as a specific case of a much more general tendency of conflicts born under conditions of inequality: the tendency to breed jealousy on the side of the privileged (those who already possess the coveted value), and envy on the side of the disprivileged (those inclined to trace the socially defined 'inferiority' of the position in which they have been cast, down to the non-possession of that value). In the cases of jealousy and envy alike, as Georg Simmel argued, 'a value is at stake which a third party actually or symbolically prevents us from attaining or keeping'.[26]

The most seminal impact of envy, consists, however, in transforming 'the ideas of the dominant' into the 'dominant ideas'. Once the link between the privileged position and certain values has been socially construed, the disprivileged are prompted to seek redress for their humiliation through demanding such values for themselves – and thereby further enhancing those values' seductive power and reinforcing the belief in those values' magic powers. It is not just the privileged who preach the need for more modernity to cure the ills of modernity; the disprivileged, on the whole, agree, with enthusiasm and self-abandon. They demand the reshuffling of cards, not another game. They do not blame the game, only the stronger hand of the adversary. By far the most numerous among the social-protest movements modernity breeds are such as demand the *redistribution* of profits, not the *revision* of profit definition or the *dismantling* of the profit-making mechanism. From competition of this kind, the authority of modernity and all its articles of faith emerge reinforced. Few people are more enthusiastic about its virtues than its victims, and few if any are so uncritical about its pretensions as those who hope for their turn in the rotation of the privilege. Thus, Molefi Asante, the Afro-American author of *Afrocentricity*, claims for the Blacks the merit of founding European civilization (through Egypt,

[26] Georg Simmel, *Conflict and the Web of Group Affiliation*, trans. Kurt H. Wolff (New York: Free Press, 1964), p. 50. Simmel goes on: 'To the envious individual it is irrelevant whether the good is denied him because somebody else possesses it or whether even its loss or renunciation by that other individual would not let him obtain it' (pp. 50–1).

and its inventions of the principles of mathematics, medicine and architecture), while the Reverend Louis Brown of Jackson, Mississippi suggests that General Schwarzkopf should take lessons of military art from (black) Hannibal.[27]

I propose that the greatest of dangers endemic to modernity lies in the conjunction of its seductiveness and non-universability. The first feature pushes it and pulls constantly towards the extremes the other feature would not allow it ever to reach; or, rather, modernity moves unstoppably toward, and beyond, the point at which the waste would transcend the ability of recycling and the dangers produced could be greater than the capacity of problem-solving. The movement seems unstoppable – since however deep and widespread are the premonitions of reaching that point, every social institution and psychological effect of modernity, let alone the market-spawn economic interests, militate against all effective change of direction.

In search of ethical solutions to modernity's problems

Hans Jonas, the ethical philosopher who dedicated most of his work to the contradiction between what morality must, and what it can do under the conditions of rampant modernization, saw the roots of the problem in the formidable powers of modern technology: the scale of possible consequences of human actions have long outgrown moral imagination of the actors. Knowingly or unknowingly, our actions affect territories and times much too distant for the 'natural' moral impulses which struggle in vain to assimilate them, or abandon the struggle altogether. Morality which we inherited from pre-modern times – the only morality we have – is a morality of proximity, and as such woefully inadequate in a society in which all important action is an action on distance.

> The good and evil about which action had to care lay close to the act, either in the praxis itself or in its immediate reach, and were not a matter of remote planning. The proximity of ends pertained to time as well as space . . . The ethical universe is composed of contemporaries and neighbours . . .
>
> All this has decisively changed. Modern technology has introduced

27 Quoted after Annick Cojean, 'Désarrois américains', in *Le Monde*, 30 October 1992, p. 6.

actions of such novel scale, objects, and consequences that the framework
of former ethics can no longer contain them.[28]

Unassisted, individual imagination cannot embrace actions of such
a scale, and see through them up to their furthest repercussions.
Neither is it called or pushed to stretch itself that far; our moral
conscience rests satisfied once responsibility for the near and dear has
been taken and fulfilled. The far-away effects of what we do or desist
from doing either remain invisible and thus unworrying, or are
presented and believed to be taken care of by agencies which neither
demand, nor would take gladly our too keen an interest, let alone
interference. We do not 'naturally' feel responsibility for such far-
away events, however closely they may intertwine with what we do
or abstain from doing. All in all – suggests Jonas – we can no more
rely on the moral capacity we have to settle the question of
responsibility for what we neither see nor know, but what really
counts among the multiple, near or distant, present or future,
outcomes of our actions.

Since what we do affects other people, and what we do with the
increased powers of technology has a still more powerful effect on
people and on more people than ever before – the ethical significance
of our actions reaches now unprecedented heights. But the moral
tools we possess to absorb and control it remain the same as they
were at the 'cottage industry' stage. Moral responsibility prompts us
to care that our children are fed, clad and shod; it cannot offer us
much practical advice, however, when faced with numbing images of
a depleted, desiccated and overheated planet which our children and
the children of our children will inherit and will have to inhabit in the
direct or oblique result of our present collective unconcern. Morality
which always guided us and still guides us today has powerful, but
short hands. It now needs very, very long hands indeed. What chance
of growing them?

Not much, at first glance. 'The very same movement which put us
in possession of powers that have now to be regulated by norms' has
'eroded the foundations from which norms could be derived'. 'Now
we shiver in the nakedness of nihilism in which near-omnipotence is
paired with near-emptiness, greatest capacity with knowing least

---

[28]   Hans Jonas, *Philosophical Essays: From Ancient Creed to Technological Man*
(Englewood Cliffs: Prentice Hall, 1974), pp. 7, 8. Jonas admits that the old
prescriptions of 'neighbour' ethics still hold – but in a close neighbourhood,
'in the immediate intimacy' of the 'day by day sphere of human interaction' –
not in the 'growing realm of collective action where doer, deed and effect are
no longer the same as they were in the proximate sphere' (pp. 8–9).

what for.'[29] It is not just that having proclaimed the self-sufficiency of human reason, modernity rejected God's claim to dictate human fate and so sapped the most solid of grounds on which moral instruction rested in the past. The roots of the present moral impotence go deeper. The 'modern movement' pulverized any ground on which moral commandments can be conceivably founded – it undermined morality as such: responsibilities which go beyond contractual obligations, 'being for' non-reducible to 'being for oneself', values interfering with the supreme precept of maximum efficacy, ends which forbid the use of potent means. Among the authorities which modernity empowers and promotes, the non-rational, non-utilitarian, non-profitable moral passions are most spectacularly absent. With the exception of Sunday sermons and unctuous homilies of vote-seeking politicians, they appear within modern view the way in which noise, the technicians' nightmare and slap-in-the-face, appears in the channels of communication.

With the inhuman consequences of the modern thrust toward a 'totally human' order on earth becoming ever more apparent, the feeling is growing that – all the denials and practical impediments notwithstanding – the actions allegedly amenable to technical evaluation only are far from being morally neutral and call for moral scrutiny; ideally, also for some sort of ethical regulation. The cancelling of spatial distance as measured by the reach of human action – that sometimes applauded, but ever more often bewailed feat of modern technology – has not been matched by the cancellation of moral distance, measured by the reach of moral responsibility; but it should be so matched. The question is, how this can be done, if at all.

The first thing to consider is the dangers which are systematically piling up as the direct, albeit unthought-of, result of the free play of means 'liberated' from goals. These dangers threaten the lives and the welfare of countless other people, distant both in space and in time, and cast in a situation which more often than not precludes all response; the danger-producing actions are as a rule uni-directional. They are not exchanges; they cannot be, therefore, limited or regulated or otherwise kept in the frame by contracts, by a mutual show of force, by negotiations or the search for consensus. I propose that nowhere closer than in the case of long-distance actions typical of our high-tech society, the unwitting targets of action match Lévinas's description of the Other as weak, vulnerable, without power; they are indeed without power since they cannot repay what has been done to them (nor for that matter reward our deeds), and vulnerable

[29] Jonas, *Philosophical Essays*, p. 19.

since they cannot prevent us from doing whatever we think worth doing; once for all, with no hope of reversing the roles, they are stuck on the receiving side of the action in which we are the only acting subjects. As Arne Johan Vetlesen points out, this circumstance demonstrates

> the utter inadequacy of any ethics which links responsibility with reciprocity. Unborn individuals cannot stand up and claim their rights; reciprocation is hopelessly beyond their reach. Yet this empirical fact . . . does not exclude them as addressees of our responsibility. Their basic right is the right to a life on an ecologically inhabitable planet; lest we be careful they will never see the light of day at all.[30]

The extension of responsibility which the 'risk society' needs and cannot do without except with catastrophic results cannot be argued or promoted in terms that are the most familiar and approved of in our type of society – those of fair exchange and reciprocity of benefits. Whatever else the sought morality is to be, it must be first and foremost an ethics of *self-limitation* (as the morality of *proximity* always was and had to be). Exactly as in the context of the 'moral party', the task of visualizing the consequences of action or inaction (and the guilt of neglecting the need of visualizing them, or not visualizing them properly), and cutting the action to the measure of such consequences, rests fairly and squarely with the actor. The excuse 'I did not know', 'I did not mean it', is not an excuse which moral responsibility at whatever level would accept (though it is an excuse admissible in a court of law, unless the ignorance referred to is the ignorance of the Law itself). Whether inside the circle of proximity or beyond, I am morally responsible for my ignorance – in the same way and to the same degree in which I am morally responsible for my imagination, and for stretching it to limits when it comes to acting or refraining from action.

The 'first duty' of any future ethics, says Hans Jonas, must be

---

[30]   Arne Johan Vetlesen, 'Relations with Others in Sartre and Lévinas: Assessing the Implications for an Ethics of Proximity' (quoted from p. 25 of the unpublished text dated January 1993). Decoupling of responsibility from reciprocity is, in Vetlesen's view, the decisive act which sets Lévinas's ethical theory against virtually all other theories. Sophisticated and carefully argued as Rawls's ethical theory may be, even there 'the appeal to "justice as fairness" is directed to each particular individual's concern for his or her own possible place and fate in the political arrangement they are admonished to evaluate for its ethical worth. In this respect, the "reversibility of perspectives" attained at the post-conventional level of moral reasoning in Lawrence Kohlberg's influential theory, fares no better. By implication, this

'Visualizing the long range effects of technological enterprise'. Ethics, I would add, differs from the present ordinary practice of crisis-management in that it must deal with what-has-not-happened-yet, with a future that is endemically the realm of uncertainty and the playfield of conflicting scenarios. Visualization can never pretend to offer the kind of certainty which the experts with their scientific knowledge and with greater or lesser credibility claim to offer. The duty to visualize the future impact of action (undertaken or not undertaken) means acting under the pressure of acute uncertainty. The moral stance consists precisely in seeing to it that this uncertainty is neither dismissed nor suppressed, but consciously embraced. Efficient performance of the task at hand (an endeavour allowing for more certainty, or at least more confidence) is subjected by a moral person to a *second degree* evaluation – by standards not necessarily specific to the task at hand and most likely to be oblivious to the direct or indirect gains and losses of its performer – and this subjection throws the gates wide open to doubts and to second thoughts that vie to be the first. One could perhaps design algorithmically prescribed, unambiguously correct ways of acting, were the task measured solely by the criteria of efficiency, or by the most efficacious use of available resources (as the technological stance prompts it to be measured). Once a moral stance is taken, however, only heuristic guidelines are feasible: rules-of-thumb that do not carry even the reassuring warranty of past habits, and cannot honestly promise more than a sporting chance of success and some hope of avoiding the worst. What future ethics should be guided by, suggests Jonas, is the *Heuristics of Fear*, subordinated in its turn to the *Principle of Uncertainty*: 'The prophecy of doom is to be given greater heed than the prophecy of bliss'. For a heuristics born of danger, and ever accumulating dangers, the 'first urging is necessarily an ethics of preservation and prevention, not of progress and perfection'.[31]

---

applies also to Habermas's tireless endeavour to accommodate the same idea – universalized responsibility in role-taking conceived as universalized reciprocity – in his discourse on ethics' (p. 22).

[31] Hans Jonas, *The Imperative of Responsibility: In Search of an Ethics for the Technological Age* (University of Chicago Press, 1984), pp. 26, 27, 31. Jonas leaves the reader in no doubt that the imperative to 'blow on cold' is implied not by the fear of technology's impotence, but of its powers: 'the danger of disaster attending the Baconian ideal of power over nature through scientific technology arises not so much from any shortcomings of its performance as from the magnitude of success' (p. 140). 'My main fear relates to the apocalypse threatening from the nature of the unintended dynamics of technical civilization as such, inherent in its structure' (p. 202).

The greatest, the most radical doom of all is, however, one that is threatened by the unconstrained rule of technological values; indeed, as we have seen before, by the innermost tendency of modern civilization. In the 'be or not to be' dilemma of our times, it is modernity itself which is the stake. Since modern values are by far the ones most solidly entrenched in the self-consciousness of our society and most intensely guarded and nourished by its institutions, the prospects for ethics advocated by Jonas – and especially in situations where it is most needed – do not look very encouraging. It remains to be seen how, if at all, the intuitively evident need of a 'morality of spatial and temporal distance' may be translated into effective social interests, and consequently into tangible political forces. The postmodern revelation of modernity's in-built morbidity may help. But it is the most salient of postmodernity's traits, the source of its strength and weakness alike, that it is suspicious of certainties and promises no guarantees; that it refuses to freeze history, in prophesies or preemptive legislation, before history takes its course.

Our collective moral responsibility, much as the moral responsibility of every man and woman among us, swims in the sea of uncertainty. Uncertainty was always the home ground of moral choice, though modern moral philosophy and adiaphorizing practice did their best to deny it in theory and repress it in deed. In this respect, the postmodern situation of ethics is not new. What is truly new, is the enormity of the stakes. If this is what postmodern self-awareness made clear to us, this new clarity may go a long way toward balancing out the blow it has delivered to our cosy, cloudless certainties.

8

An Overview: In the End is the Beginning

The reader was warned at the start of this book that no neat inventory of ethical precepts nor other props of moral self-confidence are likely to emerge from the consideration of the moral person's plight in the postmodern world. I guess that this negative promise has been faithfully kept. I doubt whether the author's and the reader's ethical confidence has much grown in the course of this exploration. And yet I believe that the frustration of certainty is morality's gain. Not the kind of gain we would wish, perhaps, and have been looking for – but the greatest gain that one can reasonably hope for, while remaining a moral person.

Is the postmodern condition an advance on the moral accomplishments of modernity? Postmodernity has dashed modern ambitions of the universal and solidly grounded ethical legislation; but has it also put paid to whatever chances modernity has had of moral improvement? In the world of ethics – is postmodernity to be seen as a step forward, or as a retreat?

I suggest that both answers to that last question are true, and that both answers are false. It is a general feature of social change that while it puts right or attenuates the wrongs of yesterday, it also ushers in new wrongs bound to become a target of curative efforts tomorrow. It is merely during the brief stopovers of todays – those half-way inns between yesterday's rocks and the quicksands of tomorrows – that putative victories are recorded, that the memory of the last day-trip is relished as an unalloyed triumph and the next day's journey shines as an ascent into bliss, and that the difference between victory and defeat appears unqualified, clear-cut and obvious.

In the most quoted of all his often quoted passages, Walter Benjamin reports the meaning he gleaned from – read into – Klee's drawing of *Angelus Novus*. The painted angel, as Benjamin saw it, is

> looking as though he is about to move away from something he is fixedly contemplating. His eyes are staring, his mouth is open, his wings are spread. This is how one pictures the angel of history. His face is turned toward the past. Where we perceive a chain of events, he sees one single catastrophe which keeps piling wreckage and hurls it in front of his feet. The angel would like to stay, awaken the dead, and make whole what has been smashed. But a storm is blowing from Paradise, it has got caught in his wings with such violence that the angel can no longer close them. This storm irresistibly propels him into the future to which his back is turned, while the pile of debris before him grows skyward. This storm is what we call progress.[1]

The dead will not be awakened, the smashed will not be made whole. The pile of debris will go on growing. Those who suffered, did. Those who got killed, will stay dead. It is the escaping from (or, rather, being blown away by) the horror of the irreversible and the irredeemable that seems to us – us who have been repelled – to be a 'chain of events'. It only seems, though; it is merely the non-relenting of the wind, which bars the return to Paradise, that makes it seem such. We are kept in flight by the force of repulsion, not the force of attraction. What we want is to get away from here. Where we hope to land (and where we do land, though only for a fleeting moment, enough for the tired wings to catch the wind anew) is a 'there' which we thought of little and knew of even less. It is the unfamiliarity of the place which will feel like a respite – until the tears of joy dry up, the eyes adjust and find the debris doing what it had been doing before – piling.

The fling would not feel like escape, though, if not for the trust – sometimes spelled out in a visionary utopia, but more often just stored in that draughty passageway which separates/links fright and despair – that there is a place where debris does not pile, where what is whole does not get smashed, while what has been smashed is repaired, and the dead are awakened or do not die at all. Such a place is the future; at least, such a place is nowhere else. If modernity, as Jean-François Lyotard suggests, sought legitimacy not in the myth of origins, not in a 'foundational act', but in the future, if living with 'a

---

[1]   Walter Benjamin, 'Theses on the Philosophy of History', in *Illuminations: Essays and Reflections*, trans. Harry Zohn (New York: Schocken, 1968), pp. 257–8.

project' was the characteristic mode of modern existence – that project, that Grand Idea at the heart of modern restlessness, that guiding lantern perched on the prow of modernity's ship, was the idea of *emancipation*:[2] an idea which draws its meaning from what it negates and against which it rebels – from the shackles it wants to fracture, the wounds it wants to heal – and owes its allure to the promise of negation. Of what life would be like without shackles or wounds, the Grand Idea of Emancipation tells little and knows less still. That life after emancipation has been lodged, after all, in the future – the absolute Other, the ungraspable and the ineffable. There, and there only, can it be considered in safe keeping – since however hard one strains one's eyes, the only sight one can catch is that of one's own vision. So the vision may stay unblemished forever, preening itself on its untarnished – untried – innocence.

Future bliss served as the cover-up for the repulsiveness of the present. The Grand Idea gave a new, modern meaning to the suffering, drained of its old sense with the dismantling of Paradise. It was now, once more, suffering 'in the name of', 'for the sake of'; as before, misery was a condition and the warrant of happiness. But the modern meaning differed from the old. Suffering was no more a trial of piety; it was now an act, an act with a purpose and a function. Modernity (whose favourite *bon mot* is that medicine does now work if it is not bitter) did not declare war on suffering: it only swore extinction to a *purposeless*, functionless suffering. Pain unplanned and unsolicited was now an abomination, and unforgivable; but if it served a purpose, if it was 'a necessary step' towards the future, pain could be – should be – had to be – inflicted. The impecunious need more penury to teach them how to get rich. Some must get less so that 'economy' may produce more. The from-hand-to-mouthers must be kicked out from their tradition-woven web of security in order to be forced to consume more for their own enjoyment. One must cut off a limb to save the body. One should sacrifice a thousand lives to save ten thousand. It is the future goodness that is but disguised as the present cruelty.

But planned and purposeful may be only the pain of today. Yesterday's pain – even if pretensions of purpose were made in its name at the time – has been proven to be purposeless and vain, since life today is no happier than it used to be then, and the blissful future remains, as before, on the other side of the horizon. Hence today's pain, the not-yet-discredited pain, is an advance over the pain of

---

[2] Cf. Jean-François Lyotard, *La Postmoderne expliqué aux enfants: Correspondance, 1982–1985* (Paris: Galilée, 1988), pp. 36, 45.

yesterday: progress marches on, we are progressing, *quod erat demonstrandum*. Perhaps progress does not mean less suffering – not yet, not at the point we have reached thus far. But it does mean paring off the *functionless* sufferings, the relentless passage from a meaningless to the meaningful suffering: it means making the world more *rational*.

With one stone of rationality, modernity killed two birds. It managed to recast as inferior and doomed all those forms of life which did not harness their own pains to the chariot of Reason. And it obtained a safe conduct for the pains it was about to inflict itself. Both achievements gave it the confidence and the courage to proceed which otherwise it would have sorely lacked. They also made the rule-governed house which modernity built hospitable to cruelty which presented itself as a superior ethics.

Moral progress?

The faculty of rationality allows one to 'make sense' out of a string of events – through presenting temporal succession as 'development', as a passage from inferior to superior states, as a chain in which each link is a means (a necessary condition or a cause) for one that comes after, and in which the later states reveal retrospectively the meaning of those which preceded them. The time-space conjured up by modern memory is linear and vertical, not cyclical and horizontal. In this time-space, 'before' means 'lower' and 'inferior'. Also, 'inferior' means 'outdated' – a relic or a hiccup of the past, a convict in a death cell awaiting execution, a zombie, an illegitimate squatter in the house of the present.

There is a carefully concealed variable, though, in that process from which the time-space emerges as the battleground between the (superior) future and the (inferior) past. This variable is power: superiority is tested and proved in victory; inferiority in defeat. The story of progress is told by the victors. The defeated stand condemned. Sometimes the defeated are brought to the court, judged and sentenced – as criminals. Most of the time they are merely pitied as terminally ill, unfit or hopelessly immature; their inferiority calls for a warden, not a judge. In neither case can the harsh treatment administered to the fallen or the about-to-fall be condemned as cruelty. On the contrary – deep down it is moral: a good deed for those who may live in a world purified of criminals, and, for the harsh-treated themselves, a lesson administered 'for their own good'.

One needs to be defeated first to be accused of immorality, and for the charge to stick. Leaders of Nazi Germany who ordered extermination have been judged, sentenced, and hanged – and their deeds, which would have gone down in history textbooks as the story of human ascent had Germany been victorious, have been classified as crimes against humanity. The verdict is safe – as much as the victory which rendered its passing possible. It will stand until cards are reshuffled and so historical memory is reshuffled to suit new hands. Unless the victors are defeated in turn, their own cruelty, or the cruelty of their acolytes and protégés, will not be committed to trial. Justice is visited upon the defeated – but since the story of justice cannot be told by anyone except today's victors, it presents the world each time as one in which immorality and punishability are synonymous.

The modern era has been founded on genocide, and has proceeded through more genocide. Somehow, the shame of yesterday's massacres proved a poor safeguard against the slaughters of today, and the wondrous sense-making faculties of progressive reason helped to keep it weak. As Hélé Béji recently observed, 'the deep malaise in the wake of the Vietnam war was not a remorse of victimising the people, but the singeing contrition of defeat'. There was no malaise if the victimization did not end in defeat. (One had not heard much breast-beating in the aftermath of the extermination of the Hottentots by the Boers, savageries committed by Carl Peters in German South Africa, or the reduction of the population of Congo from twenty million to eight million under the auspices of King Leopold II of Belgium.)[3] If there is malaise, as after the ignominious intervention in Vietnam, the lesson absorbed and memorized by the defeated is the need for more force and more effective force, not more ethical conscience. In America the shame of Vietnam boosted high-tech warfare much more than it did moral self-scrutiny. With electronic surveillance and smart missiles, people can now be killed before they have a chance to respond; killed at a distance at which the killer does not see the victims and no more has to (or, indeed, can) count the bodies.

Victors, triumphant or frustrated, do not emerge morally ennobled; but neither do their victims. As a rule, victims are not

---

[3] Cf. Hélé Béji, 'Le Patrimoine de la cruauté', *Le Débat*, vol. 73 (1993), pp. 164–5. (Béji quotes here Hannah Arendt's study of imperialism). 'There is one thing', says Béji, 'which justice shares with injustice; both need, to be exercised, all the authority of force' (p. 167). The very notion of the 'crime against humanity' would have never taken root in modern consciousness if it had not been accompanied by a convincing demonstration of might.

ethically superior to their victimizers; what makes them seem morally better, and makes credible their claim to this effect, is the fact that – being weaker – they have had less opportunity to commit cruelty. But there is no reason why they should derive from their defeat lessons different from those drawn by the frustrated victors: namely, that the safeguard against future calamity is not ethical posturing, but plentiful and powerful weaponry (though the second in no way excludes the first: the first being a useful tool to obtain the second, and the second an infallible support for the first). When their turn had arrived and they conquered Laos and Cambodia, the Vietnamese troops showed that there was little they failed to learn from their American tormentors. The genocide perpetrated by the Croats during the Nazi rule made the descendants of their Serbian victims all the more eager to kill and rape and ethnically cleanse. The memories of the Holocaust firm the hand of the Israeli occupiers of the Arab lands: mass deportations, roundings-up, hostage-taking and concentration camps are well-remembered as cost-effective. As history progresses, injustice tends to be compensated for by injustice-with-role-reversal. It is only the victors, as long as their victory stays unchallenged, who mistake, or misrepresent, that compensation as the triumph of justice. Superior morality is always the morality of the superior.

As E.M. Cioran put it, 'the great persecutors are recruited among the martyrs not quite beheaded'; a fanatical prophet of 'moral improvement' of 'morally depraved' mankind is but 'tyrant *manqué*, an approximate executioner, quite as detestable as the first-rate tyrants, the first-rate executioners'. Society, Cioran sums up, is 'an inferno of saviours'. 'All authorities have their Bastille':

> The man who proposes a new faith is persecuted, until it is his turn to become a persecutor: truths begin by a conflict with the police and end by calling them in; for each absurdity we have suffered for, degenerates into a legality, as every martyrdom ends in the paragraphs of the Law, in the insipidities of the calendar, or the nomenclature of the streets . . . An angel protected by a policeman – that is how truths die, that is how enthusiasms expire.[4]

No victory over inhumanity seems to have made the world safer for humanity. Moral triumphs, apparently, do not accumulate; in spite of the narratives of progress, movement is not linear – yesterday's gains are not reinvested, nor are the bonuses once awarded irreversible. Ever anew, with each shift in the balance of

[4] E.M. Cioran, *A Short History of Decay*, trans. Richard Howard (London: Quartet Books, 1990), pp. 5, 172, 74.

power, the spectre of inhumanity returns from its exile. Moral shocks, however devastating they might have seemed at the time, gradually lose their grip – until they are forgotten. All their long history notwithstanding, moral choices seem always to start from square one.

No wonder there are powerful reasons to doubt the reality of moral progress, and in particular the moral progress of the kind which modernity claims to promote. Moral progress seems to be threatened at the core – by the very fashion in which it is promoted. The intimate affinity between moral superiority of order and the all-too-material superiority of its guardians renders every order endemically precarious and a standing invitation to trouble: it makes the guardians nervous, and their wards envious. The first would not hesitate to coerce the recalcitrant into obedience, absolving the coercion they commit as a moral act. The second would not shirk violence, to gain for themselves the right of granting, or refusing, absolution.

The new world disorder, or re-spacing the world

The experience of insecurity is at its most acute whenever the sediment of socialization loses its solidity – and therefore the extant social space loses its transparency together with its constraining and enabling power. The spontaneous reaction to such experience is a magnified intensity of spacing efforts. Whatever stable co-ordination/ separation between cognitive, aesthetic and moral spacing has been reached in the past, now collapses.

The terms of the armistice and *modus vivendi* between the three spacings are to be renegotiated, and more probably fought for and won, anew. The potential of clash and discordance between the spacings, never fully dormant, now erupts and comes into the open. There is no effective centralized policing which could offer the precarious, continuously reproduced space an appearance of natural-ness. The feebleness of convention in which apparently tough and solid space used to be grounded is laid bare, and so the power struggle and perpetual tug-of-war are revealed as the sole reliable grounds of an orderly habitat. The task of constructing new mean-ingful social space is undertaken singly, severally and collectively; at all levels, the absence of a co-ordinating/policing agency keen and resourceful enough to arbitrate and in the end impose peace terms (that is, an *order* and binding *law* that set the standards against which all attempts at shifting the cognitive, aesthetic and moral boundaries may be cast as deviant or subversive, and effectively marginalized) leads to the endless multiplication of scattered grass-roots initiatives, adds fierceness and determination to each, and renders all agreed solution a remote prospect.

Bouts of such insecurity are in no sense novel; neither are the typical responses to them. Both are known to appear throughout history in the aftermath of wars, violent revolutions, the collapse of empires, or as concomitants of social departures too vast or too fast to be assimilated by the extant policing agencies. The present explosion of respacing efforts throughout Europe (and the never fully extinguished smouldering of such efforts in the post-colonial world) can be accounted for by the same orthodox reasons. The foundering of the *Pax Sovietica*, of the *Pax Titoica*, of the Berlin Wall, and the respacing frenzy that followed, are but the most recent cases of a recurrent phenomenon whose most vivid and best remembered pattern had been set by the Dark Ages in the wake of the collapse of the *Pax Romana*.

If the resurrection of tribalism and parochialism after the demise of the tightly policed Soviet empire, inside which pernickety oppression co-operated with insidious indoctrination in prolonging the artificial life of the moribund order, was something to be expected – the resurgence of essentially similar tendencies in the 'thoroughly modern' countries of the West took many an observer by surprise. And yet, paradoxically, the bipartite division of the world, widely and rightly viewed as the source of global insecurity, appears in retrospect as a perhaps macabre, but effective warranty of stability on *both* sides of the barricade. The broad outlines of global space were drawn with power immune to challenge and questioning – a circumstance which even the most perceptive minds obliquely endorsed through their astonishing failure to visualize the possibility of change. With the disappearance of barbed wire and tank columns that marked such outlines, unthought-of possibilities have been thrown wide open. The world chart and the local charts that drew their derivative authority from it have become fluid again: not a source of grim reassurance any more, a call to arms instead.

This momentous change could not happen at a less propitious moment. It comes at a time of what can only be called the crisis of the nation-state: of that wondrous contraption which for the last few centuries managed to tie together and 'homogenize' the processes of cognitive, aesthetic and moral spacing, and make their results secure within the realm of its triune – political, economic and military – sovereignty.

The current proliferation of units claiming a status similar to the one which has been won historically by older nation-states does *not* testify that smaller and weaker entities can now reasonably claim or strive for viability; it only testifies to the fact that viability has ceased to be a condition of nation-state formation. Most significantly, it suggests – obliquely – the *loss* of 'viability' in the old sense by such large and medium-to-large state organisms as could claim to enjoy the classical triad of sovereignty in the 'high modernity' era. The overcrowded UN building does not augur the ultimate triumph of the nationalist principle – but the coming end of the age when the social system used to be identified territorially and population-wise with the nation-state (though not necessarily, let us repeat, the end of the age of nationalism).

The way in which the world economy operates today (and there is today a genuine *world* economy), as well as the extraterritorial economic elites who operate it, favour state organisms that *cannot* effectively impose conditions under which the economy is run, let alone impose restraints on the way in which those who run the economy would like it to be run; the economy is effectively transnational. In relation to virtually any state, big or small, most of the economic assets crucial for the daily life of its population are 'foreign' – or, given the removal of all constraints on capital transfers, may turn foreign overnight, in case the local rulers naively deem themselves strong enough to meddle. The divorce between political autarchy (real or imaginary) and economic autarky could not be more complete; it also seems to be irrevocable.

Paul Valéry wrote not that long ago that 'les races et les nations ne se sont abordées que par des soldats, des apôtres et des marchands'. Though all three remain to a varying degree active, it is the traders who are active today as never before. This is precisely why the tiniest of populations may be gazed at hopefully by aspiring nation-builders as the potential suppliers of the usual quota of ministries and embassies and professional educators. ('The fundamental reconstruction of the nation', as Fichte prophetically observed, 'is offered as a task to the educated classes.')[5] Under the circumstances, we can only repeat after Eric Hobsbawm that 'there is no denying that "ethnic" identities which had no political or even existential significance. . . can acquire a genuine hold as badges of group identity overnight'.[6] And we must admit the prophetic wisdom of Michael Walzer's

---

[5]   Johann Gottlieb Fichte, *Addresses to the German Nation*, trans. R.F. Jones and G.H. Turnbull (Westport, Conn.: Greenwood Press, 1979), p. 17.
[6]   Eric Hobsbawm, 'Whose Fault-line is it Anyway?', in *New Statesman and Society*, 24 April 1992, pp. 24–5.

observation that 'if states ever become large neighbourhoods, it is likely that neighbourhoods will become little states. Their members will organize to defend their local politics and culture against strangers. Historically, neighbourhoods have turned into closed or parochial communities. . . whenever the state was open.'[7]

Paradoxically, in the era of cosmopolitan *economy* the territoriality of *political* sovereignty becomes itself a major factor facilitating free movement of capital and commodities. The more fragmented are the sovereign units, the weaker and narrower in scope is their grip over respective territories, the freer still is the global flow of capital and merchandise. The *globalization* of the economy and information and *fragmentation* (indeed, a 'reparochialization' of sorts) of political sovereignty are – contrary to appearances – not opposite and hence mutually conflicting and incompatible trends; they are, rather, coeval factors in the ongoing rearrangement of various aspects of systemic integration. Between themselves, the states police orderly conditions in localities that increasingly become little more than transit stations in the world-wide travel of goods and money administered by the multinational (more correctly: non-national) companies. Whatever has remained of economic management in state politics is reduced to competitive offers of attractively profitable and pleasurable conditions (low taxes, low-cost and docile labour, good interest rates and – last though not least – pleasant pastimes for all-expenses-paid travelling managers), hopefully seductive enough to tempt the touring capital to schedule a stopover and stay for a little longer than the refuelling of the aircraft demands.

The scramble for sovereignty (in the last account, for control over the processes of spacing) becomes increasingly a competition for a better deal in the world-wide distribution of capital. This applies to both currently observed kinds of sovereignty claims: those coming from prosperous localities like Lombardy, unwilling to share their benefits with poorer parts of the population who, as the state insists, should be treated as 'one nation'; and those brought forth by impoverished localities like Scotland, objecting to what they see as too small a share of the wealth secured by the state as a whole. In both cases the grievance is greatly helped by being economic. It is then followed by a frantic effort to collate and condense the diffuse feelings of deprivation into the image of a common fate and a common cause; by a process of collective identity-building, to be used as effective cultural capital in the struggle for the 'devolution of state power'. A

[7] Michael Walzer, *Spheres of Justice: A Defense of Pluralism and Equality* (New York: Basic Books, 1983), p. 38.

shared cultural identity is hoped to translate individually suffered deprivation into a collective effort to obtain redress.

Significant cultural differences at all times are neither 'objectively given' nor can be 'objectively obliterated' or levelled off. Cultural contents make a totality only in the form of a pool of tokens from which a volume of selections and combinations (in principle infinite) can be, and is, made. Most importantly, they serve as a raw material from which self-made identities are assembled; the truly significant cultural differences (those made visible, noticed, serving as orientation points or labels for group integration, and jointly defended) are *products* of such identity-assembling processes. (As Ernest Gellner observed, 'For every effective nationalism there are several that are feeble or dormant. Those that go down are "objectively" as legitimate as the effective ones. . .')[8] It is the presence or absence of such processes, and their relative strength, which (always contentiously) elevates some dialects to the level of languages and reduces some languages to the level of dialects; which organizes the remembered or invented past in separate or shared traditions; which, in general, prompts imitative urges *vis-à-vis* some cultural tokens and imposes a ban on embracing the others. Indeed, as Eric Hobsbawm observed, the more defunct and ineffective is the past, the more it is 'liberated' for purely symbolic, mobilizing use.[9]

Throughout the 'modernized' part of the world, identity needs tend today to become ever more acute (and, more than in the past, disjunctive) in the wake of the increasingly evident failure of the nation-states to perform their past role of identity-producers and suppliers – that is, of effective, reliable and trustworthy managers/ guards of spacing mechanisms. The identity-constructing function in which the established nation-states used to specialize may seek another carrier, and will seek it all the more zealously for the 'softness' of the available alternatives.

Insecurity and cruelty

Moreover, the paradox of the man-made collective identities of the nation-states era – the kind of identities which might hold fast only when perceived as 'given' and thus cast beyond the human power of

---

[8] Ernest Gellner, 'Ethnicity, Culture, Class and Power', in *Ethnic Diversity and Conflict in Eastern Europe*, ed. Peter F. Singer (Santa Barbara: ABC Clio, 1980), p. 260.

[9] Cf. *The Invention of Tradition*, ed. Eric Hobsbawm and Terence Ranger (Cambridge University Press, 1983), p. 4.

manipulation – has not gone away either; if anything, it has become sharper than at any previous stage of the modern era. Its solution, on the other hand, has become more difficult than ever. Identities may be safe and 'unproblematic' only inside a secure social space: spacing and identity-production are two facets of the same process. But it is precisely the great modern project of a unified, managed and controlled space which has today come under pressure and faces its critical challenge.

Ever since, at the dawn of the modern era, it had become a conscious, purposeful activity, identity-building has always contained a mix of 'restorative' and 'productive' objectives (the first category expressed in the invocation of *Blut und Boden, la terre et les morts* – the second in the requisite of patriotism, the denunciation of lukewarmness as treachery, and the demand for vigilance against the turncoats). Today, however, productive aspects come clearly to the fore – as the ostensibly firmest foundations of identity (such as territory or racial stock) have been exposed by current practice (at least in the part of the world already close to the postmodern condition) as irreparably fluid, ambivalent and otherwise unreliable. There is, therefore, a sort of 'social demand' for such 'objective' foundations of collective identities which openly admit of their historicity and human-made origins, yet nevertheless may be ascribed a supra-individual authority and a value which the carriers of identity can disregard only at their peril. Concerns with identity (that is, the uncontentious social space), complete with xenophobia they gestate in volumes inversely proportional to the self-confidence of its carriers, will in all probability seek anchor in the territory classified as 'culture' – indeed, virtually tailor-made to meet the intrinsically contradictory demand. The phenomenon described by Simmel as the 'tragedy of culture' (the contradiction between the modality of culture as product of human spirit, and the awesome, massive 'objectivity' of created culture as experienced by individuals no longer able to assimilate it) has become a hundred years later the last straw of hope for the seekers of solid identities in the postmodern world of contingency and nomadism.

The focus of, simultaneously, contentious social spacing and identity-building is now the contrived, made-up community masquerading as a Tönnies-style inherited *Gemeinschaft*, but in fact much more akin to Kant's aesthetic communities, brought into being and kept in existence mostly, perhaps solely, by the intensity of their members' dedication. Features properly belonging to the aesthetic space tend to submerge and colonize social space and drift into the role of principal tools of social spacing. The community produced with such tools comes into being and continues to exist, however ephemerically, through the combined force of individual choices. Because of in-built uncertainty, such community lives under the condition of constant anxiety and thus shows a sinister and but thinly masked tendency to aggression and intolerance. This is a community that has no other ground but the individual decisions to identify with it – yet one that needs to impress itself upon the minds of decision-makers as *superior to*, and *preceding*, any individual decision; a community which has to be built year by year, day by day, hour by hour, having the liquid fuel of popular emotions as its only life-blood. A community, therefore, which is bound to remain endemically precarious and hence bellicose and intolerant, neurotic about matters of security and paranoic about hostility and ill intentions of environment. Michel Maffesoli's neo-tribes, all the more hypochondriac and quarrelsome for being deprived of what the old-style tribes derived their security from: the effective powers to 'objectify' their ascendancy and monopolistic claims to obedience.

These 'neo-tribes' lead only a brittle life; they come into being in a moment of instant condensation – but then face daily the danger of evaporating, together with that energy of self-dedication which lent them for a time the appearance of solidity. However brief their ascendancy, it would not be possible at all were the brevity of commitment acknowledged and conceded in advance. Production must be conceived of as restoration or restitution; building new ground must be thought of as the mapping of extant continents. The counterfactuality of self-image is the prime condition of success, even such fragile and elusive success as there is. Hence the concepts drawn from cultural discourse come in handy: concepts like forms of life, tradition, community. Rejection of strangers may shy away from expressing itself in racial terms, but it cannot afford admitting being arbitrary lest it should abandon all hope of success; it verbalizes itself therefore in terms of incompatibility or unmixability of *cultures*, or of the self-defence of a form of life bequeathed by tradition. Horror of ambivalence sediments in consciousness as the value of communal cohesion and consensus that only shared understanding can bring. Arguments that wish to be as firm and solid as those once anchored in the images of soil and blood now have to dress themselves in the rhetoric of human-made culture and its values.

Thus, pardoxically, the ideologies which presently accompany the strategies of communal identity-building and the associated policies of *exclusion* deploy the kind of language that was traditionally appropriated by the *inclusivist* cultural discourse. It is culture itself, rather than a hereditary collection of genes, which is represented by these ideologies as immutable: as a unique entity which *should be* preserved intact, and reality which *cannot* be significantly modified by any method of cultural provenance. Cultures, we are told, precede, form and define (each one in its own *unique* way) the selfsame Reason which was previously hoped to serve as the main weapon of cultural homogeneity. Much like the castes or estates of the past, cultures may at best communicate within the framework of the functional division of labour, but they can never mix; and they should not mix lest the precious identity of each should be compromised and eroded. It is not the cultural *pluralism* and separatism, but cultural *proselytism* and the drive towards cultural unification that are now conceived of as 'unnatural', as abnormality to be actively resisted.

No wonder contemporary preachers of exclusivist ideology disdainfully reject the racist label. Indeed, they neither need nor deploy the arguments of the genetic determination of human differences and the biological grounds of their hereditary continuity. And so their adversaries do not advance much the contrary case, the case of cohabitation and mutual tolerance, when they insist that the racist label fits. The true complexity of the adversaries' task derives from the fact that the cultural discourse, once the domain of the liberal, assimilationist, *inclusivist* strategy, has been 'colonized' by the *exclusivist* ideology, and so the use of traditional 'culturalist' vocabulary no more guarantees the subversion of exclusivist strategy. The root of the present weakness of the so-called 'anti-racist' cause so poignantly felt throughout Europe lies in the profound transformation of the cultural discourse itself. Within the framework of that discourse, it has become exceedingly difficult to advance without contradiction (and without the risk of criminal charges) an argument against the permanence of human differentiation and the practice of categorial separation. This difficulty has prompted many authors, worried by the apparent inability of the 'multiculturalist' argument to challenge, let alone to arrest, the advance of pugnacious tribalism, to double their efforts in the refurbishing of the 'unfinished modern project' as the only rampart still capable, perhaps, of stemming the tide. Some, like Paul Yonnet[10], go as far as to suggest that the anti-racist forces, preaching as they are mutual tolerance and peaceful cohabitation of diverse cultures and tribes, are to blame for the growing militancy of exclusivist tendency – merely a 'natural' response to the 'unnatural' regime of perpetual uncertainty which the preachers of tolerance purport to install. With all its self-confessed

---

[10]   Cf. Paul Yonnet, *Voyage au centre du malaise français* (Paris: Gallimard, 1993).

artificiality – so Yonnet suggests – the original Enlightenment-inspired project of homogeneous order, with its promotion of universal values, uncompromising stance toward difference and relentless cultural crusades, stood a better chance (perhaps the only chance there ever was and could be) to replace mutual extermination with peaceful coexistence.

The 'Other', as we have seen before, is a by-product of social spacing; a left-over of spacing, which guarantees the usability and trustworthiness of the cut-out, properly spaced-up habitable enclave; the *ubi leones* of the ancient maps signifying the outer frontiers of human *habitat*. The *otherness* of the Other and the security of the social space (also, therefore, of the security of its own identity) are intimately related and support each other. The truth is, however, that neither of the two has an objective, real, or rational 'foundation'; the sole foundation of both, as Cornelius Castoriadis put it,

> being belief in it and, more specifically, its claim to render the world and life coherent (sensible), it finds itself in mortal danger as soon as proof is produced that other ways of rendering life and the world coherent and sensible exist. . .
> Can the existence of the other as such place *me* in danger? . . . It can, under one condition: that in the deepest recesses of one's egocentric fortress a voice softly but tirelessly repeats 'our walls are made of plastic, our acropolis of papier-mâché'.[11]

The voice may be soft, but it takes a lot of shouting to stifle it. Particularly since the inner voice is but an echo of loud voices all around – each peddling an altogether different recipe for a world both meaningful and secure. And since shouting is the only thing one can do to promote one's cause: each voice is a voice of reason, each recipe is rational, it is always one rationality against the other, and reasoned argument would help little. Each recipe has good reasons to be accepted, and so at the end of the day only the pitch of voice and the size of chorus offer a guarantee of being in the right. I shout, therefore I am – is the neotribal version of the *cogito*.

Postmodern tribes are brought into their ephemeric being by explosive sociality. Joint action does not follow shared interests; it creates them. Or, rather, joining the action is all there is to the sharing. Joint action deputizes for the absent force of law-supported socialization; it may rely on its own force alone, and solely on its own it must accomplish the daunting task of structuration – that means to assert simultaneously its own identity and the strangehood of the

[11] Cornelius Castoriadis, 'Reflections on Racism', trans. David Ames Curtis, in *Thesis Eleven*, vol. 32 (1992), pp. 6, 9.

strangers. What used to surface on carnival occasions, to be a momentary rupture of continuity, a festive suspension of disbelief – becomes the mode of life.

Postmodernity has two faces: the 'dissolution of the obligatory in the optional'[12] has two apparently opposite, yet closely related effects. On the one hand, the sectarian fury of neotribal self-assertion, the resurgence of violence as the principal instrument of order-building, the feverish search for home truths hoped to fill the void of the deserted *agora*. On the other, the refusal by yesterday's rhetors of the *agora* to judge, discriminate, choose between choices: every choice goes, providing it is a choice, and each order is good, providing it is one of many and does not exclude other orders. Tolerance of the rhetors feeds on intolerance of the tribes. Intolerance of the tribes draws confidence from the tolerance of the rhetors.

There are, of course, good reasons for the present reticence of the rhetors, once only too eager to discriminate and legislate. The modern dream of the happiness-legislating reason has brought bitter fruits. The greatest crimes *against* humanity (and *by* humanity) have been perpetrated in the name of the rule of reason, of better order and greater happiness. A mind-numbing devastation proved to be the issue of the marriage between philosophical certitude and the arrogant self-confidence of the powers-that-be. Modern romance with universal reason and perfection proved to be a costly affair; it also proved to be abortive, as the great factory of order went on producing more disorder while the holy war against ambivalence spawned more ambivalence. There are reasons to be wary of modern promises, and suspicious of the tools alleged to make them true. There are reasons to be chary and heedful of philosophical certitude; and there are reasons to consider such caution prudent and realistic, since the appointed marriage partner of universal certitude – the powers boasting universalizing ambitions and resources to support them – is nowhere to be seen.

But the reticence itself is costly. Just as the modern adventure with order and transparency bred opacity and ambivalence, postmodern tolerance breeds intolerance. Modern etatization of social space spawned oppression massive and condensed; the postmodern

---

[12] Alain Finkielkraut, *Le Mécontemporain: Péguy, lecteur du monde moderne* (Paris: Gallimard, 1991), p. 174. Finkielkraut continues: 'Désormais *post-moderne*, l'homme contemporain proclame l'égalité de l'ancien et du nouveau, du majeur et du mineur, des goûts et des cultures. Au lieu de concevoir le présent comme un champ de bataille, il l'ouvre sans préjugé et sans exclusive à toutes les combinaisons.'

privatization of social spacing spawns oppression scattered and small-scale, but manifold and ubiquitous. Coercion is no more the state's monopoly, but this is not necessarily good news, as it does not mean less coercion. The grand certitude has dissipated – but it split in the process into a multitude of little certainties, clung to all the more ferociously for their puniness. One wonders what sort of service is offered to the uncertainty-stricken world by (to quote Castoriadis's pithy characterization) 'the intellectual boy-scouts of the past few decades, who preach both the rights of man *and* the idea that there is a radical difference between cultures that forbids us from making any value judgments about other cultures'[13] – though many such cultures, having avidly and joyfully embraced Western guns and video-recorders, show amazing reserve when it comes to the borrowing of such Western inventions as *habeas corpus* or citizenship.

There is no easy exit from the quandary. We have learned the hard way that while universal values offer a reasonable medicine against the oppressive obtrusiveness of parochial backwaters, and communal autonomy offers an emotionally gratifying tonic against the stand-offish callousness of the universalists, each drug when taken regularly turns into poison. Indeed, as long as the choice is merely between the two medicines, the chance of health must be meagre and remote.

One may say, however, that both corrective therapies tend to turn pathogenic for the same reason. They both accept and tolerate their objects, be they 'bearers of the rights of man' or 'faithful sons of the people', in any capacity but one: that of moral selves. Autonomy of the moral self is one capacity that neither of the two would admit gladly, since both encounter it as an obstacle to any certainty, including the kind of certainty they are bent on securing or protecting. If either had its way, the outcome would be strikingly similar: disqualification and then gradual extinction of moral impulses and moral responsibility. It is precisely this effect that debilitates and incapacitates in advance the only forces which would stand a chance of arresting the treatment at a point where it turns murderous. Once expropriated or excused from moral responsibility, subjects know no more when (to quote Bertrand Russell again) to start screaming.

As far as the prospects of safeguarding human lives against cruelty (something which both the modern project and its postmodern rejection promised, though each sniffed the roots of cruelty under a different tree) are concerned, it does not matter much who is in charge of social spacing and whose charts are proclaimed obligatory; it does not matter either whether it is the cognitive, or the aesthetic

---

[13] Castoriadis, 'Reflections on Racism', p. 10.

spacing which structures the human habitat. If anything does matter, it is the redemption of moral capacity and, in the effect, re-moralization of human space. To the likely objection 'This proposi-tion is unrealistic', the proper response is: 'It had *better* be realistic'.

Vagabond and tourist: postmodern types

The predicament of contemporary men and women has been often compared to that of the nomads. (I myself, in my previous work, compared the plight of 'postmodern nomads' with that of 'modern pilgrims'.) The metaphor, however, does not survive closer scrutiny. Unlike the settlers, nomads are on the move. But they circle around a well-structured territory with long invested and stable meaning assigned to each fragment. Unlike pilgrims, they do not have a 'final destination' which plots in advance their itinerary, nor a privileged place to which all other sites they traverse are but stations. But they still move from place to place in a strictly regular succession, following the 'order of things' rather that composing that order as they move in and dismantling it again as they move out. Nomads, therefore, are a flawed metaphor for men and women cast in the postmodern condition.

Vagabonds or vagrants offer more apposite a metaphor. The vagabond does not know how long he will stay where he is now, and more often than not it will not be for him to decide when the stay will come to an end. Once on the move again, he sets his destinations as he goes and as he reads the road-signs, but even then he cannot be sure whether he will stop, and for how long, at the next station. What he does know is that more likely than not the stopover will be but temporary. What keeps him on the move is disillusionment with the place of last sojourn and the forever smouldering hope that the next place which he has not visited yet, perhaps the place after next, may be free from faults which repulsed him in the places he has already tasted. Pulled forward by hope untested, pushed from behind by hope frustrated. . . The vagabond is a pilgrim without a destination; a nomad without an itinerary. The vagabond journeys through an unstructured space; like a wanderer in the desert, who knows only of such trails as are marked with his own footprints, and blown off again by the wind the moment he passes, the vagabond structures the site he happens to occupy at the moment, only to dismantle the structure again as he leaves. Each successive spacing is local and temporary – episodic.

But there is one more metaphor which fits postmodern life: that of the tourist. Perhaps only together the vagabond and the tourist are capable of conveying the full reality of that life. Like the vagabond, the tourist knows that he will not stay for long where he has arrived. And as in the vagabond's case, he has only his own biographical time to string together the places he visits; otherwise, nothing orders them in this rather than another temporal fashion. This constraint or paucity rebounds as the experience of pliability of space: whatever their intrinsic meanings, whatever their 'natural' location in the 'order of things' – they may be pushed aside and allowed into the tourist's world solely at the tourist's discretion. It is the tourist's aesthetic capacity – his or her curiosity, need of amusement, will and ability to live through novel, pleasurable, and pleasurably novel experiences – which appears to possess a nearly total freedom of spacing the tourist's life-world; the kind of freedom which the vagabond, who depends on the rough realities of the visited places for his livelihood and who may only act to avoid displeasure by escaping, can only dream of. The tourists pay for their freedom; the right to disregard native concerns and feelings, the right to spin their own web of meanings, they obtain in a commercial transaction. Freedom comes in a contractual deal, the volume of freedom depends solely on the ability to pay, and once purchased, it has become a right which the tourist can loudly demand, pursue through the courts of the land and hope to be gratified and protected. Like the vagabond, the tourist is extraterritorial; but unlike the vagabond, he lives his extra-territoriality as a privilege, as independence, as the right to be free, free to choose; as a licence to restructure the world. What may be (what probably is, when you come to think of it, but then why should you think of it?) the routine quotidianity for the natives, is for the tourist a collection of exotic thrills. Restaurants with their strange-smelling dishes, hotels with strangely dressed maids, strange-looking memorials of somebody else's historical dramas, strange rituals of someone else's daily routines – all wait docilely for the tourist to cast his eye over, pay attention to, derive pleasure from. The world is the tourist's oyster. The world is there to be lived pleasurably – and thus given meaning. In most cases, the aesthetic meaning is the only meaning it needs – and can bear.

One more feature unites the lives of the vagabond and the tourist. They both move *through* the spaces other people live in; these other people may be in charge of the spacing – but the outcomes of their labours do not affect the vagabond, and especially the tourist. With the locals, the vagabond and the tourist have but the briefest and most perfunctory of encounters (*mis*-meetings, as described in previous chapters). Like a theatre performance, the most dramatic and impressive of contacts are securely encased between the wings of the stage and between the rise and the fall of the curtain – inside the time and place designated for the 'suspension of disbelief' – and guaranteed not to leak through them and spill over (unless fondly preserved, at the tourist's discretion, as memorable adventures, as private property – in most cases confined to the safe-keeping of photographic paper or, better still, to the not-so-lasting storage of erasable videotape). Physically close, spiritually remote: this is the formula of both the vagabond's and tourist's life.

The seductive charm of such a life is that it comes with the solemn promise that the physical closeness will not be allowed to get out of gear and slide into moral proximity. Particularly in the case of the tourist, the guarantee is very nearly foolproof. Freedom from moral duty has been paid for in advance; the package-tour kit contains the preventive medicine against pangs of conscience next to the pills preventing air sickness.

One thing that the vagabond's and the tourist's lives are not designed to contain, and most often are excused from containing, is the cumbersome, incapacitating, joy-killing, insomniogenic moral responsibility. The pleasures of the massage parlour come clean of the sad thought about the children sold into prostitution; the latter, like the rest of bizarre ways the natives have chosen, is not the punter's responsibility, not his blame, not his deed – and there is nothing the punter can do (and thus nothing he *ought* to do) to repair it. Nowhere as much and as radically as in the tourist mode is the uniqueness of the actor disavowed, erased, blotted out. No one but the tourist is so blatantly, conspicuously dissolved in numbers, interchangeable, depersonalized. 'They all do the same.' The wobbly tracks are well trodden, kneaded by countless feet; the sharp sights rounded up by countless eyes; the rough textures sanded to a gloss by countless hands. Moral proximity, responsibility, and the uniqueness – irreplaceability – of the moral subject are triune; they will not survive (or, rather, would not be born) without each other. Moral responsibility vanishes when 'everybody does it', which, inevitably, means also that 'everybody can do it', even if the latter came together with 'no one does'. The tourist is bad news for morality.

In the postmodern world, the vagabond and the tourist are no more marginal people or marginal conditions. They turn into moulds destined to engross and shape the totality of life and the whole of quotidianity; patterns by which all practices are measured. They are glorified by the chorus of commercial exploiters and media flatterers. They set the standard of happiness and successful life in general. Tourism is no more something one practices when on holidays.

Normal life – if it is to be a good life – ought to be, had better be, a continuous holiday. (One is tempted to say that what Bakhtin described as 'carnival culture' – those cyclical fairs of public morality-breaching, meant as a break in routine, as a momentary suspension of normality and reversal of normal roles designed to let off the accumulated steam and make normality bearable – itself turns into the norm and the routine. It is now the well-spaced and short-lived public rituals of collective empathy with other people's collective calamities that have taken over the function of therapeutic 'norm reversal' once performed by the carnival culture in its orthodox, Bakhtinian sense.) Ideally, one should be a tourist everywhere and everyday. In, but not of. Physically close, spiritually remote. Aloof. Free -- the exemption from all non-contractual duties having been paid for in advance. Ideally, with the moral conscience having been fed a sure-fire dose of sleeping pills.

Politics faithfully records, follows and reinvigorates the trend. Moral issues tend to be increasingly compressed into the idea of 'human rights' – folkloristically translated as the right to be left alone. The dismantling of the Welfare State (once an operative reflection of the principle of universally shared responsibility for individual weal and woe) – a prospect still few years ago deemed unthinkable by the most perceptive of minds – is now taking place. The welfare state, wisely, institutionalized *commonality* of fate: its provisions were meant for every participant (every citizen) in equal measure, thus balancing everybody's privations with everybody's gains. The slow retreat from that principle into the means-tested 'focused' assistance for 'those who need it' has institutionalized the *diversity* of fate, and thus made the unthinkable thinkable. It is now the taxpayer's privations that are to be balanced against someone else's, the benefit recipient's, gains.

Altogether different principles are embodied in, say, a child benefit for every parent, and child benefit for indolent parents alone. The first makes tangible the bond between public and private – community and individual, and casts the community as the pledge of the individual's security. The second sets the public and the private against each other, and casts the community as the individual's burden and bane. The loss of the first would be resented by most, as only for a few is it likely to be balanced by the gain from reduced taxation. The loss or curtailment of the second would be welcome by all except the few who bear the loss. In almost every chapter of the Welfare State the invisible dividing line between the first situation and the second has been passed, and what used to be a collective insurance against individual disasters has turned into a nation divided between the premium payers and the benefit recipients. In the new constellation, services for those who do not pay are bound to be resented by those who do pay – and calls to reduce them or abandon them altogether would find an ever growing number of willing ears. If the installation of the Welfare State was an attempt to mobilize economic interests in the service of moral responsibility – the dismantling of the Welfare State deploys economic interest as a means to liberate political calculation from moral constraints. Moral responsibility is once more something that 'needs to be paid for', and hence something one can well be 'unable to afford'. To be a Good Samaritan, one needs money. If there is no money, one need not worry about not being a Good Samaritan.

The dismantling of the Welfare State is essentially a process of 'putting moral responsibility where it belongs' – that is, among the private concerns of individuals. It spells a hard time for moral responsibility; not only in its immediate effects on the poor and unfortunate who need a society of responsible people most, but also (and perhaps, in the long run, primarily) in its lasting effects on the (potentially) moral selves. It recasts 'being for Others', that cornerstone of all morality, as a matter of accounts and calculation, of value for money, of gains and costs, of luxury one can or cannot permit. The process is self-propelling and self-accelerating: the new perspective leads inevitably to relentless deterioration of collective services (the quality of the public health service, of public education, of whatever is left of public housing or transport), which prompts those who can to buy themselves out from collective provisions – an act which turns out to mean, sooner or later, buying themselves out of collective responsibility.

It is a 'your value for my money' situation: citizenship means getting better service for less expense, the right to pay less into the public kitty and get more from it. Responsibility does not come into it either as the reason or as a purpose. The ideal for the citizen is a satisfied customer. Society is there for individuals to seek and find satisfaction for their individual wants. The social space is, primarily, a grazing ground, the aesthetic space is a playground. None allows, nor calls for, moral spacing. The written or unwritten citizen's charter of consumer society underwrites the status of the citizen as a tourist. A tourist always, on holidays and in daily routine. A tourist everywhere, abroad and at home. A tourist in society, a tourist in life – free to do his or her own aesthetic spacing and forgiven the forgetting of the moral one. Life as the tourist's haunt.

Postmodern wisdom, postmodern impotence

The postmodern perspective offers more wisdom; the postmodern setting makes acting on that wisdom more difficult. This is, roughly, why the postmodern time is experienced as living through crisis.

What the postmodern mind is aware of is that there are problems in human and social life with no good solutions, twisted trajectories that cannot be straightened up, ambivalences that are more than linguistic blunders yelling to be corrected, doubts which cannot be legislated out of existence, moral agonies which no reason-dictated recipes can soothe, let alone cure. The postmodern mind does not expect any more to find the all-embracing, total and ultimate formula of life without ambiguity, risk, danger and error, and is deeply suspicious of any voice that promises otherwise. The postmodern mind is aware that each local, specialized and focused treatment, effective or not when measured by its ostensive target, spoils as much as, if not more than, it repairs. The postmodern mind is reconciled to the idea that the messiness of the human predicament is here to stay. This is, in the broadest of outlines, what can be called postmodern wisdom.

The postmodern habitat offers little opportunity to act upon postmodern wisdom. The means to act collectively and globally, as the global and collective welfare would demand, have been all but discredited, dismantled or lost. All comings-together and joining-forces are moves in the zero-sum game; their success is measured by the tightness of the resulting divisions. Problems can be handled only locally and each on its own; only such issues are articulated as problems, which can be handled in that way. All problem-handling means building a mini-order at the expense of order elsewhere, and at the cost of rising global disorder as well as depleting the shrinking supplies of resources which make ordering – any ordering – possible.

It has become commonplace to aver that ethical problems of contemporary society may only be resolved – if at all – by political means. The question of relationship between morality and politics hardly ever leaves for long the agenda of philosophical and public debates. What is, however, attended to, publicly scrutinized and most hotly discussed is the morality of the politicians, not the morality of politics. It is how the persons in the public view behave, not what are they doing – their personal morality, not the ethics they promote or fail to promote – the personally corrupting, not socially devastating, effects of political power – the moral integrity of the politicians, not the morality of the world they promote or perpetuate – which seem to exhaust or nearly exhaust the morality-and-politics agenda. There is nothing wrong with the public interest in the moral purity of those who occupy public places; people invested with public trust need to be trustworthy, and prove it. What is wrong is that, with all the attention focused on the moral integrity of the politicians, the moral deterioration of the universe they administer may well go on undisturbed. The morally unimpeachable politicians may, and do, preside over dissipation of moral responsibilities and lubricate the mechanisms which undermine, marginalize and rule out of court moral concerns. Morally clean politicians may, and do, cleanse policies of moral duties.

The morality of politicians is an issue altogether different from the moral impact of their politics. (Most gruesome and gory tyrants of our age have been selfless ascetics.) But, moreover, politics is no more what the politicians do; one may venture to say that the politics which truly matters is done in places far away from the politicians' offices. As Patrick Jarreau commented in his review of a recent study of *les politocrates*,

> politics is everywhere, be it in urbanistics, school curricula, film produc-
> tion, contaminating the haemophiliacs with the AIDS virus or housing the
> homeless. At the same time, on the other hand, politics gives an
> impression of being nowhere, at any rate not there where it would be in its
> right place, at the reach of the citizens' vote: not in the Parliament, where
> the deputies and even the senators busy themselves, amidst an almost
> universal indifference, with problems which do not reach the public except
> through the mediation of spokesmen or experts of the day selected by the
> media; nor in the meetings of local councils . . .; nor in the political parties,
> which lose their militants and whose efforts to revive the debate about
> ideas remain idle.[14]

But the moral crisis of the postmodern habitat requires first and foremost that politics – whether the politics of the politicians or the policentric, scattered politics which matters all the more for being so elusive and beyond control – be an extension and institutionalization of moral responsibility. Genuine moral issues of the high-tech world are by and large beyond the reach of individuals (who, at best, may singly or severally purchase the right not to worry about them, or buy a temporary reprieve from suffering the effects of neglect). The effects of technology are long-distance, and so must be the preventive and remedial action. Hans Jonas's 'long-range ethics' makes sense, if at all, only as a *political* programme – though given the nature of the postmodern habitat, there is little hope that any political party competing for state power would be willing, suicidally, to endorse this truth and act upon it.

[14] Patrick Jarreau, 'Le Politique mis à nu', in *Le Monde*, 12 February 1993, p. 27.

Commenting on Edgar Allan Poe's story of three fishermen caught in the maelstrom, of whom two died paralysed with fear and doing nothing, but the third survived, having noticed that round objects are sucked into the abyss less quickly, and promptly jumping into a barrel – Norbert Elias sketched the way in which the exit from a non-exit situation may be plotted. The survivor, Elias suggests,

> began to think more coolly; and by standing back, by controlling his own fear, by seeing himself as it were from a distance, like a chessman forming a pattern with others on a board, he managed to turn his thoughts away from himself to the situation in which he found himself . . . Symbolically representing in his mind the structure and direction of the flow of events, he discovered a way of escape. In that situation, the level of self-control and the level of process-control were . . . interdependent and complementary.[15]

Let us note that Poe's cool and clever fisherman escaped alone. We do not know how many barrels there were left in the boat. And barrels, after all, have been known since Diogenes to be the ultimate individual retreats. The question is – and to this question private cunning offers no answer – to what extent the techniques of individual survival (techniques, by the way, amply provided for all present and future, genuine and putative maelstroms, by eager-to-oblige-and-profit merchants of goods and counsels) can be stretched to embrace the collective survival. The maelstrom of the kind we are in – all of us together, and most of us individually – is so frightening because of its tendency to break down the issue of common survival into a sackful of individual survival issues, and then to take the issue so pulverized off the political agenda. Can the process be retraced? Can that which has been broken be made whole again? And where to find an adhesive strong enough to keep it whole?

If the successive chapters of this book suggest anything, it is that moral issues cannot be 'resolved', nor the moral life of humanity guaranteed, by the calculating and legislative efforts of reason. Morality is not safe in the hands of reason, though this is exactly what spokesmen of reason promise. Reason cannot help the moral self without depriving the self of what makes the self moral: that unfounded, non-rational, un-arguable, no-excuses-given and non-calculable urge to stretch towards the other, to caress, to be for, to live for, happen what may. Reason is about making correct decisions, while moral responsibility precedes all thinking about decisions as it does not, and cannot care about any logic which would allow the approval of an action as correct. Thus, morality can be 'rationalized' only at the cost of self-denial and self-attrition. From that reason-assisted self-denial, the self emerges morally disarmed, unable (and unwilling) to face up to the multitude of moral challenges and cacophony of ethical prescriptions. At the far end of the long march of reason, moral nihilism waits: that moral nihilism which in its deepest essence means not the denial of binding ethical code, and not the blunders of relativistic theory – but the loss of ability to be moral.

As far as the doubts in the ability of reason to legislate the morality of human cohabitation are concerned, the blame cannot be laid at the doorstep of the postmodern tendency to dismiss the orthodox philosophical programme. The most pronounced manifestations of – programmatic or resigned – moral relativism can be found in the writings of thinkers who reject and resent postmodern verdicts and voice doubts as to the very existence of a postmodern perspective, let alone the validity of judgements allegedly passed from its vantage-point. Apart from value-signs added (often as an afterthought), there is little to choose between ostensibly 'anti-postmodern', scientific recordings of the ways and means of 'embedded selves', and the arrogantly 'postmodern' declarations that 'everything goes', given enough space and enough time. There is little disagreement between them as to the assumption – authenticated by the long managerial efforts of modern times and the realities of the social habitat these efforts managed to produce – that in order to act morally the person must first be disowned of autonomy, whether by coercive or purchasable expertise; and as to another assumption (which also reflects the realities of the contemporary mode of life), that the roots of action are likely to be assessed as moral, and the criteria to assess the morality of acts, must be *extrinsic* to the actor. There is little difference between two ostensibly opposite standpoints in the way they disallow or neglect the possibility that it may be precisely the expropriation of moral prerogatives and the usurpation of moral competence by agencies extrinsic to the moral self (multiple agencies, contestant and combative, yet equally vociferous in their claims to ethical infallibility) which stand behind the stubborn unassailability of ethical relativism and moral nihilism.

There is little reason to trust the assurances of the expropriating/usurping agencies that the fate of morality is safe with them; there is little evidence that this has been the case thus far, and little encourag-ment can be derived from the scrutiny of their present work for the hope that this will be more of the case in the future. At the end of the ambitious modern project of universal moral certainty, of legislating the morality of and for human selves, of replacing the erratic and

unreliable moral impulses with a socially underwritten ethical code –
the bewildered and disoriented self finds itself alone in the face of
moral dilemmas without good (let alone obvious) choices, un-
resolved moral conflicts and the excruciating difficulty of being
moral.

Fortunately for humanity (though not always for the moral self)
and despite all the expert efforts to the contrary, the moral conscience
– that ultimate prompt of moral impulse and root of moral responsibility – has only been anaesthesized, not amputated. It is still there,
dormant perhaps, often stunned, sometimes shamed into silence –
but capable of being awoken, of that Lévinas's feat of sobering up
from inebriated torpor. The moral conscience commands obedience
without proof that the command should be obeyed; conscience can
neither convince nor coerce. Conscience wields none of the weapons
recognized by the modern world as insignia of authority. By the
standards which support the modern world, conscience is weak. The
proposition that conscience of the moral self is humanity's only
warrant and hope may strike the modern mind as preposterous; if not
presposterous, then portentous: what chance for a morality having
conscience (already dismissed by the authority-conscious mind as
fickle, 'merely subjective', a freak) for its sole foundation? And
yet. . .

Summing up the moral lessons of the Holocaust, Hannah Arendt
demanded that

> human beings be capable of telling right from wrong even when all they
> have to guide them is their own judgment, which, moreover, happens to
> be completely at odds with what they must regard as the unanimous
> opinion of all these around them. . . These few who were still able to tell
> right from wrong went really only by their own judgments, and they did
> so freely; there were no rules to be abided by. . . because no rules existed
> for the unprecedented.[16]

What we know for sure is that curing ostensible feebleness of moral
conscience left the moral self, as a rule, disarmed in the face of the

[16] Hannah Arendt, *Eichmann in Jerusalem: A Report on the Banality of Evil*
(New York: Viking Press, 1964), pp. 294, 295. In *Modernity and the Holocaust*
(Cambridge: Polity Press, 1989), pp. 177–8, I suggested that Arendt's
statement articulates the question of moral responsibility for *resisting* socialization and any other pretenders to extra-individual adjudication on the
ethically proper. What the Holocaust, that extreme manifestation of modern
spirit and practice, brought to the surface, is the truth blurred and diluted
under 'normal' circumstances: that morality may, and often should, express
itself 'in *insubordination* towards socially upheld principles, and in an action
openly defying social solidarity and consensus'.

'unanimous opinion of all these around them', and their elected or self-appointed spokesmen; while the power which that unanimous opinion wielded was in no way a guarantee of its ethical value. Knowing this, we have little choice but to place our bet on that conscience which, however wan, alone can instil the responsibility for disobeying the command to do evil. Contrary to one of the most uncritically accepted philosophical axioms, there is no contradiction between the rejection of (or scepticism towards) the ethics of socially conventionalized and rationally 'founded' norms, and the insistence that it does matter, and *matter morally*, what we do and from what we desist. Far from excluding each other, the two can be accepted or rejected only together. If in doubt – consult your conscience.

Moral responsibility is the most personal and inalienable of human possessions, and the most precious of human rights. It cannot be taken away, shared, ceded, pawned, or deposited for safe keeping. Moral responsibility is unconditional and infinite, and it manifests itself in the constant anguish of not manifesting itself enough. Moral responsibility does not look for reassurance for its right to be or for excuses for its right not to be. It is there before any reassurance or proof and after any excuse or absolution.

This is, at least, what one can find out looking back at the protracted modern struggle to prove – to make real – the opposite.

Index